730 and a Wakey

FRANK T BENKO

Frank Benko was born in Hungary in 1946 and migrated to Australia at the age of ten. After an unsuccessful first attempt to complete his matriculation at Bentleigh High School in 1964, he worked as a clerk for the Postmaster  General's Department while finishing those studies at University High School. Compulsory National Service followed in 1967, and this included a nine-month period of service in Vietnam.

Upon discharge from the army, he enrolled at Frankston Teacher's College and has subsequently spent the bulk of his professional career teaching children in primary schools. He also spent three years teaching both youngsters and adults at the Police Cadet and Police Recruit Academies while completing a Bachelor of Arts Degree at Monash University. These studies engendered a lifelong interest in reading, writing and in history.

Frank married Kristina in 1974 and they live in the eastern suburbs of Melbourne. They have two children, Danielle and Stephen, and in 2006 became grandparents for the first time.

Published in Australia by Sid Harta Publishers Pty Ltd,
ACN: 007 030 051
23 Stirling Crescent, Glen Waverley, Victoria 3150 Australia
Telephone: +61 3 9560 9920, Facsimile: +61 3 9545 1742
E-mail: author@sidharta.com.au
First published in Australia 2009
This edition published 2020
Copyright © Frank Benko 2020
Cover design, typesetting: Chameleon Print Design

The right of Frank Benko to be identified as the Author of the Work has been asserted in accordance with the Copyright, Designs and Patents Act 1988.

All rights reserved. No part of this publication may be reproduced, stored in a retrieval system, or transmitted, in any form or by any means without the prior written permission of the publisher, nor be otherwise circulated in any form of binding or cover other than that in which it is published and without a similar condition being imposed on the subsequent purchaser.

Benko, Frank
730 and A Wakey
ISBN:1-921642-25-4
EAN13: 978-1-921642-25-8
pp432

Dedicated to the 50 000 Australians who served there, the 500 who died there and the thousands of others who, in one way or another, have been permanently scarred by their experiences in Vietnam – and are still serving and paying all too high a price for what was eventually achieved.

Given the vagaries and shortcomings of memory, this story is, to the best of my recollection, an accurate accounting of what happened to me during the two years as a Nasho in the Australian Army and is therefore my perspective on events at the time. Not a single word is intended or designed to discredit or belittle anyone and if errors of fact or errors in chronology exist, those are undoubtedly mine.

The names, dates and times of departures of those mentioned in Chapter 17 have been purposely fictionalized.

Contents

Part A 5
Puckapunyal Basic Training

Part B 67
SME: School of Military Engineering Corps Training

Part C 121
CARO: Central Army Records Office
JTC: Jungle Training Course

Part D 165
Vung Tau, Vietnam

Part E 381
Discharge

Part F 391
With hindsight …

Introduction

Contemporary jargon might call it a footprint. It is that lasting impression of a single event or combination of moments that will occur during the course of even the most staid and humdrum of lives which will leave a profound mark with its singular importance, or in their significant totality. These can be so powerful and influential as to affect the rest of one's life as much, if not more, than any other series of experiences will ever be capable of doing.

In my case, for better or for worse, such defining events started in 1967 when, as a young boy, I was conscripted into the Australian Army. We were at war in the late 60s and part of my army service included a period in Vietnam. Halting the spread of communism in that unfortunate land, in response to the politically favoured 'Domino Principle' of the time, was a key factor in the Australian Government's foreign policy.

The cumulative effects of the sights, sounds, smells, and the feelings of joy and bitterness of those two years, have had as much of an effect on my life, subsequent character, and current mindset, as any others to have occurred before or since.

So, reader, if you are willing to join me in a retelling of

what happened and if you are willing to be my companion on this somewhat self-centred and some will say self-indulgent journey, then I ask that you engage in a game of pretence.

Whatever your current age or situation in life, pretend to be a youngish twenty-one. Become one who is from a comfortable middle-class, migrant background. You have finished studying for your Matriculation Certificate and are just starting to get accustomed to what you thought would be your permanent job in life, with some uncertainty about your long-term future still enduring.

Be religious in that you still accept the vaguely possible existence of a higher being. Have a positive work ethic. Be ambitious, broke, and painfully lacking in self-confidence. Be physically healthy. You have just ended a two-year relationship with a girlfriend and are romantically unattached, so yearn for a radical change in that aspect of your social relationships, but be reasonably optimistic about your potential abilities. Above all, have an abiding sense of respect for what your elders say and do. Consequently, you are impressionable, even naïve, and easily swayed by clever or devious logic. Be politically uninformed and unmotivated, but owing to parental influences lean somewhat to the right. Become one who totally accepts conventions, rules and the words of those in authority, and be content in the belief that, like it or not, it is your unquestioned duty to do whatever society and your government expect of you in a time of any 'substantial need'.

If you are able to pretend some or all of these things, then you are almost me, as I would have been in 1967.

Additionally, be ready to tolerate whatever will be on offer, no matter how unpalatable that might turn out to be, because henceforth, your life and the manner in which you live it are literally in others' hands. You are no longer in control!

Now with these similarities in our backgrounds, beliefs, feelings and general characteristics, what are you going to do? Would you have acted differently those many years ago in 1967?

My reaction and behaviour at the time, no matter how helpless and impotent they now seem to have been, were tacit acceptance and obeisance.

Part A

Puckapunyal – Basic Training

Chapter 1

Wednesday, 1 February 1967, was a typically hot and humid Melbourne summer's day. The sky was somewhat overcast and the drive from the family home in East Bentleigh towards the city had been uncomfortable and stifling. While on the outside I was sweaty and bothered, inwardly I was a cold, shivering bundle of uncertainty. Luckily we found a parking space quite near the Olympic Swimming Pool built some twelve years earlier for the 1956 Melbourne Olympic Games, and from there it was a short walk to the assembly hall next to the cycling velodrome. Although the call-up papers contained a map marked with street names and arrows indicating the spot to which we had to go, we didn't need that because days earlier I had driven past the very building to which we now headed, to ensure I knew exactly where I had to be when the big day came. That day had indeed come and as my parents and I locked the car and I handed the keys back to my father, we saw several small and some larger groups walking towards one common point. One member of each group carried a suitcase, while women embraced or held the hands of loved ones – mothers embracing sons, wives embracing husbands, girlfriends embracing boyfriends. One could well have been at a railway station or an airport, instead of in busy Swan Street, Richmond. My parents and I smiled at each other as we regarded this unusual sight and, with my father voluntarily manoeuvring my seemingly overlarge suitcase under his arm, the three of us joined the converging throng.

Inside the hall, seats had been arranged in rows and as we entered there was less noise than one might have expected from the large crowd already assembled. Very few had taken advantage of the seats provided and the groups we had noticed outside remained as separate units wishing to be alone, each taking up an unoccupied share of space in the room. Speech was muted, movement kept to a minimum and here, too, last minute intimacies were being exchanged.

We followed this example and found our own private sanctuary near the far wall, a short distance from the doorway.

From this vantage point, it was easy to see who was arriving. The similarities were quite striking. Each newly arriving group had, as a member, one young boy who, on the surface at least, was about to show everyone that he was not affected in any way by what was happening and what might lay ahead. He was the one to smile and laugh the loudest at the jokes that were told, to monopolise most of the conversation, to sound assured, and to appear to be the one least concerned. Surrounding each of these boys was a pale father pretending, like his son, to be in control of his emotions and a mother on whose face the effects of a recent sleepless night were not completely masked by the makeup and lipstick freshly applied in the car. Many of the boys had arms entwined in those of girlfriends or wives who cried freely, while younger brothers and sisters, perhaps unaware of the significance of the moment, held sheepishly onto their mothers' hands.

As ten and then twenty minutes went by, I began to feel somewhat uneasy, wishing that we had not arrived so early. Most of what my parents and I thought we wanted to say to each other had already been said and now the periods of silence began to feel quite uncomfortable. I suddenly wanted the parting and the emotion of that moment to be over.

Just as it seemed that the interminable wait would continue, there was a sudden flood of new arrivals, louder than any before, accompanied by photographers and television crews. This was a surprise, for although the first few intakes of Nashos had received a lot of publicity in the years before, mine was the seventh such intake, and the newsworthiness and novelty had, we thought, worn off. Some moments later, we saw the reason for this unusual and unexpected media attention.

One of the boys joining that day was a well-known footballer from the St Kilda Football Club, Carl Ditterich. Anyone who lives in Melbourne or even visits it in winter will know of the adulation showered upon players and the heroic status to which supporters of the local game elevate some football personalities. The media interest in Carl was therefore easy to understand. He was a very tall and strong player and with his flowing blond hair, had made a name for himself as a ruckman who could dominate a game both with amazing skills and with aggression. As I now watched him being pursued by the interviewers and cameramen, I was suddenly very happy with my own anonymity. He fielded some of their questions, inane as they sounded, posed for one or two photos, and then stalked off gruffly to a far corner of the hall.

'How do you feel about the army, Carl?'
'How will this affect your football career?'
'Will you be playing football for the army?'

'How do you feel about getting your hair cut, Carl?'

His answers were curt and flung back over one shoulder and it was obvious that he, too, was showing the worry and uncertainty of the moment. The last thing he needed or wanted at that time was the sort of intrusion that now pursued him. I admired him for the manner in which he handled the situation and wondered if I could have done it with similar flair.

Thankfully, the time soon came when an officer of some rank ascended the stage and in a booming voice that was a portent of things to come, addressed the crowd which had become quite noisy as a result of the cameras. Conversations stopped almost immediately. All eyes turned towards the stage and we listened nervously. His instructions, delivered in resonant monotone, were short and to the point. We were told to make our final farewells, after which we were to assemble at different locations around the room as indicated by signs on the wall. Curiously, I had not noticed those before. We were further told that, after having our names checked, we would be embarking on buses for the journey to Puckapunyal. One might have surmised that we were already a finely-tuned squad, for there was an immediate response. Wives stole a final hug and parents embraced their children again. As I kissed first my father and then mother, I noticed that her earlier stoicism had melted and there were tears in her eyes, too. This had always had an adverse effect on me and my own eyes began to water.

'Don't cry, I'm only going sixty miles away, not to the end of the world,' were, I think, my parting words.

Surnames beginning A to D grouped near the front of the hall. I joined them. In a few moments, some forty names had been checked off a list. We were told to stay together when we went outside, as we would be travelling on the same bus. Before leaving through a side door, I looked back but my parents had gone. I felt more than just a little deserted.

Outside, an odd collection of pale and hesitant boys was ushered onto buses, some in shorts, others wearing thongs, one in his leathers and still carrying a bike helmet, and those even less appropriately dressed in a shirt and a tie. I had been tugging at my tie all morning. My deodorant wasn't working. I sensed it and thought others did, too. There was no conversation at all and, in a few minutes, my bus pulled out into Batman Avenue. Many families, having discovered the direction the buses would take, had made their way across to the Yarra bank and as we passed the greyhound track my heart lifted as I noticed that my parents were among them. We waved to each other and then the vehicles crossed Swan Street Bridge for the journey north.

Chapter 2

After the heat and tension of that morning, the air-conditioned coach was heavenly bliss. The nervous expectations of the previous hours disappeared in its coolness. We drove through the city and had the distinct feeling that everyone on busy Swanston Street was looking at us as we passed. We motored up Royal Parade, onto Sydney Road, and finally reached the Hume Highway. Once we passed the Ford Motor Works in Broadmeadows, we had left Melbourne behind.

The silence in the vehicle became eerie and somewhat unnerving. Short of a casual glance at or a handshake with the person who might have sat next to us – which was usually accompanied by a murmured introduction – little had been said by anyone. The whine of the engine filled the cabin, only to be broken in its pitch by the change of gears and speed as we passed through Kilmore and Broadford. Everyone, it seemed, was immersed in private thoughts.

For my own part, I couldn't help but mull over the very same thoughts that had occupied so much of my time in recent months. I knew that whatever lay ahead would be of permanent significance in my life and the uncertainty of what that might be made me both nervous and filled me with eager anticipation at the same time.

I was aware of my shortcomings and limitations. I knew that from a political viewpoint, I probably wasn't totally informed, nor was I a sufficiently motivated political individual to ensure that I had studied and weighed all the facts. My parents' Hungarian, anti-Communist opinions had influenced my thinking and as such, I tended to accept the government's claim that halting the spread of Communism in Vietnam, in response to the politically-favoured 'Domino Principle' of the time was necessary. Consequently, the notion that I would have raised a conscientious objection to being conscripted never entered my mind. Serving my country in a time of need was a duty I felt I needed to fulfil and therefore accepted the inevitability of the draft's outcome.

Privately, I considered myself to be a youngish and impressionable twenty-year-old and that recognition, together with the knowledge that there was a growing dissent among many of my own age about what we were doing in Vietnam was sufficient to make me question whether I was, in fact, right. Additionally, I was still sufficiently religious to wonder if He might have agreed with what was happening over there. In short, I wasn't absolutely convinced that I was doing the right thing.

On the other hand I had just finished the final year of high school, had resigned from employment that I wasn't particularly sorry to leave, was fit and healthy, broke but ambitious, had what I thought was a positive work ethic and, in spite of a personally worrying lack of self-confidence about my physical capabilities in terms of what the army might require, I was optimistic about my potential to succeed. I also wanted to experience and grab my share of the excitement and adventures that I thought the military would provide.

But above all else, my ready acceptance of rules and conventions and an abiding sense of respect for the words of my elders and those in authority were all mitigating factors that convinced me that, on balance, I needed to be on *that* bus *that* day!

The six coaches carrying the entire crew motored north on the Hume in single file. Several miles south of Seymour, we branched to the left onto the road leading to Puckapunyal. Compared to the fairly sharp details that remain in memory about the early hours of that day, I recall very little about the trip itself, except that one individual, sitting several seats ahead of me on the left, spent most of the hour-and-half of the journey looking out the window, quietly sobbing. No one spoke to him as far as I could tell, for indeed he sat alone. When we reached our destination, he became another face among many hundreds and I don't know who he was and can't remember ever seeing him again. Perhaps I could have sat next to him or approached him in some way, but I didn't. The object of so much earlier attention, Carl, sat somewhere towards the rear of the bus and I noticed at one point that he was just as alone and quiet with his thoughts as the rest of us were with ours. I distinctly remember being very pleased, though, that the painful parting from the family, which I had dreaded, was finally over.

The military police on motorbikes whose reflections I had first noticed in the shop windows back in Melbourne accompanied the convoy of buses all the way – two in front and two behind. They led us through the military township of Puckapunyal itself. The unusual sight of the colourful MPs on bikes, escorting six coaches, must have been what everyone in the city had been ogling some time before. This realisation somewhat deflated my ego, which had earlier whispered to me that everyone, knowing who we were and where we were going, was paying us quiet, personal homage as we passed. We drove along streets that had what appeared to be quite normal houses with triple-fronted brick veneers of the era. We later discovered these to be the enlisted men's married quarters. Seeing these was a surprise for, in my naïveté, I truly expected to find nothing but the semi-circular, corrugated iron barracks that I had seen so often in *Sad Sack* comic books and in television's version of the same sad, incompetent soldier, *Gomer Pyle*.

The buses finally stopped on a large, empty, gravel-surfaced area, where they lined up in true military fashion, each dead in line with the one ahead.

The area where we alighted turned out to be the battalion parade ground and if only we had known how many foot-blistering hours we were to spend on that hallowed and hated plot, we might have *debussed* and walked upon it even more awkwardly than was now the case. The term *debus* was the first 'army-ism' we heard, but we shouldn't have been surprised to hear the word, for later we learned to *en-truck* and *de-truck* as well. The army had its own rules, its own reason for doing things, and even its own language, it seemed. Perhaps an economy of words was considered to be a desirable army characteristic, but I just wished they had told us to get off the bloody bus. It seemed such a preferable and simpler term to use. As we mingled after *debussing*, I spoke to some of the boys who had been on my coach. We wondered whether the military police had been there to make sure we wouldn't get lost, to make the whole process appear more regimented, or to ensure that no one tried to get deliberately lost. We decided that it was most likely to be the latter of these. I presume that not a single soul did in fact get lost or try to escape, for after another roll call all were present. We picked up our belongings yet again and, after lining up, were marched in shaky rows of three to our new quarters.

We would soon think longingly of the triple-fronted brick

veneers of the married quarters, or the comfortable homes we had just left when we saw the sheds or boxes in which we were to live. The existing training facilities of the army were severely inadequate to cope with the increased numbers to be trained when conscription was introduced. In haste, therefore, two completely new complexes were constructed, one in Kapooka in New South Wales called 1 RTB, the First Recruit Training Battalion; and the one at Puckapunyal in Victoria where we had been taken, called 2 RTB.

These prefabricated, rectangular buildings were no doubt better than those used for training purposes in World War II and we should not have complained, but for a group of boys who that morning had just left family homes, perhaps private bedrooms and wall to wall carpets, these huts were strange, uninviting, stark, and smelt of mould despite the heat of the day.

The rest of that first day and all of the second was spent in a mind-numbing whirl. Everything was new, unusual, unaccustomed, and downright foreign. Not a moment of time for relaxation or private thought was offered as a frenzy of administrative matters and a host of introductory procedures were ceaselessly thrust on us. Excerpts from letters I scribbled on the first two evenings offer some ideas about the confusion and the newness of it all.

1.2.67

My Dear Parents,

Since arriving we've been running madly from here to there – collection of clothing, making of beds, lunch, cleaning of shoes, polishing of boots and what boots they are! You should see the size and weight! Then we saw the dentist, two of mine need filling. Injections, then a half hour orientation walk around the camp involving lessons on which is our right and which is our left foot, back for dinner, followed by a two hour long psychology test. We get up at six tomorrow, lights out is in five minutes, so more tomorrow.

2.2.67

Up at six, roll call in pyjamas or naked as we happened to be at the time of waking, shower, shave, breakfast is at a quarter to seven, I'm surprised at the food, it's really good. The clothing we got yesterday included an overcoat and it was almost 100 degrees outside, mind you – beret, slouch hat, four pairs of socks, two pairs of boots, stacks of underwear both winter and summer.

We also got three shirts, three trousers, sweater, and tennis shoes. With the exception of boots and shoes, every single stitch is green. We look ghastly in green underwear, but I suppose we'll get used to it. This morning, we had a blood test and more marching, left foot right foot garbage. We went for a training run and we were given our rifles, bayonets and got a hair cut. Quite a few pale necks are already being scorched pink by the sun. There are sixteen of us in a hut in four groups of four, and there are four huts altogether so that makes sixty-four in my platoon. One corporal is in charge of one hut, so altogether the boss of sixteen of us. All is fine so far, I only wish he wouldn't yell so bloody much. None of us is deaf!

When the corporal steps into the hut, the first one of us to spot him has to stand up quickly and yell, 'Stand fast!' At this, the other fifteen yell likewise and we all stand at attention until he yells and gives the next command. It's weird when this happens; something like a television comedy, only this is real. Thanks for waiting around so long yesterday morning. I really appreciated you being there when we left Swan Street!

In life, we are given lots of numbers that define and identify us. Birth certificates are numbered, as are registration numbers on cars, licences, taxation papers, telephones, houses, insurance certificates, deeds, and a host of other official documents. We don't commit many of these numbers to memory because there is often no need, but by the end of my second day in the army, my personal service number of 3790533 had become deeply etched in my mind. The corporal had promised us everlasting hell if any of us should happen to forget these important and permanently identifying numerical monikers.

It was the first of many such ultimatums issued in those first few days and the litany of rules, the do's and don'ts which were to guide our very existence, became the new focus by which our lives were to proceed from that time. Without apologies or explanations, we were informed to forget who we were or who we had been, for ahead of us lay work and effort which would make us into entirely different, fitter, healthier, and superior individuals to those who had entered camp only a day before. Being in no mind to argue the toss or the point, we accepted the proposition without question.

On 2 February 1967, a letter was sent to parents and families by the army administration. It was thoughtful, reassuring and a nice touch which must have been welcomed by its recipients. (Page 195)

Chapter 3

The fifteen strangers who became my section and hut mates were not strangers for very long. We soon found that personal fears, inhibitions, and uncertainties about our current situations were not at all unique. The move from home and the sudden thrusting into a new environment were equally taxing on all. My own fears about an inability to complete difficult tasks and worries about competing with others whom I thought would be bigger, fitter, and stronger than I was were put to rest by the discovery that the majority were not bigger or even fitter, and that I could manage if I worked hard. The new tasks put before us had to be performed equally by everyone and as I sweated through a three-mile run in boots in a hundred degree heat, so did everyone else. The discomforts, as well as successes, were not selective but universally shared. Whenever my father had spoken about his army experiences, it had been this oneness and sameness of circumstance that he had often mentioned and it was that very fact that now began to bind us and formed the comradeship that was to be such an essential ingredient in the successful completion of those things that lay ahead.

In those early days, punishment was measured out harshly,

but always equally. The section of sixteen or the platoon of sixty-four as the case may be, was ordered to do twenty push-ups if someone's boots were not shiny, or if some blanket corners were not tucked sufficiently tightly under a mattress. Hospital corners on beds and their immaculately folded appearance was a particularly hot item with our section corporal, and if one of the sixteen beds was faulty or not to his total satisfaction, all of them had to be remade. Litter that was left carelessly anywhere around the hut resulted in the automatic penalty of a five lap run around the parade ground. For serious and capital crimes, like buttons being left undone, wardrobe doors left ajar, or, heaven forbid, tardiness in going to formation by just one of us meant that all could expect some form of retribution, generally exacted by the dreaded section corporal. If anyone higher in the pecking order, such as the company sergeant major was to note one of our indiscretions – like a handkerchief hanging slightly from a pocket – we quavered in fear as strips were torn off the entire section or platoon for such a blatant disregard of army discipline. At first, this seemingly unfair treatment made us wary and suspicious of each others' actions, but it also forced us to take particular care in everything we did. No one wished to be responsible for the punishment and suffering of others. This treatment not only sparked the notion of unity and the necessity of doing things for the good of the group, but also helped forge swift friendships based on mutual dependence and assistance. It was the ultimate affirmation of the maxim that 'a friend in need is a friend indeed.' It was simply the army way!

Apart from the peculiar word *debussing*, the expression *emu bob* entered my vocabulary for the first time. The sight of sixty of us, all in a straight line, heads bowed, bobbing and searching for the smallest scrap of inconsequential rubbish on an already spotless, windswept parade ground must have seemed hilarious, if not ludicrous, to an outsider. To us, it was holy-writ work, ordered by our corporal and yet another bloody form of punishment we were forced to endure for someone's error or omission. We grumbled and complained quite vocally when the opportunity presented itself, but only until it was a personal mistake that got others into strife. Then we would silently plead for mercy and understanding, knowing that if looks from the others could kill, we would be dead many times over. Of course, it was not long before each one of us had contributed in some way to the growing list of extra work duties meted out to the group. With each act of such apparent bastardry by those in charge, we complained more vociferously, cursed more, worked more, and bonded more closely. In fact we got up together, showered and shaved together, ate, polished, ran, stood, sweated, cursed and ached together, and so began to think of ourselves as one. The deliberate ploy, of course, was to make of us a unit of sixty-four, rather than remain as we had begun, a unit comprised of sixty-four individuals. My correspondence home reveals that even as early as the second or third letter, the first person plural regularly replaces the first person singular as I tell my parents what we are doing.

6.2.67

We help each other as much as possible, because by 6.30 in the morning, 12.45 in the afternoon and 5.15 in the evening, the hut has to be ready for inspection.

Yesterday, Sunday, was a day off usual training, but we were cleaning from 8 in the morning until 9 at night and I'm not joking! More shoe polishing, floor washing and waxing, three times, washing of walls and windows, packing and re-stacking of wardrobes – all because this morning, the Company Sergeant Major, the CSM, was to hold an inspection. The rotten dog spent all of three minutes walking through our hut and after ripping apart three beds and emptying a larger number of drawers claiming that they were the filthiest he had ever seen, he left grumbling about the overall mess in the place. Honestly, we had made it so tidy you could have eaten off the floor! So that was the end result of thirteen hours of work we put in. We felt like telling him to do a better job himself if he wasn't happy with what we'd done. Of course, God save us, we actually said no such thing.

As a young teenager, I loved reading adventure stories like *The Count of Monte Cristo* and *The Three Musketeers*. The Musketeers' cry of 'All for one and one for all' seemed particularly applicable to our situation. While the Count relied upon his individual abilities and craft to escape the dreaded Château d'If and exact revenge on those who had cheated him, Porthos and friends made a team and it was the collective ability of the group, comprised of their individual skills, which eventually overcame difficulties.

One of the main objectives of basic training was to quash individuality and to break our spirits in the process. This was achieved through the use of tedious, demanding, and repetitive physical harassment. Having altered, if not completely destroyed individual endeavour and ambition, a new form of collective spirit began to replace that which had existed before and this fresh ideal was specifically cast in the army's mould. Self-interest and personal welfare were replaced by the more desirable notions of the military common good. The selflessness of Athos and the mateship of Aramis often came to mind during those ten weeks as we gradually and almost imperceptibly lost some of our previous character traits, absorbed the new teachings, and subconsciously became 'army broke'. It was a slow, calculated, and almost insidious process, but one that got results.

As I had written in detail to my parents, each hut was built for sixteen recruits and they were partitioned off into four identical quarters, there being four beds in each quarter. The simple rule was that all lights had to be extinguished by 10.45 pm, at which time an appropriate piece of music was played over the public address system. According to age-old military custom, this finale to a day was marked by the blowing of a trumpet and by the time the final notes sounded, each light in each quarter of each hut in the company had to be switched off. One night, the light in one quarter of my hut was several moments late – perhaps five second at most. One of the boys had been returning from the toilet, had slipped on the steps leading up into the hut, and had been that amount of time too slow in reaching for the switch. Within a scant ten seconds thereafter, our corporal, whom we now despised with a serious intensity, burst through the door. Naturally, we sprang out of bed to the accustomed yelling of 'Stand fast!' He ordered the lot of us outside.

'Ladies, since you're this slow in undressing and getting into bed, you obviously need more practice! You have exactly two minutes to get into physical education gear and be lined up here again!' He screamed this like some demented animal.

We knew he was serious. We roared inside, ripped off our pyjamas, flung open the wardrobe doors, dragged out the shorts, socks, singlets and sandshoes that comprised the physical education outfit, got changed, and in the process destroyed the arrangement of tidy clothing in the wardrobes that moments earlier had been militarily straight and neatly arranged. The two minutes given for this task was ample and in an almost conceited and self-congratulatory manner, the lot of us lined up outside well within the allotted time.

'Since you're so bloody good, you now have three minutes to get into full battle dress, you horrible little people!' By now, he was bellowing.

In we ran again. Off came the shorts and sandshoes. Out of the wardrobe came the freshly polished boots, gaiters, thick socks, trousers, jacket, and belt with the highly polished keepers, shirt, tie, and slouch hat. Getting all of this on in three minutes might have been possible, but putting it all on with army precision was an impossible task, and the bastard waiting for us outside knew it. But that, of course, was the whole idea. The last of us to make formation outside did so at the end of about five minutes.

'I told you that you needed practice! My lame grandmother could have done this faster! Jockstraps, overcoats, and boots! You have one minute! Go!' Now, he roared.

As we ran back in again, we wondered if the bugger could ever have had a grandmother and assured ourselves that if he did, and if she were lame, it was probably because she chased him around all the time with an axe. We were totally at his mercy. Whatever little novelty this late night exercise had at the start was soon completely gone. We ripped off the neatly-pressed battledress, threw it on the bed with the previously discarded pyjamas, shorts, sandshoes, and associated items, and grabbed the overcoats. This time we all made it back in one minute.

'So you can do it, after all! Well now, ladies! If the hut passes inspection, you can all go back to bed and dream about being back in your mothers' arms again!' By now, he was slobbering in his usually abhorrent way.

Needless to say, the hut looked like a battlefield and did not pass his blasted inspection. Clothes had been thrown around everywhere, chairs upended in the mad rush and hats and rifles were lying on the ground. Every cardinal rule governing military neatness and personal order had been broken. The corporal was positively gushing with smug pride and satisfaction as the torment continued for another half hour and he made us jump like trained fleas, running in and out, changing clothes, all at his private whim.

The point in all of this was certainly not to see if we could be in full battle dress in three minutes, or if we could change into a sports outfit in two, but to ensure that we wouldn't actually make it. The five extra seconds of burning light globe simply provided the army training system with the opportunity to impose a little more pain and collective discomfort upon us, thereby building the team and emphasising the importance of interdependence. The lesson was not to dress quickly, but to accept orders without question, no matter how stupid or purposeless the orders might have seemed.

It was the same object lesson for which I was the helpless and sacrificial lamb another day. My crime had been to forget to button my shirt pocket. The tirade came unexpectedly as we were standing in formation. It had the desired effect on all.

'Recruit Benko, front and centre!' he bellowed.

Being front and centre meant that one had to take a step forward, turn right or left as necessary, and march to the front and to the centre of the formation using an exaggerated arm motion in the process. In this way, one was in full view of the group and open to close and embarrassing scrutiny not just by the corporal, but by everyone else as well.

'What do you call that, Recruit?' said he, pointing to the button on my pocket.

'A button, sir, I mean, Corporal,' was my weak reply.

'Is it done up?'

'No, Corporal!'

'Why not, Recruit?'

'I must have forgotten to do it, Corporal!'

'What do you mean you forgot to do it, Recruit? Should a worthless little grub like you be allowed to get away with such forgetfulness?'

'No, Corporal!'

'You are a forgetful, moronic little ass! What are you?'

'A forgetful, moronic little ass, Corporal!' I shouted at the top of my lungs as the faintest ripple of laughter came from behind me.

'I can't hear you!' he roared back.

'A forgetful moronic little ass, Corporal!' I screamed again.

'Will you ever be this forgetful again, Recruit Benko?'

'No, Corporal!'

'I still can't hear you!'

'NO, CORPORAL!' I yelled much louder.

'Return to formation! Now, the man who thought that was funny and laughed, front and centre immediately.'

Having finished his sport with me, he now continued the process with another who had been stupid enough to smirk and laugh when I had been the object of ridicule. He was now made to feel similarly worthless.

'Recruit Yewen, you're a tall streak of pelican shit! What are you?'

'A tall streak of pelican shit, Corporal!'

'I can't hear you!

'Recruit Trowse! Do you know that when you march, you move with all the grace and ease of a pregnant hippo? How do you move, Recruit Trowse?'

'With all the grace and ease of a pregnant hippo, Corporal!'

'I can't hear you!

'Recruit Addams! Why are you staring at me as though you've suddenly fallen in love? Get your beady little eyes off me, you insignificant bit of flea shit! Do you understand me clearly, Recruit Addams?'

'I understand, Corporal!'

'I can't hear you!'

And so continued the verbal barrage and his reading of the gospel for that particular day. Corporal Gowans, our section corporal, certainly had an unusual gift for words and an interesting and varied vocabulary. Even though he might have been yelling at us only inches from our faces, it was difficult at times not to burst out laughing at his choice of phrases. Those, added to the sight of the dilated pupils, wide eyes, and distended carotid arteries on either side of his neck, made the whole situation seem funny. But the fear of an obvious reprisal, should any of us have actually laughed or smirked, was sufficient impediment to an expression of mirth at such times. Gowans was about thirty-five, a lance corporal, and was a regular army man with almost twenty years of service. He was always immaculately dressed and pressed, and while only a scant five feet six inches high, he could tear us down with a glare and his voice carried sufficient authority to make us quiver and obey instantly. At first, we feared and then grew to hate him with a passion. Strangely, though, by the end of basic training in April, the feeling became one of sincere respect. By that time, we would have been happy to do just about anything that he asked because he had changed and remoulded our attitudes, opinions, and even characters in the army's style. How proud we were on the last Sunday at the march-out parade, as we strove and tried our best to do his section and him, full justice. That weird thought, though, hardly entered our minds as we stood outside that awful night in jockstraps, boots and overcoats, being berated and cursed by someone who looked and acted as though he had been birthed by one of the Harpies from Greek mythology and fathered by Vlad the Impaler, and who seemingly enjoyed inflicting as much pain, discomfort and personal grief as possible on anyone who was available and at his immediate mercy.

Chapter 4

The result of the democratic and random selection system used for National Service was reflected in the wide variety of boys with whom I found myself. Among my closest friends were several clerks, a quantity surveyor, a plumber, an insurance agent, and a baker's apprentice. Further afield there were cooks and a taxi driver, several training to be mechanics when the call-up came, the professional footballer already mentioned, farmers' sons, and even a trainee model. Many of these boys, recruits, or ex-civilians as we preferred to think of ourselves, were not at all happy to be new members of Her Majesty's Australian Armed Forces.

Although I had been quite prepared to leave my former place of work, others had apprenticeships and budding professional careers interrupted by the draft. By law, former employers were obliged to take us back at the end of two years, but many of us realised that the cost in seniority and other promotional opportunities would be substantial, perhaps irretrievable. In addition, many had political, social, personal, and religious objections against our enforced military service and there was consequent bitterness in the minds of many of my new mates. Those who objected most harshly found that their first few months were made harder by their negative, doggedly wilful opposition to the new rigours. While it was the hope of some, in the weeks immediately after enlistment, that appeals would be approved and that a discharge was imminent, the fact was that of the 1200 boys who comprised the seventh intake at Puckapunyal in 1967, only three or four were successful. The reality was that, like it or not, we were army fodder for the next two years and there was very little that any of us could do to alter that fact. The malcontents who continually fouled up, deliberately failed tests, and refused to co-operate were not rewarded in the way they would have wished. A discharge was not an available option. Their attitude brought extra grief and hardship on themselves and initially on us all. Resistance to rules and orders by any of us was met with an even greater degree and severity of resistance by the army.

12.2.67

Each day we have five or six different training sessions. The first is always physical training, running, push-ups, rope-climbing or general calisthenics. By the end of ten weeks, we have to run the mile in seven minutes or we fail and have to repeat basics. We must be able to do at least thirty push-ups and twenty full arm chin-ups.

Second, we have weapon training. Disassemble the rifle, reassemble it, cleaning, loading and so on. We have to be able to load the magazine in thirty seconds or we fail.

Third, there is marching. There is always a lot of bloody marching. Full dress, backpack loaded, rifle, boots, hat, the works. Believe me, a 7.62 millimetre, ten-and-half-pound

Swedish, gas-operated, self-loading rifle gets heavy after a mile or two.

Incidentally, we have to memorise useless stuff like that. We also get a daily lecture on tactical warfare – whatever that may be – and I still can't understand it and yesterday we got one on Vietnam. After that, we're back to drilling, which is more marching. Left foot, right foot, right turn, about face, wheel, how to stand, how not to stand, look up, look down – it's a circus more often than not. The bloody hot weather is not helping!

The worst part of the whole thing is that for each different activity, we're only given a few minutes to change into an entirely different outfit. This bloody army is fixated on dress! I'm thinking of asking the corporal for a raise! The $63.80 a fortnight is nowhere near enough for all this!

You won't believe this final indignity! Yesterday, Gowans took my electric shaver during inspection, removed the head, tapped it on the table and when some tiny hairs fell out from between the blades he called me a filthy little swine for not cleaning it properly! So this filthy little swine of yours is not allowed to use it for the next week, I'm shaving with soap and razor. Like I said, it's a weird circus!

From 6.00 in the morning until 8.00 at night, every moment of our waking day was timetabled for a lesson or activity of some sort. Even our so-called spare time from 8 in the evening till lights out at 10.45 was spent in preparation for the next day, and the unannounced visits by the corporals into huts during these supposedly free hours became less surprising with their regularity. Each time one of them appeared, we would have to go through the tedium of standing at attention while they rifled through our belongings. They read private letters if those happened to be within easy reach, searched through drawers, threw out neatly stacked shirts and trousers so we would have to fold them again and generally ensured that we got no respite from being constantly on edge. We were forever expecting the unexpected, constantly active and there was simply no chance to relax, ever.

What made the situation worse was that summer of 1967. The weather bordered on the unbearable. Melbourne can sometimes experience two or three days of continuously hot conditions close to 100 degrees in February, but that's ultimately relieved by a cooling, southerly change. The flat, central Victorian plains surrounding Seymour and Pucka are too distant from the sea to benefit greatly from southerlies. In the first three weeks, the temperature never seemed to fall below ninety and was often over the century. Climbing vertical ropes with sweaty palms, calisthenics, and five-mile runs, were totally exhausting in such weather for the majority who had spent a fairly lazy, sedentary life until then. The fact that some of us literally fell out from a column of running men, heaving, retching and gasping for air, made little difference to those in charge. We were berated for collapsing, were given only a moment to catch our breaths and then had to continue as though nothing had happened. Even the hardened, fitter, country boys found the going difficult and were just as close to tears as any of us when, in the evenings, we had to remove blood-soaked socks caused by broken blisters and new boots that had not yet been broken in.

Rope-climbing was both literally and metaphorically my greatest downfall. It might have been the lack of strength in arms and wrists or an inability to co-ordinate an upward motion of the arms with a simultaneous grip on the rope with feet and thighs. Whatever my shortcomings, I could not drag myself further than three or four yards off the ground before sliding unceremoniously back again. After being roared at for not pulling my finger out of my anal orifice, I would again reach the dizzy height of four of the twelve yards required and fall in another heap at the feet of the snarling corporal who was enjoying my awkwardness. I marvelled at the gymnastic ability of those who could attack the rope and, in a fluid, repetitive motion, pull themselves to the top and, with similar ease and agility, come down again. Then there were those who could repeat the procedure several times without fully descending or touching the ground at all. Then there was me.

'If we can't get you to climb that rope, Recruit Benko, we'll get you to climb up something else,' came, yet again, the threatening venom from Gowans.

When the entire battalion of 1200 recruits had been assembled for the first time from all parts of Victoria and South Australia, we were put into four companies, aptly named A B C and D. Each company was made up of four platoons and each platoon was in turn split into four sections. There being sixteen of us in each hut, this meant a total of about seventy-five huts. Visible from both the front and rear entrances of every hut, we could see an almost perfectly shaped, hemispherical hill a few hundred yards from camp. It was about 200 yards high, completely devoid of trees or shrubs and in the heat of that current summer, even the grass was totally burnt off.

Apart from its unusual contours, what made it immediately noticeable was a curious, dome-shaped, stone construction at the very summit. From our vantage point below, it looked very much like the nipple on a woman's breast pointing seductively towards the sky. Appropriately, therefore, this was called Tit Hill. As yet another available form of army bastardisation, we were required to run up this bare hill, touch the nipple, and run back down again as punishment for an incomplete or unsatisfactory performance. As one who had trouble climbing ropes, I was given plenty of opportunities to climb and to touch the tit.

'What's it going to be today – the rope or the tit, Recruit Benko?'

For about three of us in the platoon, including me, it was always the tit. I was getting quite proficient at saluting and visiting that small patch of elevated Puckapunyal.

The monotony of the daily gymnastics, lectures and drill was broken in the third week of our stay at the Pucka holiday camp. It was my platoon's turn for kitchen duty.

The Mess, as the army very appropriately calls its dining hall, was enormous. For an establishment that large, the organisation of the three daily meals was so smoothly arranged that the entire battalion, eating in several strictly-scheduled short shifts, could complete eating any of these meals in one hour. The logistical appropriation of the hundreds of loaves of bread; the scores of packets of bacon rashers; the hundreds of cartons of eggs; and the huge quantities of meat, vegetables, milk and cereals, was a joy to behold. The food that was required at any moment appeared as if by magic, was served and the refuse disappeared, again as if a wand had been waved. Watching the cooks prepare the gargantuan meals in cauldrons that rivalled baths for capacity was a sight in itself, and their readiness was always timed such that a snaking queue of ravenous mouths appeared on cue to consume it.

The work we were required to do was hard and the hours in the kitchen even longer than those spent in normal training, but at the time we were happy to be in the relative coolness and comfort of the mess and not in the blistering heat of the parade ground. The first shift for eating breakfast arrived at 6.45 am, so our day began at the earlier time of 5.45 am. The last shift finished eating the evening meal at about 7.30 pm, but we remained till nine o'clock cleaning the tables, washing floors and pots or preparing whatever else was required by the cooks for the next day. The very welcome compensation for such long hours was as much food as we could eat and the gloriously icy cordials and milk that were constantly on tap. Days earlier, during a three-mile run, we would have killed for a cupful of cold cordial and it hadn't been available. Now we had it by the gallons. After nine o'clock, it was back to the huts for the daily washing of clothes, polishing of boots, and the ironing of shirts and trousers for the following day. Many times in those first weeks, I silently thanked my mother for her earlier insistence that, as young children, my brother and I learned how to care for ourselves completely. She made us help clean the house, cook, iron our clothing, and do those things which were generally regarded as being women's work. Those few and previously despised skills now stood me in good stead and I was often able to help others who had never touched an iron or folded a shirt, get ready in time for an inspection or for lights out.

At the end of the fourth week, we got our first full day off for visitors' day. We had just spent a demanding and strenuous month without a break and we were exhausted. The time had passed quickly in many respects, yet it also seemed like ages since the farewells on 1 February. Very early that morning, the usual tiredness seemed to have deserted us and we dressed eagerly in the army's best summer finery – the polyester shirt, trousers, tie, and highly spit-polished black shoes. Their toes were gleaming even more than usual if that was at all possible, for we were determined to make as much of an impression on our families by choice, as we had to make on the inspecting corporals by force. Parents, wives, and sweethearts had been asked to report to the orderly room and as they arrived from Melbourne, Adelaide, or even further afield, our names were called on the loudspeaker to go and meet them. I felt comically stupid at having to march at attention on the footpath around the parade ground towards my grinning parents. Arms had to be rigid and lifted to shoulder height, thumbs on top, toes pointed forward with backs held straight. Slouch hats were worn and we had been warned, under threat of execution, not to break into a trot or cut any corners of the platoon's parade ground when approaching our families. Happily, everyone else was strutting in the same manner as I was. Otherwise, I might have broken the army's cardinal rule and sprinted across it to embrace my parents, brother, aunt, and uncle.

We had a glorious day. There was much that the family wanted to know, news that my letters had not contained and there was much I wanted to tell. A lot of it was no doubt coloured in the telling for effect, but if I exaggerated to excess, they probably knew it anyway and didn't let on. Although we were not allowed too far from camp, we drove towards Seymour – which was the given limit – found a shady spot on the banks of the Goulburn River, and ate the food my parents brought from home. The fried chicken and potato salad were delicious. Two of my mates, whose families could not visit them that day from as far away as Adelaide, came with us and we felt relaxed, without pressure for the first time in a month. The tight, restricting shackles had been momentarily loosened and the natural freedom we had always taken for granted was suddenly recalled, welcomed, and valued if only for a few, brief hours.

We sat by the river on some blankets, kicked a soccer ball, took photos, enjoyed the food, talked about what had happened to each of us in the past month and in every sense of the word enjoyed a picnic atmosphere that was so different to the artificial and controlled atmosphere of recent weeks that it was a salve for the soul.

Chapter 5

'A gun is the thing that you tuck into your underpants. This is called a rifle!'

So began the very first lesson on the L1A1, SLR. The standard issue rifle in use by the Australian Army was a Swedish designed weapon, the L1A1, Self-Loading Rifle. Its technicalities, such as the 7.62mm ammunition it used and specifications with respect to manufacture, weight and muzzle velocity, were of little interest to me, even though I was obliged to commit the facts to memory. At the time, all I cared about was that it was bloody heavy to carry and that the bullets came out the business end extremely fast. I was uncomfortable around weapons. To that point in my life, I had never fired anything apart from an air rifle that a friend had once let me try. We didn't have a rifle at home. I had never hunted and never had the slightest inclination to do so. I was very uncomfortable and nervous with my SLR for weeks before it became an accustomed companion.

Corporal Gowans placed the water-filled twelve gallon drum at the base of the sand dune, walked back to us, cocked the rifle that was not a gun, aimed, and fired three shots. The bullets left three neat, circular holes in the front of the drum through which the water now dribbled. At the back, however, three wider, star-shaped holes had appeared, and by the time we walked to where it had been placed, the drum had emptied of water.

'It will do the same to a man! A small hole in the chest and a gaping bloody hole in his back,' the good corporal explained.

With an obvious passion for the topic, he then described the mechanics of how a bullet – the projectile – upon leaving the barrel flies straight through the air in a spinning motion, but begins to tumble end over end once it meets any resistance such as a body. This tumbling, as it passed through the drum, had therefore caused the much larger holes at the points of exit. It was a thought-provoking and sobering explanation for those of us who were unaccustomed to firearms. I wasn't alone in my ignorance and naïveté about what we had just witnessed. The notion of a small, pointed lump of lead tumbling at very high speed and tearing through my living flesh, or that of any other person, was quite unpalatable and sickening. The new understanding that my SLR and I could easily inflict such damage on someone, made the reality doubly unnerving.

This initial hesitation and unsteadiness soon passed and after several days of shooting, albeit with wavering hands and sporting the obligatory sore shoulder from the recoils, I gained sufficient confidence and skill to become a reasonably good shot. This was especially true from the prone position when we were lying on our stomachs and in which I was able to anchor my trembling hands sufficiently. That nervousness and unsteadiness invariably spoilt my aim from the standing position.

Caring for the rifles became the single most important priority in the army's long and distinguished list of many other priorities. It even surpassed the maddening emphasis that had, to that stage, been placed on neat and correct dress. We were inculcated with an obsessive need for our weapons' maintenance, their safety, their supreme standing in the order of all things and, I daresay, even in the comfort they required when out of our hands. Brushing and keeping the exterior surfaces free from dust, removing and oiling the bolt, using the pull-through to ensure that the interior rifling of the barrel was spotless, and checking the tension of slings, had to be done several times a day. Even God could not help the recruit whose rifle was found to be dusty, misplaced, or, heaven forbid, rusty! The dust gave us the most concern, as the hot winds of March kept sweeping through camp. Our rifles became the constant companions which were never to leave our sight and which were to be pampered and cared for as much as we had ever cared for anything else in our lives. The presence of that lump of wood and metal weighing down my hands and shoulders, leaning next to my bed and being constantly carried while marching, walking, or even going to the toilet, finally brought home the significance of what we were doing and what we might, in reality, be asked to do in the future.

For me, the absolute low point of the ten-week long recruit course came in the sixth week. On one particularly bloodthirsty day, after we had spent several hours on the rifle range honing our skills with the SLR, we were introduced to another, smaller weapon – a lightweight sub-machine gun, the F1. This despicable, yet remarkable piece of engineering brilliance had a single tubular bolt which was its only moving part and fired at the rate of about six rounds a second. With hardly any recoil, its only negative tendency was to pull slightly upwards and to the left when fired. Held at the waist and properly aimed, it could demolish several wooden targets with a single burst from a distance of twenty yards. We were told that it was the ideal weapon for the close combat that had been experienced in the jungles of Vietnam.

After lunch, we marched to the bayonet range for a further helping in the manly art of how successfully one could shove a long knife into someone's guts. Running forward with bayonets fixed to the end of the rifle barrels, we had to plunge the blade into swaying, straw-filled sacks suspended from beams, pull out the blade, smash the swinging sack with the butt of the rifle, and then run to the next sack to repeat the process. A guttural, animal-like scream was not only preferred, but even required during this process. Of the many despicable things asked of us, this was the one to which I most objected and found the most difficult to perform with anything other than utter revulsion. To complete this totally demoralising and perfectly shithouse day, we were made to run back to camp that afternoon with rifles held above our heads shouting, 'Kill! Kill! Kill!'

Despite total physical exhaustion, I didn't sleep much that night. The following day, we were to throw our first live grenade. I was strangely both petrified and at the same time keen for the experience. In the short space of six weeks, I had been made to do things that had seemed quite improbable and unthinkable during my previous twenty years. While inwardly we objected to much of what was happening, we obeyed, followed orders, and shot, garrotted and pretended to kill on command. The army's methods and practices were beginning to work on us recent clerks, bakers, farmers and students.

Chapter 6

I recall a story my father once told me about an experience he had during his army service that exemplifies the degree of bastardisation that can occur. Towards the middle of his basic training, aching desperately to get away from the rigours of camp life and enjoy a short period of leisure and private recreation, their superiors asked the troops one Saturday afternoon if they would like to go out that night to see the sights in the local town. Naturally, all showed a healthy interest in the suggestion and were promised time off for that purpose the same night. By eight o'clock, dressed in the army's finest threads, they were loaded aboard transports and driven to a hill some miles from camp that overlooked the town in question. The troops, with quizzical looks on their faces lined up as ordered, at which point the officer-in-charge strode to the front of the ranks to fulfil his promise.

'Over there you can see the steeple of the church. Running north to south is the main road and the bright lights you see towards the centre of town is where the cinemas and shops are to be found. You can probably see a large hall next to the brightest light and that's where the local girls are going tonight for the Saturday night dance. Now that you've seen the sights, back on the trucks! We have more drill sessions and inspections to complete tonight!'

Thankfully, such a dirty trick was not played on us. At long last, the countdown reached four, then three, two and finally one and a wakey. Our first proper leave was only a day away! When a very young child wants to know how long it is until Christmas or a birthday, a parent's answer might well be that it's only six more sleeps. We adopted a similarly child-like expectation or countdown towards a major event such as leave. We counted the remaining days just as fervently as a child might have counted the days until Christmas or the end of a school term.

What a marvellous feeling it was, sitting in a friend's car, being able to drive through the previously forbidden boom gates and out of the recruit battalion's secure area when the one day, and finally the wakey, had passed. It was as if for six weeks we had been imprisoned and had just then been granted time off for good behaviour and the consequent freedom to walk out the front gate. It was a similarly liberated sensation to be travelling south and unaccompanied along the Hume Highway whereas only weeks earlier we had travelled north under military police escort. Reaching the city and alighting from the car in Swanston Street, I felt as if all eyes were on me. They were ogling my uniform that was immaculately pressed, my spit-polished shoes that were at their lustrous best and my haircut which, for the first time, felt uncomfortably short amongst those sporting the long-haired fashion of the current era. Just the same, I relished the pure vanity of the moment. I boarded a Frankston line train for the trip to Moorabbin and sat in the carriage with a straighter posture than ever before.

It was nothing short of delightful to be at home again, in familiar surroundings, and to be pampered for a day-and-a-half. Apart from seeing my parents and brother again, the most powerful images remaining are the sight and feel of carpet under my feet, comfortable furniture in which to sit, pictures on the walls, and coloured flowers in the garden. Needless to say, the home-cooked meals were also very easy to tolerate.

There was, however, a surrealistic air about this visit home. I knew I was welcome and the visit was there to be savoured and enjoyed, but its very temporary nature made the house and home seem strangely different, somewhat colder, as though I was only a visitor and didn't really belong as I had done before. Puckapunyal was an increasingly impacting reality on my life that a thirty-six hour absence could not suddenly remove from the conscious mind.

10.3.67

We got back to camp without incident. Andrew's small Prefect made heavy going of the journey, especially going up Pretty Sally with five of us on board. I showed them around a little until the duty officer told me off. They left for the return journey about an hour ago. Understandably, Andy was very interested in the layout of the place. I was one of the first to get back. The hut felt weird being empty like that. Many thanks for the special attention you gave me yesterday. The fruit I brought back has been hidden in my overcoat pockets. Maybe there it won't be found and confiscated. One of the boys brought a guitar back with him and quite a few are sitting around singing quiet songs, so it seems I'm not the only one feeling a bit low.

I had known Andrew for years through our parents' mutual friendship, and although he and I lived in Elwood and East Bentleigh, respectively, we had spent some time together and had become quite friendly. Being only a year younger than me, the prospect of National Service was heavy on his mind as well. He was glad, therefore, to drive me back to camp that Sunday so that he could sneak a peek at what might lay ahead of him in the not too distant future. Little did either of us know at the time that in about seven months, I would make another trip to Pucka to watch the march-out parade of the ninth intake of Nashos and that Andrew would be a part of that.

By the middle of March, only four weeks of basic training were left and as the days passed, increasing pressure was applied. Sessions set aside for physical activities became even longer and drill practice in particular was now more demanding. By this time, many of us had satisfied the requirements for shooting with the SLR and F1. We had shot the necessarily accurate spreads at both twenty-five and fifty yards and had shown that we could disassemble, clean, reload, and reassemble both weapons within specified time limits. We continued the slow and painful process of ensuring that everyone ran the mile in the required time and that dress and general kit preparation and maintenance were up to the army's exacting standards.

'Not one bastard in my section is failing this course as long as I can draw breath, because if I see any lazy little individual not doing his best, his life will not be worth living! Is that plainly understood?' the corporal would bellow.

'Every one of you will pass or else! I'll not tolerate failure! Never have and never will,' the platoon sergeant boomed.

'My company always performs at one hundred percent,' the CSM would add when it became his turn to threaten us.

It seemed that as the rank of those in control of our lives rose, fewer and fewer words were necessary to convey an identical message. We understood, believed, and obeyed them all unquestioningly. After all, what options did we have? None at all! As more of us passed our tests in such diverse skills as night-compass marching, estimation of distances by night and day, swimming one hundred yards fully clothed, rope-climbing, drilling, running, or grenade throwing, pressure was put on us to help those in difficulty. The competitive element that had been constantly encouraged between the sections, platoons, and especially the four companies, meant that we had to spend all of our precious spare time helping train the weaker runners, or those like me in trouble with the ropes. There was a developing urgency in us to ensure that our immediate superior, Corporal Gowans, be shown to his immediate superior, the Sergeant, to be doing an outstanding job with us. Exactly when this unexpected transformation in attitude, from hatred and distrust to respect and admiration had occurred, we could not say. We had, however, formed a bond with the Corporal to the extent that we now wanted to win the section and platoon prize for best drill and best dress for him, rather than for any other selfish, personal, or other collective reason.

Other changes had also emerged. Taking rifles apart, loading magazines, or polishing shoes, became a competitive game we began to enjoy, rather than remain the hated chores they had once been. Eight or ten of the best runners would take out the fatties and pace them around the perimeter of the camp to ensure improvement and an acceptable running time by them, while some boxing and working with weights was suggested by others to assist those like me cope with the rope. Six weeks earlier, we would have thrown up in disgust at the thought of voluntary physical exertion. Now we did it fairly contentedly, in the belief that we were doing the section, the platoon, and the company some possible good by such effort. The ulterior, backhanded training methods employed were working superlatively well.

Having portrayed themselves as emotionless automatons in the early part of our training, our instructors now began to show that a real, human side to their characters actually existed. Instead of barging into the hut, upturning beds and leaving with a snarl as though they had just encountered inferior, alien life forms that had to be trodden underfoot, corporals and sergeants actually spoke to us as if we were of this Earth. They began to show an interest in such things as the fact that Warren was married only a few weeks before enlistment and was therefore suffering more than most from homesickness, or that Richard's parents were facing ruin as a result of drought on their orchard in the Goulbourn Valley. Perhaps they had known all along that Jim's mother was seriously ill, or that Shane's younger sister had won a scholarship to one of the best girls' schools in the state, but they had never acknowledged that we actually had a private existence outside the army and had never shown the slightest degree of interest in anything but that which lay within the bounds of the Puckapunyal camp. For the first time they asked, listened, and at times even opened up about their own private situations.

We had been deliberately treated, for a short period, as specimens on the lowest rung of the evolutionary ladder and now that there was a relaxation in this very strict and suffocating regimen, we felt almost honoured and certainly thrilled to listen to them tell us about their recent army experiences. This subtle, yet clever shift in treatment style was not only greatly appreciated, but received the expected response in the form of much greater efforts on our part. They followed the old saying that they could, 'Kick us in the guts till we bled and hurt, for after that slaps on the face would feel almost like congratulatory kisses.' They were bloody clever, all right! They knew how to get results.

This new attitude was, however, carefully monitored and rationed so that it was actually nothing more than a changed teaching tool. Care was taken so that this new familiarity would never actually border on intimacy. The instructors were still very much in charge and continued to remind us of that fact. At the end of a half an hour of seemingly friendly conversation, we were still required to stand to attention as they left, with the customary reminder that inspection would, of course, be held as usual in the morning.

While the individuals with the most influence upon our daily existence were undoubtedly the section corporals, it often seemed that there were more Chiefs than Indians on our reservation and that every adult whose path crossed ours was an instructor or a superior of some description. As such, they were either to be saluted or not or perhaps avoided, if at all possible. It took us a long time to become accustomed to the hierarchy of ranks and the protocols appropriate to each.

As recruits, we were definitely on the lowest rung of the ladder. We knew it because the notion was repeatedly reinforced in our training. We also knew that at the end of basic training we would be promoted to the second rung comprised of almost similarly unimportant low lives as privates, bombardiers, signalmen or sappers. Only the names differed, but these were all still the lowest ranks in the particular Corps to which we would be ultimately assigned. The third rung was occupied by the non-commissioned ranks who wore their rank insignia on the sleeves of uniforms. This group comprised the lance corporals, corporals, sergeants and staff-sergeants, whom we had to address by rank, never call 'sir', and were not ever to salute. This mob's higher echelon was made up of the Warrant Officer group, Classes 1 and 2, who had to be addressed as 'sir', but, again, never saluted.

Above them on some Olympian pinnacle which was beyond our current view, sat the commissioned ranks that were always to be addressed as 'sir' and absolutely always to be saluted. This group included Second Lieutenants, Full Lieutenants, Captains, Majors, Colonels, and even some higher immortal beings upon whose lofty ranks we were not yet allowed to ponder. Commissioned officers wore rank insignia proudly on their shoulder epaulettes. Whenever we moved around the camp area, it was always difficult in those early weeks to decide whether to salute, march stiffly to attention without saluting, say 'sir', call the officer's rank, or simply say nothing in the hope that by being silent we wouldn't be noticed. Unfortunately, we never went unnoticed and many were the push-ups and other various penalties we paid for erring in our choice of response.

There was one individual, however, who didn't leave us in two minds about how to respond when he approached. Of all the non-commissioned officers we met at Pucka, the weather-beaten face of this one stays most vividly in my memory. He was the highest ranked non-commissioned officer of the RTB, in charge of all drill and parades. On our third day at Pucka, when we were still petrified and uncertain about most things that occurred, the whole battalion of all recruits was assembled in a hall. We were ordered to sit at attention with fists clenched, one resting on each knee, with backs and shoulders as straight as we could make them. After some minutes, by which time this unnatural pose and the silence of the room had become quite weird, an abnormally erect and sombre figure strode loudly to the centre of the stage. He made an extraordinarily exaggerated left turn and slammed his right foot into the wooden planking as he spun around to face the quivering lumps of jelly seated before him in the auditorium. His bearing, manner, and awesome presence with shiny yardstick under his left armpit made us fear him without even knowing why we ought to.

He boomed in a deep baritone, 'During these ten weeks and in the months to follow, you will come across men of many ranks whom you will obey because they are your superiors. I, however, am the Regimental Sergeant Major of this battalion and I am the closest thing to the Almighty you will ever meet in this army!'

The RSM seemed to look at each of us personally as he expressed this undeniably simple thought, and the look in his eyes appeared to challenge us to doubt its sincerity. Charlton Heston playing Moses, commanding the parting of the Red Sea could not have uttered the words more forcefully or convincingly. We immediately believed and accepted the RSM's exalted station in life and trembled whenever our paths crossed. We never ever made the mistake of saluting him, or of forgetting to call him 'sir' – very loudly!

Chapter 7

'Company! Attention!'

Left legs are lifted with a jerky motion and the thighs brought parallel to the ground. Then, as if on loaded springs, left feet are driven back into the ground and a simultaneous movement of the right arms bring the rifles from their forward-leaning positions to be vertically in line with the body.

'Company! Shoulder Arms!'

Right hands fling rifles upwards, left hands shoot across in front of the body and grab the barrels, while the freed right hands clutch rifles near the stock, with barrels now resting against the right shoulders. Followed by a mental count to two, left fists fly back to be dangling on the left side of the body.

'Company! Dressing by the right! Right dress!'

The front row of each platoon takes one step forward. A pause to the count of two and left arms shoot horizontally outwards, marking off the required arm's length between each man. A pause to the count of two is followed by an orderly but swift shuffling of boots on gravel as each man casts strained and furtive glances ahead to perfectly align with the body in front. This is done while keeping the face turned to the right, similarly aligning the torso with those to the right.

'Company! Eyes front!'

As one, all arms in the front row drop and heads snap back to face the front again. The company is now in perfectly straight rows of three, ready for the inspection.

One can watch with admiration the apparent ease with which a skier descends a slope, the skill with which a rally car driver negotiates a difficult curve or the agility with which a hurdler clears the obstacles ahead. The practitioners of these arts display a degree of readiness and of ability which only comes from the confidence that prolonged practice and repetition have taught. The ease of the performance is in the viewing and not in the execution. So it was with our drill. The turns, wheels, synchronised pumping of arms, stops and the interspersed motionless periods of a military parade might seem simple, but only to the viewer, not the performer.

Similarly, when cars line up at the red lights of a traffic signal they are in single file. When the light turns green, the first car moves off, to be followed a moment later by the second, then the third and so on. But what would be the likely outcome if each of ten drivers in a single file engaged gears and tried to move off at the same moment that the light turned green? Chances are that many bumper bars would need radical repairs. Not so, however, with professional driving teams who practice their art and that particular manoeuvre, and perform it successfully. To get ten, fifty, or twelve hundred recruits to step off simultaneously with their left feet on command and to do it successfully without a crashing of bodies is very much a learned and practiced skill.

Starting as sections, then platoons, companies, and finally as the whole battalion, our incessantly repetitive drill sessions had been designed to achieve the dual aims of making us act and behave as a single unit and to ensure that we could perform successfully during the two-hour parade marking the end of basic training. Now, in the eighth week, the four companies joined for the first time so that the battalion could try to strut its military stuff. With the RSM on the rostrum at the front, in charge of all traffic and indicating with yardstick the direction the official party would take, we again went through the double circumnavigation of the battalion parade ground, first in slow and then in quick time. Even from within the body of the march, it felt good and at the end we thought we had done well. Satisfactory for us, however, meant that it was barely passable for the RSM, so after doing it once more, we were promised we could have seconds or thirds the following day and every day thereafter until he thought it was satisfactory. With the march-out being only two weeks away, we didn't mind the threat, the heat, the flies, or the dehydration and exhaustion that saw a number of us faint. The end was tantalisingly in sight.

28.3.67

In the last few days we've had the tests. Rifle and sub-machine gun are OK; I scored forty-two out of a possible fifty. In PE the 100 yards, long and high jumps were good, but the rope got me. I actually made it to the top and down, but the second time got only halfway and just hung there like a helpless, skinned carcass until I slid down. I'll have to do it again.

The platoon is working well and our drill is fine. The march-out, which will be on television, will give us orgasms when we see it and those are the sergeant's words, not mine. The fruitcake you sent disappeared in minutes when the boys got a whiff of it.

This morning was a scream. We had to attack and capture an enemy position while under fire. An old Owen Gun was firing live ammunition about ten yards above our heads while we crawled and cut our way through mud, water, cow patties, wombat droppings and barbed wire to get to the objective. Small explosive charges were set off as we passed certain points. My ears are still ringing. We got mud up the barrels, not to mention ears and nostrils. You should have seen us at the end of this! A more pathetic, bedraggled lot was never seen. A photo would have been worth taking.

It's still damned hot and last Sunday's laziness was repaid with an early morning compass march and a three mile run. On the run, corporal thought Barry wasn't trying hard enough, so he loaded his backpack with rocks. Barry carried an extra stone and a half and he was totally buggered, pretty much like the rest of us. My bed was shortsheeted again last night, but I know who's doing it, I'll get him back.

One of the boys is on a charge! He got two weeks confinement to barracks and a $30 fine – something to do with illegal visits to the married quarters and not his own I might add. How did he have the opportunity, time or the strength is what we're wondering. We're also getting a bit uptight about the Corps we'll be given! I'm of course hoping and praying it won't be Infantry! I'm not the only one! Incidentally, Barry cannot get home to Adelaide this weekend and I hope it's all right if he comes home with me?

See you at the weekend and then at the march-out...

Chapter 8

Barry came home with me for that final weekend's leave and we spent a wonderful Saturday night together. Neither of us was terribly worldly, but feeling particularly taut and terrific in our uniforms, we borrowed the family car and drove into the city in search of some action. After an obligatory walk around the block, which in Melbourne consists of the square bounded by Swanston, Elizabeth, Bourke, and Collins Streets, we decided to have a few drinks at the London Hotel, which boasted a Saturday night band, a dance floor, and had the reputation of offering potential female companionship. As thousands before us and no doubt a similar number after, we soon left the London consoling ourselves in the firm belief that traditionally, sailors had always been more successful in matters related to the ladies than soldiers anyway. By ten o'clock, the city had reached its accustomed dead and dreary state and, with St Kilda providing the only remaining nightlife, we headed that way.

The bond of friendship between us had sprung from an altogether small and unimportant incident that had taken place weeks earlier. To ensure that we would be as healthy as possible should we ever be sent to fight overseas, we were inoculated against smallpox during the early weeks of training. The effect of this injection causes only slight discomfort in young children, but is much more debilitating and taxing on adults. As it was, I happened to be one of the few to have already received a smallpox needle as a child, prior to migrating to Australia in 1956. Consequently, the effect of this booster on me was negligible, causing nothing more than a sore arm and a slight headache. Many others, Barry included, developed high fevers, painful sores, dizziness, and an extreme lethargy. Nonetheless, training with its customary physical demands continued unabated for all, with many of my friends vomiting, some fainting, and suffering substantially in the days that followed the injection. During this period, I helped a few close mates, polishing their boots, pressing their greens and cleaning their rifles to take some of the pressure off them. Barry responded very positively to this act of friendship and, as a result, we became what is colloquially known as best mates.

The friendship was at its best and most open this particular Saturday night and we shared jokes and spoke about the events of the past and the coming weeks as we drove towards St Kilda. Within days, we were to be assigned to a Corps and there was some uncertainty in our minds about what that would entail. Sharing mutual concerns about what might lie ahead was a great help. We became more serious very quickly as a Fitzroy Street strip joint beckoned. Emblazoned in large letters out the front we could see TITS painted on the window, standing for the more innocuous name of 'This Is The Spot.' Following a lengthy period of titillation, the audience was rewarded with a very scant glance at an uncovered breast, after which the dancer or performer was quickly ushered off stage, as though a hungry mob would attack and ravish her if she stayed too long. It was tacky, but for us at the time it was breathless entertainment and we were delighted to pay the price of admission. We drank some more, ate the food dished up by bored waiters and then walked along the Lower Esplanade above St Kilda Beach before going home. Given everything that we had been through during the previous two months, it was, in all respects, a great night of fun and comradeship.

Barry and I were both assigned to the same Corps, the Royal Australian Engineers. Consequently, there wasn't a total parting of the ways, even though he went to Wodonga for Corps Training and I was sent to Sydney. We corresponded several times in the immediate months after Pucka, but there was inevitability about the ending of the friendship, as there would be about many others I would make during the two years. Years later, Barry and I met again in civilian life as surveyor and teacher, respectively. While there was still mutual respect and remembered fondness, the closeness of that Saturday night was unfortunately long gone and was never recaptured.

The news that I had been posted to the RAE provided one of the happiest and most relieving moments of the entire ten-week basic training period. I had dreaded the prospect of becoming an infantryman – or 'grunt', as they were affectionately called. Not only were infantry regiments in great demand for overseas service, but the physical demands of the corps training and eventually of the job itself were infinitely worse than that which we were just completing. I was sufficiently honest with myself to recognise that I was not the physically-endowed specimen who could handle those rigours easily. Thankfully, the army in its wisdom had also noted these shortcomings of mine and I was thrilled to accept its decision that made me a Sapper in the Engineers, rather than a Private in the Infantry. I was not the sole, thankful recruit that day.

Understandably, those receiving the news that most of us had feared were philosophical. They reasoned that the die had already been cast on 1 February when they were conscripted, so being made a grunt simply meant that their fortunes had reached their lowest ebb and could only improve from that moment on. While that reasoning helped to soothe hurt feelings temporarily and camouflaged anger that often bordered on despair, for many, this conclusion unfortunately turned out to be inaccurate. Within months, we read of the death in Vietnam of one of our friends from the seventh intake who had been posted to an infantry regiment.

For those very few who had taken to the army as a duck takes to water, the infantry posting was welcome news, for they had already resolved to re-enlist after two years and had military careers in mind. In any case, I suspect that genuine opinions and feelings were suppressed and under tight control that day as we either congratulated or consoled each other about what had been mapped out for us. I, for one, wanted to scream my delight at the top of my voice!

Unlike most workplaces in which the majority of labourers are at the coalface performing the precise job for which the organisation exists, the army is a ponderous and bottom-heavy system, resembling a squat, wide-based pyramid. We were informed as part of our early orientation that to support each infantryman fighting in the front line or those at the apex of the pyramid required at least seven others behind the lines – those at its base. The cooks, the drivers, the signalmen, the engineers, the clerks, the plant operators and even the doctors and dentists in uniform performed their travail for the sole purpose of keeping those fighting men in the front line. Thus, a very large and complex organisation existed to support the smaller band of fighting troops, which was the active Infantry force. It was for this reason, we were told, that conscription was necessary and introduced by the government in the first place.

Thoughts about army composition and political objectives were far from our minds, though, on Sunday, 9 April 1967. We were marching out, determined simply to impress the huge gathering of family and friends who had positioned themselves around the parade ground. Thousands had come, many from interstate. Those closest who had farewelled us on 1 February were there, as well as the grandparents, uncles, and friends who came to show their support. We dearly wanted to show them just a small portion of what we had been doing during those recent, difficult weeks. As promised, television crews were on hand, reporters buzzed the area, and even the weather was forgiving in providing just a warm, rather than an unbearably hot day. We were going to be magnificent, we had been told, and I believe it was a grand sight, even if I could only judge so from within the body of the march. Watching Andrew's march-out as a spectator months later, I was impressed by the co-ordination of movement to music, the colour, the crunch of boots on gravel, the looks beneath slouch hats, but especially by the pride beaming from those serious faces. This was the culmination of ten weeks of bloody hard yakka, after all, and pride was the most fitting and obvious emotion.

The parade was not without incident. During the long period of 'at ease', which lasted for an hour while speeches and inspections were made, two of our number fainted. Much to the initial amazement and eventual disgust of onlookers, they were left prostrate on the ground until an opportune moment presented itself and marshals collected the boys. I seem to remember that two rifles were dropped and hastily retrieved as fingers became numb holding onto them for so long. I discerned an icy intake of breath from the platoon sergeant as one of our rifles hit the gravel, but we smiled inwardly with smug satisfaction, knowing that he couldn't rant and rave at the miscreant on that occasion. We knew, though, that he would afterwards! Although my group, 7 Platoon of B Company, had made a fair fist of the parade, we didn't win the prizes for best platoon or company, which was disappointing, but I was certainly proud to have been a part of the whole process that had brought us this far.

The wise old heads among the spectators were still seen to be nodding their silent approval. The army had changed us considerably in a very short time. Undeniably, it had made us fitter, probably healthier, more self-reliant, and confident, while totally accepting of the dependence we now had on one another. We were certainly regimented, but in a constructive, positive way.

The transformation was complete.

We were soldiers.

Chapter 9

We knew that the previous weekend had been our last leave from Pucka and that in about three days we would be moved to various destinations around the country for Corps Training. Those of us going to Sydney or further north were also told that the day of the march-out would be the last opportunity to spend time with family and friends. For the first time, however, we were allowed to show family members around and in the huts which had been such a large part of our lives till then. A light lunch was also provided for everyone in the mess.

As I was showing my family and friends through the hut, I laughed out aloud when my mother suggested that I should go to the orderly room and ask if I could have leave that night. I assured her that this was simply not possible. Her further serious insistence that I do so began to worry me, especially when she went outside and made moves in that very direction, saying that if I wouldn't, then she would go and ask. When I physically tried to hold her back and explained that it was simply not possible for anyone to have leave that day, she finally confided that leave had in fact been prearranged for me. I didn't and then couldn't believe what I was hearing!

On the one hand, the thought of spending another night at home before going to Sydney was fantastic, yet we had been specifically told that leave would not be granted to anyone. My mother's strange behaviour was soon made clear when she explained that the special circumstance of my twenty-first birthday being in six days time had been considered and accepted some weeks earlier by the Commanding Officer as grounds for special leave. Without my knowledge, the family had arranged this wonderful surprise. I was ecstatic, for I truly had been granted one night's leave.

I left the orderly room with the overnight pass clutched in my sweaty palms. A slight twinge of guilt accompanied me on the trip to Melbourne, for as far as I knew, I was the only one from the platoon to leave Pucka that day. I had intermittent visions of the wind-down following the march and what the boys would be doing after their visitors had left.

My parents had invited a huge number of friends and relatives who crowded into our home. That evening and subsequent night were full of emotion, some happy, some not, but everything about the occasion was loud. A mountain of food, plenty of drink, music, and dancing, made for a very memorable coming of age party.

A rather subdued and tired crew of three of us arrived back in camp a few minutes before my leave ran out at six the next morning. My father and I were particularly tired but happy, while a family friend who had done the job of driving us wanted to hurry back and continue proceedings at the party. The hut was freezing when I entered and I felt a little off-balance and guilty again in spite of the greetings and friendly questions about the birthday party. For the first time since 1st February, I had not been involved in whatever everyone had done the previous night and I didn't know how things had worked out after the march-out. That bothered me and was the cause of my unease.

There was a bustle of activity going on as the boys were beginning to clean the barracks and pack. Also, for the first time that I could recollect since that starting day in February, everyone was wearing a jumper, for the weather had changed and the hut was strangely cold and uninviting. Things might have looked the same, yet they felt disturbingly different.

Mentally, I think we had already started leaving Puckapunyal behind.

PART B

SME: School of Military Engineering – Corps Training

Chapter 10

One by one, the groups were summoned over the loudspeaker. Grabbing brown sausage bags into which we had stuffed the sum total of our current worldly belongings, we threw a thumbs-up sign to those having to wait a bit longer, and were gone. First to leave were those going to Adelaide. Then, those headed to Hobart boarded trucks which took them to catch their respective train connections in Seymour. In true army fashion, we were hounded out of bed at six with the warning that a great deal had to be done that day, so we needed to hurry. 'Make haste and do things slowly,' was a motto the army could have adopted with all sincerity as its recruiting slogan. We were ready by seven. The first to leave didn't depart until eleven and, as it happened, the largest contingent – which included my group heading to Sydney – left at two in the afternoon.

The final departure from Puckapunyal was an anti-climax after the high emotion of the march-out. It was also quite subdued, for we hadn't realised the strength of the bonds of friendship that had been forged until it was time to depart. The knowledge that, in all probability, we wouldn't see each other again made the farewells more difficult. In the end, most of us chose to say very little, but simply picked up bags and walked out when it was our turn. We didn't even bother to exchange addresses or make arrangements to meet sometime in the future. This was best left undone and we accepted whatever fate had in store for us during the remaining twenty-two months.

A train had been reserved to take the many hundreds of us to Sydney and, with eight squeezed into a cramped compartment, we couldn't sleep. Mostly we talked, smoked altogether too much, and played cards. At Central Station in Sydney the next morning, we were further separated into different groups and buses heading to various destinations and camps around the Harbour City and we also said goodbyes to those going further north to Brisbane. Two buses made the hour long trip to Liverpool, south-west of the city, to the rather grandly-named 'School of Military Engineering' – or SME as it was better known.

There was a remarkable difference between our arrivals at SME and Puckapunyal some months earlier. Pucka had been hot, isolated and the reception hectic and almost frightening, while everything at SME was totally different. The school itself was just one of a number of army establishments outside the township of Liverpool. It was within walking distance of such dearly missed things as shops, pubs, and female pedestrians, while also possessing other reminders of a normal way of life like cars, traffic lights, footpaths, and people who wore clothes that were coloured something other than green. The weather at this time of year was comfortably cool and the corporals who met us as we got off the buses were actually civil in their welcomes. We thought we were suddenly in heaven yet immediately wondered how much longer such bliss could last.

The physical appearance of the place was also quite pleasant. After passing through the imposing front gate, we drove up a tree-lined avenue of about a hundred yards and negotiated a roundabout, in the centre of which were planted some roses. Beyond those, the road continued further ahead and we could see barracks on either side. The officers' mess was to the left at the roundabout and to the right was a neatly parked array of plant equipment, the size and like of which I had not seen before. Huge bulldozers, front-end loaders, and graders were lined up in true military fashion, with not a wheel, scoop, or blade more than an inch out of line with any other. The small parade ground, our mess, and some classrooms were set behind and amongst the barracks. In all, the camp presented a pleasing aspect of manicured lawns and well-tended shrubbery. There had been some rain earlier that morning and the moist pines that receded towards the back of camp gave off the delightfully fresh scent of a forest. The hot, windy, and dry desert that was Puckapunyal seemed a long way away.

The comfortable barracks also added to our generally relieved state of mind. Unlike the tin-roofed, prefabricated huts at 2RTB, we found ourselves in a substantially large, solid, double-storied building. One half of the ground floor comprised a common room with chairs that actually offered some degree of comfort and a table tennis table, dart board and television that promised the possibility of recreation. The rest of that floor and the upper level comprised the dormitories. To cap off these gloriously unexpected luxuries, the rooms were set up for two men in each so that we could finally enjoy a bit of that elusive element called privacy that we had lost so suddenly on 1st February.

After the obligatory parade and roll call, we were assigned

to particular barracks and rooms and only then did we come across the single disappointment of an otherwise perfect day. Our opposite numbers from the 7th intake, New South Wales, 1 Recruit Training Battalion had arrived some hours before us and had already been given some of the choicer rooms nearest the showers. This, though, could not spoil the positive feelings which the place generated. The rest of the day was ours, the first full parade for 1 Troop of the Engineers Corps Training Squad having been called for seven the next morning. After lunch, we tried out the ping pong table, immediately drew up a roster for a knockout competition, and played some darts. These very simple pleasures enjoyed in the army's time provided us with great satisfaction. It was the first working day in ten weeks that we had been given, without reservation, to pass alone and without military harassment. By early evening, the Victorian contingent was dead tired from the previous night's travel and we drifted to bed early, feeling quite comfortable and confident about the next day.

15.4.67

Before going on about anything else, many thanks for the party. It was a great surprise and I just hope that you're not still working cleaning up the mess. I'm 21 today! I said my farewells to Barry and Wayne and if they're as happy at their new place as I am here, then all is well with them. We didn't see much of Sydney itself, but apparently there is more opportunity for leave here than there was at Pucka, so we'll see some of it soon.

SME looks great with green bushland in the middle and a river a few hundred yards behind us. I'm sharing a room with a boy from Hobart. We've hardly had time for introductions, but we'll get along fine. Incidentally, the boys at Pucka knew that I had left to go home for the party. They bought me the Parker pen I'm using to write this letter. They were great! I'll see you as soon as it's at all possible.

Chapter 11

'Three days ago, you were the scum of the army. You were recruits. You've proven yourselves to be worthy of the uniform you wear and now you're soldiers, but I assure you that you're not yet worthy of being called Sappers. In the next ten weeks it's my job to make sure that you also earn the right to bear the title of Sapper in the Australian Corps of Engineers.'

Those were roughly the words thrown at us by Warrant Officer Polkinghorne at seven the next morning. There was a universal and just audible groan of *here we bloody go again*. The starch must have been used by the gallons when his clothes were washed, for the creases in this warrant officer's shirt and trousers looked sharp enough to slice bread. If we had formulated any sudden misconceptions during the previous day that Corps Training was to be a holiday camp, those were soon dispelled. We were again back in their clutches, back at the mercy of instructors and physical fitness fanatics.

Our complete situation was laid out clearly during the introductory lecture that very morning. The basics were behind us, but the specifics pertinent to the Corps of Engineers now had to be mastered. With a gloating in his voice that he hardly tried to suppress, the corporal informed us, however, that the basics would not be completely ignored. They would be further refined and even improved by the SME experience, he assured the Troop. I could distinctly hear anew the crunch of boots on gravel as he uttered these revelations about the close order drill we would have to continue.

In a nutshell, engineers in the army did two things as we were further informed.

'We build whatever is needed to be built and we blow up or demolish whatever is no longer required to be standing.'

The simplicity of the two notions contained in that statement made us smile at the time. The prospect of constructing things especially appealed to me because I was unfamiliar with any of the trades and what that work would entail, while the notion that we would be able to blow things up no doubt elevated the heartbeats of everyone listening at the time. On the surface, it sounded like a fun ten weeks ahead. Consequently, in the days that followed, we settled in at SME to learn about building and dismantling the things within the purview of the Royal Australian Engineers. The first thing my troop built was food. 1 Troop was given the first week's duty in the kitchens.

There were forty of us in the troop and ten of us, including me, were scheduled to work in the officers' mess, with the others having to slave away in the larger, enlisted men's mess. If ever there was a convincing recommendation or a positive incentive for becoming an officer in the armed forces, it would have to be for the cuisine offered to them. They certainly ate well. The quality of the ingredients, the preparation, and presentation, were all first class. Well-schooled army chefs worked in spotless surroundings on prime cuts of meat, daily delivered fresh vegetables and dairy products, preparing a la carte meals for the very few mouths that visited this mess. The plates that we delivered to the tables were attractively and artistically presented, as we young sappers in training, wearing funny little white waistcoats and pretending to be qualified waiters added that further touch of class while serving the officers.

As a child, my favourite cartoon character had always been the hapless Sad Sack. I greatly enjoyed reading about his unchanging fortunes, as after each misdemeanour which he could never avoid, he was given KP duty by the sergeant, which invariably involved the peeling of mountains of potatoes. But just like the prison inmate who discovers that his work on the inside will never involve the manufacture of car number plates – another childish misconception of mine – I was amazed to find that I didn't have to peel a single potato.

A contraption – not unlike the spin dryer on a washing machine trough – did the peeling for us. In the main, we cleaned, washed, vacuumed, served at tables, swept, and were treated as cheap, hired help by the cooks, much the same as we had been thought of by the cooks at Puckapunyal. The glaring and important difference here, however, was in the far superior quality of the pots and their contents, which we got to sample before and after each meal. The work itself was easy, but the hours again very long, with most of us on duty an hour before breakfast, and having to stay until everything was packed away and tidied after the evening meal. The grind continued during that first week and it felt just like the dawn-to-dusk hounding to which we had become accustomed and had been part of life since 1 February. It was now nearing the end of April and we had only enjoyed four complete rest days since enlistment. I was beginning to think that my two years would be spent either in a kitchen or on a parade ground, doing some senseless, repetitive task. This changed abruptly the very next week and some semblance of sanity returned to life.

With the commencement of the training itself, our days now ended at half past five and we were free from then until six in the morning. After eleven weeks of strict regimentation during which every hour of the day was planned out for us, we at first had difficulty occupying ourselves in these new, free hours. It was almost as if we had forgotten how not to be on edge, how not to be expecting a surprise inspection and how to act when there was nothing that needed immediate attention – in short, how to relax. The lights of Liverpool beckoned, as did those of Sydney itself, and we began to make trips to both. After seeing the Harbour Bridge, King's Cross, Paddington, The Gap, and other tourist spots two or more times, we ended up staying in camp both to save money and to study for the weekly tests. As at Pucka, the sword of Damocles was hung above our heads. A standard had to be met and tests passed satisfactorily, or we could expect to have to repeat specific weeks or indeed the whole ten-week course if that was necessary. To a man, we didn't wish this even on our greatest enemy, so the required effort was put in by all to ensure a successful march-out from SME on 14 June. What lessened our load on this occasion was the fact that, by now, most things we did had become, by force of army dint, a collective effort which made their successful completion an easier task.

26.4.67

The waiters' outfits we wore in the officers' mess were in use again yesterday. About sixty retired engineers came to SME to celebrate Anzac Day and to have a really good lunch. The majority of the group was made up of WWI veterans who were too old to take part in the city march. We felt a little guilty about our own complaints as we listened to them recount tales of their hardships and sacrifices so long ago. Some were in uniform and were they ever proud-looking and ramrod straight as the Last Post was played! I was glad to have been rostered to wait on them. It was a privilege.

Twice now, you've hinted in your letters that I don't write enough about the actual work we do, so I made a copy of this six-week program from the notice board to give you some idea of the variety of stuff involved in this 'Engineering Corps' business of ours.

- Basic bridge building and watermanship, knots, hashings, hitches, anchorages, block and tackle, derricks, boat orders, paddling drills, improvised floatation.
- Equipment bridging and rafting, loading of stores both day and night, aluminium footbridge, site preparation.
- Water supply and purification methods, testing water for chemicals, tower construction using tubular steel.
- Mine warfare, igniter principles, mine sense, mine-laying and breaching, detectors, recovery of mines, booby traps and mechanisms.
- Demolitions, service explosives and their uses, safety precautions, electric ignition, fuse preparation, charge firing.
- Field defences, compressors, wiring drills, chain saws, field geometry, construction of weapon pits, sandbagging.

I honestly don't know what half of this means yet, but we all will soon enough I guess. There is also some talk about a mock-up of a Vietnamese village here in camp, which we'll get to see later, and of some heavy-duty demolition work we do in Week 5 according to the plan.

One of the guys I introduced to you in Pucka broke his ankle some days back when he fell off a bridge we were building. He's out of action for quite a while and will have to do the course with the next intake in July, the poor bugger!

My parents had obviously noticed an important missing element in the letters I wrote home and I remember discussing it with friends at the time. Rather than writing to our families about the details of our daily lives, which is what they wanted to know, our correspondence was somehow deliberately biased against army matters and favoured those things we did outside of working and training hours. We wrote about friends, about weekend visits, people we had met, money concerns, trips away, the next leave and consistently about the next visit home. Strangely, whenever work or training got a mention, the detail was always diluted, the description very balanced and, in all respects, gentler and more palatable than the harsher reality which existed. Whether this was done intentionally to shield our families and so minimise the worry they would have to endure about us, or to ensure that we didn't relive distasteful experiences by retelling them in our letters, is a matter for conjecture.

Undoubtedly, though, in my letters, even at this early stage, the emphasis was always on the next job, the next step, the future, and not on the quite unpleasant reality of the past or the present. Although not consciously stated verbally or found in the writing, I know that the mental countdown had already started.

Thirteen weeks had gone and about ninety were still left.

Chapter 12

Each troop was under the control and leadership of two corporals and one second lieutenant. Mine had been assigned an officer in his early twenties who was a physical fitness fanatic. He had developed an unfortunate passion for jogging. Late in the evenings, we would watch him footslogging past our barracks and out the front gate of SME into Liverpool Road. He would return an hour later looking almost as fresh as when he left. Rabbit, as we unkindly named him as a result of the jogging, put in quite a strenuous day by joining us for drill, calisthenics, long-distance running, and the other physical jerks and exercises that were part of our everyday life. We were amazed to see that on top of that, he voluntarily pushed himself further in this way. As the days passed and our confidence grew, it became part of our nightly entertainment to rush to the windows as he appeared and wave our encouragement for him to run even faster. He would wave back. Feeling particularly daring one night, some idiot yelled out to him to get his knees up higher as he ran. As this was what we were constantly told to do during our runs, we thought the comment was funny. Rabbit obliged by doing just as asked and we cheered him as he passed the roundabout on his way out of the school.

The shrill, unaccustomed sound of a whistle reverberated through the barracks as we tumbled out of bed to an almost forgotten yell.

'Get up, you sods. Outside in formation, running gear, three minutes. Move!'

We managed the task quite easily, for we hadn't lost the skills of dressing quickly and at a moment's notice. We wondered, however, what Rabbit could possibly have wanted at 5.30 in the morning. We really should have known better.

'I couldn't help noticing the degree of interest you've all taken in my running. As it happens, I not only run at night, but a few miles before breakfast as well. Lately, I've been feeling a bit lonely during the morning sessions. Since you gentlemen are not busy at this time of day, I'll allow you all to keep me company. In rows of three, left turn! Double time! Quick march!'

I guess we should have seen it coming all along. Perhaps that one person's comment might have been the decider, or perhaps Rabbit would have done this to us whatever the circumstance. It didn't really matter either way, because for some of the rest of our time at SME, we were fated to have the pleasure of accompanying Rabbit on his morning constitutionals. The worst part was that the other troops were not accorded a similar privilege and it bothered the hell out of us that they were able to stay in their warm beds until the more civilised time of six. Out the front gate, a left wheel and up a deserted Liverpool Road we would run, with Rabbit leading us, a pack of angry, almost snarling dogs, while he would call the tune with a distinct laugh in his voice.

'Gentlemen, we're turning around in ten minutes. Stop

yapping, Sapper Fox. You'll need that energy later. Isn't the air magnificent at this time of day? Take a deep breath! Just imagine how enjoyable breakfast is going to be! I can almost smell the bacon. Get those knees up, Sapper Illingworth! You know how important that is, don't you? After this tiny hill it's all downhill, gentlemen. Great feeling to be alive isn't it?'

He would rave on in this way during the course of each run and his use of the word 'gentlemen' only made his mockery more caustic and harder to accept. The mention of Illingworth made us all throw a stern and knowing glance in his direction. Illingworth just stared stoically at the ground passing under his feet.

Yet in spite of these taunts and the discomfort of the morning runs, of all the commissioned officers that we had come across to that stage, and certainly of all those with whom I had dealings during the two years, Rabbit was the one I respected most. He never expected anything of us that he didn't do himself. If a new manoeuvre or lesson was being taught, he would jump in ahead of the corporals to show us how it ought to be done, especially if it involved any danger with explosives or was a difficult, physically demanding activity. It was just a bit more painful therefore to have this officer bring against me the only charge that I ever copped. The same charge was levelled by Rabbit at about ten of us.

By mid-May, the mornings were quite cold and at 5.30 it was downright freezing. To be sure, we warmed up after the first half mile, but the business of jumping out of bed, pulling on shorts, waiting in the frosty air while everyone assembled and knowing, in particular, that ours was the only troop that had to do so, made the exercise doubly despised. Rabbit was a man of dependable habits. Once the run started, he would trot behind us for about thirty seconds and then sprint ahead to lead the column of threes out of the SME gates. He would then lead the rest of the way, looking back only occasionally to see that the troop was not spreadeagled all over the road. Then, as we re-entered the school, he would allow us to break ranks and a mad rush would ensue as we all tried to be the first in the showers. There was never another roll call at the end of the run. Thus we were provided with an opportunity to try to evade his daily torture.

Our table tennis roster was prominently displayed in the common room for all to see. Our 'beat the Rabbit' roster was not. This unwritten list showed which of us, on what days, would try to make up the last three in line when we were summoned for the run. These last three, jogging at the end of the troop would be out of Rabbit's view as we left the school grounds and at least two of them, if not all three, could nip behind the bushes that skirted the front entrance. After waiting for a minute till the troop was out of sight, they could then run back to the barracks for an extra bit of sleep. That was the theory and the plan, and for most of a week it was highly successful. About ten of us, including me, got the chance to outwit Rabbit and the system. We revelled in the sweetness of the victory. During the early part of the second week, however, we felt so confident that we tried to rescue five or six a day instead of three. It turned out to be our downfall.

Rabbit had apparently not noticed two or three missing from the group, but he was certainly awake to more. One day, he halted the troop, counted heads, and, realising that a certain number was missing, ordered an immediate march back to camp. Those who had ducked the run that morning were informed at breakfast that they were to be charged for disobeying a lawful command. When this became general knowledge, there was only one proper thing to do. We fronted

Rabbit and the others who had previously cheated him also owned up to that fact. He showed little surprise and only scant emotion, but did voice his disappointment, informing us that we were all going to be similarly charged. I felt worse for having cheated him than I did about the potentially costly consequences of the charge. I think we would all have preferred to hear him rant and rave, as was the usual custom of the other instructors. This man's calm acceptance of the facts was disarming and preyed on my conscience quite unexpectedly.

For the next few days, we dreaded the summons that we knew would require our presence in the Commanding Officers' rooms. Strangely, the call never came. We were certain that a fine would be the least of the penalties that might apply, while a period of confinement to barracks would be both a more distasteful and a more likely outcome. But the matter seemed to have been forgotten and none of us was eventually called to hear the charges laid against us during the remainder of our time at SME. We reasoned that Rabbit might have taken honesty into account and withdrawn all charges, or that his superiors might even have advised him that charging upwards of a dozen men over such a trivial matter might not be totally and militarily expedient. Whatever the reason, there was complete silence on the subject. Needless to say, none of us dodged the morning runs thereafter and, if anything, we now ran with a spirit and a gusto that wasn't there before. Rabbit looked around more often, we thought, but he needn't have. He had gained such a degree of respect from us that we would not have cheated him again.

Our two corporals were, we thought, in their mid-thirties and seemed very knowledgeable about matters related to the Corps. Without ever referring to notes, they instructed us in surprising detail on dozens of subjects as diverse as bridge building, water safety, tunnel excavations, fencing, road construction, mine-laying, explosives, as well as the more accustomed and by now truly hated skills of shooting, marching, and close order drill. Apart from the latter few, to me much of this was completely new, interesting, and informative.

I had always been a totally useless handyman at home. As young boys invariably do, I listened to friends who would rave on for hours about the universals and differentials on their cars, or the relative performances of Ford or Holden engines. While I nodded my head in polite agreement, I rarely knew what they were talking about. When working on cars, if one was to ask me to hand him a Phillips-head, I would probably reach for the spanner. I would look at an array of tools and almost certainly choose the wrong one for the job required. For me, working on a car meant washing it, vacuuming the inside and occasionally polishing the beast. I despised being covered in grease from hand to elbow. Things electrical were a complete mystery and the first time I successfully changed a fuse wire was a day I used to recall with immense pride. Out of ten nails, I would bend nine before driving one in straight, while a natural laziness restricted the amount of pick and shovel work I ever did. As a consequence, I rarely hammered, sawed, planed, or shovelled anything.

In short, the Corps of the Royal Australian Engineers got a real dud when my posting was made.

At SME, however, I wasn't given the chance of opting out of any part of the course, so like it or not, skilled or not, I competed with mechanics, carpenters and plumbers on their terms and in their particular fields of expertise. Initially I was – as I suspected I would be – a monumental failure. I had no trouble in passing the written examinations at the end of each week, but my practical performance with tools in the field was less than impressive. I could easily memorise the sequence of steps involved in the assembly of an eighty-ton Bailey Bridge and could visualise how the parts fitted together, but handling and actually bolting and attaching those parts in reality was another matter. Teamwork being the essence of any group activity however, I eventually found my niche in the gangs, as we spent many days in building and disassembling rope, aluminium, arc-mesh and other types of bridges. Although not a foreman or leading hand in any sense of the words, I used to organise, sort and call out the names of parts as they were needed and helped to carry them back and forth as others took care of the actual assembly. I supplied some brains and brawn, they the manual dexterity. I got an immense amount of satisfaction out of these sessions, perhaps more than the others did. They were accustomed to erecting, creating, and building different structures. But these were the very first things I had ever had a hand in constructing that didn't fall down afterwards.

The feeling was great.

Early in the morning, under the watchful eyes of Corporals Walsh and Bettiman, we would requisition the necessary parts from stores, load them aboard trucks, or carry them to the river behind the school. A section of the river was normally closed to civilian craft. We would spend the rest of the day seeing how many ways there were of getting personnel and equipment across the forty-yard stretch of water. Most of the bridges were assembled from parts that reminded me of a giant Meccano set. Precisely matching sections of footings, steel rods, wire mesh, and aluminium sheeting were held together by custom-made nuts and bolts. Pieces were never welded, for they needed to be taken apart at a moment's notice. Since the assembly was commenced and took place from one bank only, the ever-lengthening span we constructed snaked further and further out across the river, resting on pontoons placed at regular intervals. In this way, the structure finally reached the far bank. First, a few of us would walk gingerly across to test its strength and if it held, others followed. We would strut rather proudly from end to end admiring our work, basking in the afterglow of a successfully completed job. On occasion, a bridge didn't hold as an improperly secured section would falter when under stress. It was for this reason that several days were spent on water training, water confidence, and methods of rescue. We wore life jackets at all times, but cursed their bulk as they made movement and the work more difficult. By the end of two weeks when we graduated to the construction of the celebrated Bailey Bridge, eight-ton trucks could drive safely across our bridges in complete safety. We had cause for well-earned pride on those occasions.

The most unique and hair-raising bridge we built was relatively simple in design, easy to construct, and could be completed in less than an hour. It first involved two of us swimming or rowing across to the opposite bank, dragging two thin lines tied to our belts. These lines were attached to lengths of rope, which in turn were attached to thick, steel cables. When these cables were eventually hauled across and secured to two rigid posts on the far bank, the same was done at the points of origin. Thus we had two taut cables, about two yards apart, stretching from bank to bank, approximately a yard above the water. At this point, a jeep fitted with modified wheel hubs would manoeuvre onto the cables and simply motor across using its four-wheel drive, suspended just above the water. The sensation of moving across water in this way was fantastic, but we shuddered at what might have been if one of the cables, or both, had snapped or come loose. These cables could also be modified to support a swinging footbridge by reducing the lateral distance between them. Once this was done, specially moulded planks, grooved on one side to match the cables, were put on top one by one to form the path. It was often quite comical to watch others holding on for dear life, especially when a larger number tried to cross simultaneously. As more of us stepped on and were not sufficiently careful to avoid sideways movement, the initial sway of the structure became accentuated. Helplessly we would stand there as the period of the swing slowly increased and approached its zenith. There was nothing we could do to stop the outcome, as a correction to one side would inevitably result in an increased swing to the other. At such times, we often took a dunking and would fall in, accompanied by the raucous laughter of those watching from shore. It took us many attempts before we learned how many of us and how quickly we should move from one side to the other to counter-balance the sideways sway. Crossing these bridges was sometimes a more difficult process than assembling them, but it was always a lot of fun.

The weeks we spent in and around this river were most enjoyable and educational for me. At times, we froze on chilly mornings when our clothing got wet, but at such times all we needed to do was recall the heat of Puckapunyal and we felt better immediately. We even had the chance to motor up and down the river, piloting the three powerboats the school owned, something that very few of us had done before. Spirits were high. The room checks, drill, spit polishing of shoes and boots, push-ups and rifle practice continued unabated, but by then they had become almost second nature and not the all-consuming and troublesome chores they had been earlier.

After my third week in Sydney, I flew home on the weekend to surprise the family. I felt like the returning prodigal son. Winter uniforms had been issued, and unlike the battle dress which was modelled on the British army's outfit of the same name, our Australian dress uniform with its many shiny buttons was quite different and looked very smart. We had by now all developed a sense of great pride in our appearance and began to understand why so much emphasis was placed on correct dress. Taking pride of place on my uniform was the Engineers' lanyard; a dark woven cord placed under the right epaulette, with its loose end tucked into the right top pocket of the jacket. On the collar, just above the lapels were two, shiny, Engineers' insignia bearing the word 'Ubique,' the Latin word for *everywhere*, signifying that as Engineers we would serve in all places.

Again, I strutted, rather than walked past people at Essendon airport and Flinders Street Station. I was confident in my conceit that everyone was staring at me with envy and wished that they might be wearing my new magnificent threads.

Chapter 13

10.5.67

The plane arrived back in Sydney on time so that, by nine o'clock, I was on the train for Liverpool. I got to camp before midnight but didn't even unpack. Andrew is obviously uptight about his impending enlistment – he had a lot of questions at the airport.

Thanks for a great, although short weekend. If only they were longer and more frequent. We've been out on the boats again and spent two nights camping by and crossing the river on a variety of bridges we built at night. We really appreciated the shower after forty-eight hours in the bush! I told you about Mark who broke his ankle recently? A group of us will visit him in hospital this coming weekend. 4 Troop killed us yesterday in a basketball match. The score was 18 to 2.

The big news is that we need to start thinking about postings for after we leave here. Our preferences are restricted to Commands, such as Southern Command for Victoria, Eastern Command for New South Wales, and so on. I'll try for Victoria of course and if I'm successful it might be Pucka, Victoria Barracks, Broadmeadows, Richmond, etc. Hopefully, one of these will come through and I won't end up in Cairns or way over in Fremantle. We find out about these postings in about three weeks. I also hope that this is a wise decision, but I'll be asking for a clerical job. The problem is that even though I've got my matriculation, I don't have any trade qualifications or that much experience. Most of the guys here are plumbers or mechanics and their placement will be easier than mine. Unless I specify that I want a desk job, I might just end up in Cairns or Port Headland digging ditches for the monsoons or laying bridges across swollen rivers.

Anyway, I'll write more about that later. Wish Greg the best of luck for this weekend's fencing competition in Hobart.

My younger brother Greg, at fifteen, was already a very accomplished sportsman. Blessed with sharp eyes and extremely quick reflexes, he had made a name for himself in fencing, with two Victorian Junior Titles to his credit. Early in 1967, he had entered the Victorian Open Championships for the first time and won, and this was the forerunner, he hoped, of many Australian titles and his future wish to represent Australia at the Olympic Games. The Rabbit became quite interested in Greg's progress, when he discovered that the brother of one of his charges was so successful. It seemed that apart from his army duties and jogging, he also fenced on a competitive basis. God only knows when he had the time.

My roommate, Terry, also had words to say about Greg, although his were much less complimentary. The poor guy had not been home to Tasmania for over two months and he couldn't stand the thought of anyone else going there while he was unable to do so. He was rather put out, therefore, when I told him about the fencing tournament in Hobart to which Greg was going.

I don't think we ever used the word homesick in private conversation, nor any other word for that matter to describe the emotion, but the feeling was an ever-present reality. It didn't hurt like a toothache, there was no temperature or illness, but it was nonetheless a gnawing, persistent, and painful companion. To be sure, we were no longer children, but the longing for the friendlier, accustomed sights and sounds of home is not restricted solely to a child's realm of thought and perception. In spite of the relative freedom we now enjoyed at SME, the distances separating us from those with whom we most wished to be, were often damned in our hearts. In my case, 560 miles of Hume Highway kept me from Rae Street, East Bentleigh. For Terry, it was the same highway, with the Tasman Sea added for extra anguish. Homesickness was not a product of unhappiness, disillusionment, or even loneliness, but simply the result of our enforced separation from the families we missed. If, as civilians, we had made the conscious decision to move interstate for employment or for business reasons, the emotion would not have been such a significant part of our experiences. But ours was not a conscious, voluntary choice. That fact made all the difference and was, I believe, the genesis of some of the distrust and eventual hatred that developed in us against those who had missed, and in particular against those who had deliberately avoided the draft. They continued to live in the relative comfort and safety of a home, while we were forcibly removed from ours, put in some degree of danger, and ordered to perform tasks that we would not ordinarily have chosen to do. The blatant unfairness of that situation was a constant source of angst, nurturing suspicions and jealousies between 'us and them'. These emotions festered during the weeks and months that comprised our two-year stint.

Melbourne, in winter, is generally not a very pleasant place. Yet in the middle of the winter of 1967, I thought of her balmy summer nights, her tree-lined boulevards, her beaches, the football matches I was missing, the grandeur of St Kilda Road, and all the other attractive aspects she possessed. In particular, I thought of the family and friends that were a part of her, yet far from me. When at home, I seldom made the effort simply to walk up and down our street, but now I ached for that opportunity and felt sorely disadvantaged at being prevented from doing so. This wasn't childishness, petulance, or immaturity, just plain homesickness.

We didn't get around to visiting our friend in hospital the following weekend. An offer we could hardly refuse was put to three of us which we gratefully accepted. A boy from Melbourne who had flown down with me some weeks earlier had driven his car back to Sydney and decided to drive home again to surprise his fiancée. We were delighted to share the cost of petrol, so six of us in all set off on Friday night, quite content in the knowledge that of the next three nights, two would be spent travelling on Highway 31. We reached Melbourne at five on Saturday morning and hitched from the city in our respective directions with the understanding that we would be picked up from beneath the Flinders Street Railway Station clocks on Sunday night. That would give us about twelve hours to return to SME by morning roll call on Monday. The thirty-six hours spent at home, we reasoned, was indeed well worth the twenty-four spent in the car, given the surprise element of the visit.

It was still dark when I crept into the house that Saturday

morning and crawled quietly into bed without waking anyone. The family's joy at finding me there so unexpectedly the next morning more than justified the trip. Everything else happening that weekend just turned out to be an added bonus.

Three of us, accompanied by fathers, waited under the clocks of the railway station on Sunday night. We strained for a glimpse of the blue Holden in the heavy traffic passing along Flinders Street, but it was already an hour late. To say that we were becoming worried both for the welfare of our friend and our own hides should we end up being absent without leave would be understating the fact. The sudden, surprise visit home took on sombre and threatening undertones. A two-tone Ford pulled up in front of us and out jumped the familiar figure for whom we had been waiting. The poor guy had crashed his car on Saturday night and had to borrow his father's second car to get us all back to Sydney. Gladly, neither he nor his fiancée had been injured in the accident. As we drove away from the kerb several hours later than originally planned, I sent a silent prayer skywards in the hope that the rickety old bomb managed the journey safely and on time. It was a quarter to six as we drove through the SME gates and had fifteen minutes to strip, dress in greens, and be in time for roll call at six. In spite of the damage to the car, which was fully insured and eventually repaired, and our own exhaustion throughout Monday's sessions, we agreed that given the same circumstances, we'd do the journey again.

The weekend further reinforced the limitless nature of parental concern, love, and willingness to sacrifice for their children's welfare and why we missed them so much.

The content – and, therefore, the direction of the next fortnight's lessons – changed abruptly. The building and construction components of the course were superseded by their diametrically opposed notion. The question was in fact put to us. 'In how many ways can one destroy something by the use of explosives?' We studied the design and function of anti-tank and anti-personnel mines. We pored over books and films that dealt with the effectiveness of dynamite, TNT, and gelignite. Booby traps, Claymore mines, fuses, detonators, and detonating cord terminology occupied our minds. The highly specialised Bangalore torpedo, intended as a weapon for breaching barbed wire and concrete obstacles, was brought into class and we were treated to a lecture on the destructive capability and explosive force of a mixture of super-phosphate and diesel. Finally, we were shown some frightening examples of the explosive charges and booby traps that were currently in use in Vietnam. We sat through the lectures of those first few days, fascinated by what we saw and heard and tremendously eager to experiment with our newly discovered 'toys'. For once, I looked forward to the practical, rather than the theoretical test at the end of the week.

The nervousness with which I first handled a live mine was reminiscent of the same uncertainty with which I had thrown my first grenade. The potential power of the small lump of material in my clammy hands was enough to set the imagination racing. I conjured up a multitude of images that all dealt with maimed and splintered body parts, freely flowing blood, and shards of protruding bone. The fear of the consequences of what might happen if we should make a mistake was terrifying and it compelled us to be, if anything, overcautious and to follow instructions too literally to the letter.

At first, all our laying and lifting of mines was done with dummies. Our instructors, having taught the same procedures to many groups of Sappers previously, had the wisdom and foresight to ensure total competence on our part before we were allowed to handle the real things. We were taught about the tried and tested patterns of concealment of mines that had been successful in previous wars. To illustrate a point, the troop was told to walk across a sandy field. Having crossed, we had to look back and examine the tracks we left. The footprints revealed that we had automatically walked across the central part of the field and that we had followed each other, as sheep, in clearly defined lines as soldiers on the march often do. This was so apparent that on a sloping portion of the field, separate groups of us had even converged on each other and ascended in single file, footstep on footstep. The illustration showed that the laying and concealment of a minefield required deliberate planning and could be determined by such things as terrain, weather or even the type of enemy for whom the mines were intended. With the explosive contents and detonators removed, one half of the troop experimented by laying random, zigzag, circular or V-shaped patterns of mines and the other half would then attempt a crossing without setting any of them off.

It seldom did.

We made a game out of the first mine-laying session – which was only a practice –and lasted less than half a day. Like children playing Cowboys and Indians and shooting each other with pretend six shooters or bows and arrows, we cheered and clapped when one of our pretend mines zapped a member of the other half. As in all fair games, the other side then got its innings, and it was then our turn to try to stay alive. The seriousness of the whole exercise was soon brought home to us, however, as on occasion we would drop or accidentally step on a mine that we had laid. Apart from the vociferous and loud public admonishment from the vigilant corporals or Rabbit that this entailed, such accidents also showed the importance of care and the utter respect that mines and explosives demanded. It should be, as we discovered, by no stretch of the imagination, either funny or a game.

Locating, defusing, and lifting mines, though, became the epitome of tedium. We would inch forward hour after hour, bayonets in hand, prodding and probing the ground, searching for the metallic click that indicated a find. Muscles ached and sweat poured from foreheads despite the cold weather as we traversed the practice field. When one of us was 'killed' in this process, he would be removed from the exercise to watch the remainder trying to complete a crossing. It was an embarrassing and guilt-ridden removal, for the error had let the group down, but at times we hoped to be zapped, just so that we could stand up and ease the screaming pain in our legs. At times, only as few as eight might survive from an original twenty starters. It was an exacting, mistake-prone, and difficult exercise and we were only using dummies. Once located, the mine had to be exposed by the careful removal of soil covering it. Fingers were the most sensitive tools for this, while a shaving brush was handy for sweeping off the remaining loose dirt. With the plunger and detonator now visible, a pin was inserted below the plunger, which neutralised the mine. That procedure alone could take half an hour and steady hands were required. We were also told that the length of time the mine had been in the ground could even determine if the explosive contents of the casing had become unstable. Old, unstable explosive could blow in spite of the plunger being rendered inoperable.

We learned not only about mines and explosives in those few days, but also about our own patience, the degree of application we could bring to the completion of a task and about the exact levels where our frustration peaked, at which point we could no longer continue with any assurance of safety. The dangers lurking behind the type of work we were doing was highlighted on the third day by a demonstration of the real thing. Standing some hundred yards away behind barriers, we watched heavy metal panels thrown skywards as Corporal Bettiman detonated an anti-tank mine under several rusting car bodies that had been brought there for that purpose. The hollow thud of the blast reverberated from the building surrounding us and we felt the sudden shock wave pass through the air. There were no laughs and certainly no merriment by this time. We had witnessed, first-hand, the destructive nature of this powerful stuff and we were astounded by its power. The dual thoughts that we might have to do that to someone in the future, or alternatively to have someone do it to us, were totally sobering.

No less frightening were the anti-personnel mines, which looked very much like cans of baked beans one might buy at the supermarket – similarly sized but without the coloured labelling. If disturbed, they had sufficient explosive force to cripple a man. The more devious of these exploded upwards only, catapulting dozens of sharp metal fragments into the feet, upper legs, and abdomen. Perhaps the one we found to be the most objectionable was the spring-loaded type, which jumped out of the ground once the pressure of a foot had been removed from it. Then, at knee height, it exploded, cutting the victim's legs literally in half. Many of these had been found in the jungles of Vietnam and also hidden at the bottom of tunnels and wells. As we listened to these tales of horror, it wasn't at all reassuring to hear the corporals tell us that the enemy used such mines and 'immoral tactics' – whereas we did not. That subtle, moral distinction was, I think, lost on 1 Troop at the time, because to that point all our training and lessons had been directed towards learning about all those things that could kill and destroy the enemy. The manner of that killing and, more importantly, the 'legality or morality' behind it, had not entered our minds until that moment.

Chapter 14

The landscape resembled the moon's surface. The astronauts who we knew were training at NASA to walk on the moon had not yet managed that wonderful feat, but we had seen many photographs of the moon taken by orbiting satellites to be able to draw the comparison. Great grey craters were gouged out of the earth and car-sized clods of clay were scattered around. Boulders were balanced precariously on the oblique sides of trenches and the place was totally devoid of life. In one corner of this scene was an undamaged concrete bunker with a flagpole beside it and in the middle ground were shattered remains of other structures which had been ripped apart with great force. The bent and tortured steel reinforcements protruding from concrete slabs bore testimony to the strength of the blasts. Individual pieces must have weighed tons, but appeared to have been carefully placed in their present, leaning positions on the edges of craters and steep inclines. It was quite literally an alien-worldly sight.

We were at the demolition range some miles from SME in the hills outside Liverpool. Three trucks had transported us to this forlorn place, two of them carrying expectant Sappers eager to experience a 'big bang', while the third was loaded with the wherewithal that would create the bang. All three flew red flags and the front of the first and rear of the third were emblazoned with the words 'Danger' and 'Explosives'. Upon arrival, Rabbit immediately placed another red flag on the pole beside an undamaged bunker and we assembled there for final instructions. Basically, we were to put into effect that which we had been learning during the previous fortnight. The third truck contained varying quantities of TNT, gelignite, dynamite, mines, detonating cord, and Claymores. By early afternoon, we had to set these explosives at selected points around the range, insert the necessary detonators, link each charge using hundreds of yards of detonating cord and subsequently blow everything up. The result would show the effectiveness of each explosive, as well as our skills in their correct placement. This was a day for which we had been truly waiting.

Lessons during the previous week had touched briefly on the chemistry of explosives, as well as on their most productive placement and destructive capabilities. We were also made to handle live mines and dynamite to ensure that we had the confidence to work with them later on. There was an admission from the corporals and Rabbit that the day involved a considerable risk, but as one of them had said so eloquently when he noticed our reticence and nervousness with the stuff, 'What's the point of trying to get your driver's licence if you've never sat behind the wheel of a car and have never driven in heavy traffic or on slippery roads? Sooner or later you simply have to do it.'

With great trepidation at first, and then with slowly increasing ease, we handled the tubes of putty-like gelignite – which were relatively safe – and the cuboid-shaped blocks of dynamite which, if dropped, would have blown us into the next world. As part of his rehearsed act, Corporal Walsh scared the living hell out of us when he dropped a half stick of gelignite into a flame and yelled for us to run. Several hearts missed beats, but none more than mine as we scattered in all directions. As object lessons go, this was most successful because it proved the point that the stuff was really safe – that it could be cut, burned, or even hammered without harm as long as it wasn't jarred into life by a firing detonator. We felt relieved, foolish perhaps for having bolted, but had learned something new. The corporal pointed out very forcibly, though, that the same characteristics didn't apply to the other explosives with which we were working. So, after carefully unloading the truck of its unstable cargo, we split into three groups and set about the assigned tasks for each.

As we walked around the range and descended into craters, we saw evidence of earlier carnage. Some of the depressions were eight to ten yards in diameter and up to three deep. At the bottom were strewn huge slabs of concrete, with the tubular, steel re-enforcing jutting out menacingly in places where the slabs seemed to have been ripped apart by a giant hand, as easily as one might be able to pull apart soft tubes of putty. Some of them weighed tons and it was under the larger sections that we dug holes and laid our charges. Under the watchful gaze of Corporal Walsh, we hauled the explosives across this pockmarked surface to their final destinations. Having secreted several, one and two pound blocks of dynamite under a slab, we prepared another hole for gelignite.

To me, there seemed little rhyme or reason for the final positioning of charges, although one would have to assume that there was a master plan we followed. The real purpose of the day was to give us the experience and opportunity of handling and using explosives. That we certainly did. After inserting the required fuses, we moved to another crater to repeat the process. The three sections into which we'd been divided were each supervised by one of the instructors and while there appeared to be randomness in the way each operated, they took careful note of each charge, its placement, and accurate disposition. At the end of about four hours, scores of charges were set and ready for detonation.

In the afternoon, we were taken to a remote corner of the range for a special demonstration. A hundredweight bag of granulated super phosphate was poured into a deep hole after about two gallons of diesel had been hand-mixed through it. Loose soil was then placed on top and we dragged several larger pieces of concrete over to cover the area. A detonator and one end of a short length of detonating cord had been left in the mixture, the other end of which showed above the ground. It was now time to hook up every charge we had laid and to join all cords to one common point, in readiness for the finale.

Under normal circumstances, almost anything can serve as a fuse, from a rag soaked in petrol to gunpowder, or a normal, slow burner made from Hessian impregnated with wax or powder. The purpose of the fuse is simply to provide a small impetus or blast, which then sets off the main charge. The state of the art fuse at the time was detonating cord. This tubular, pliable material, about the same thickness as a pencil, didn't burn as most fuses do, but when activated by a small electrical input, exploded instantaneously along its entire length. Connected to a detonator inside other explosives, it caused those to blow as well. The exact statistic is debatable, but I remember being told that about a mile of this cord could explode in about three seconds. Wrapped a few times around the trunk of a tree, the cord alone could sever the trunk, felling the tree.

We spent the next couple of hours unravelling hundreds of yards of this detonating cord and connecting it to every explosive we had placed on the range. Starting from the super phosphate, we fanned out in three directions, weaving the cord in and out of the explosives so that ultimately two ends were brought back to the bunker. As a final addition to what we had done, two Claymores and a Bangalore torpedo were also hooked into the system. The Claymore was a devastating piece of work. Curved slightly, its plastic mass was impregnated with hundreds of tiny pieces of shrapnel similar to ball bearings. Being fairly small, it could be easily hidden near frequented paths. When detonated, the concave internal surface was blasted outwards in an instant, hurling the shrapnel forward at great speed. As such, it could cut off a man's leg or even disembowel him should he receive a direct hit in the stomach. To show us the effect, sheets of paper held up by sticks and some cans were positioned a few yards in front of the Claymores. The Bangalore was a tube about three yards in length and about four inches in diameter. The explosive was encased in this tube and, being long and thin, the whole thing could be pushed quite easily into a barbed wire obstacle or underneath a stone construction such as a gate or fence. Being a shaped charge, it exploded in an outward arc of 360 degrees.

When all was finished, everybody was ordered back to the bunker. The two loose ends of the detonating cord were wired onto a small generator. The roll was called again to make sure that everyone was present and the moment had finally arrived.

Corporal Bettiman rang the sentry at the front gate to inform him that we were blowing. He pushed a button on a control panel and a siren sounded. He then motioned to us to open our mouths and, as we did, he pushed another button. The noise was every bit as loud as I had expected. The sudden change in air pressure swept through the bunker and it felt as though it had passed right through one's body. The open mouths compensated for the sudden change in pressure that could otherwise have damaged our eardrums. I felt myself lurch slightly forwards and then back again as the force of the blast disturbed and rippled through the air. The ground reverberated as though a thunderbolt had burst above our heads and a moment later we heard its echo rebound from the nearby hills. Then it became deathly silent. The corporal pushed the button again to check if any charge had failed to explode, but there was no other audible response. We were ordered outside to examine the results of our labours.

At first glance, the range looked unchanged. Large craters and disturbed earth were everywhere as before. But as we ventured further, the changes became noticeable. We had just spent six hours trudging across this field and we had mentally noted the size, shape and location of holes and assorted mounds. Many were now larger, others not there at all. The concrete block in the centre had been picked up and hurled at least ten yards, for it was no longer hanging precariously on the edge of its crater, but lying on its side on level ground. As we moved to our respective thirds of the range, the changes became more apparent. The shattered slabs now looked even more grotesque as freshly twisted, rust-free shards of re-enforcing showed through in new places and moist, darker coloured earth wrenched from deep below was evident everywhere. It was both fascinating and frightening to pore over the changes that had occurred in the split second that the power was unleashed. We identified metal parts and concrete slabs that we had marked using particular colours twenty – and even thirty – yards from their original positions. Even some of those coloured markings showed the tortured results of being rent asunder. By far the greatest surprise was in the area where the superphosphate had been buried. The small hole we dug for it was now a yawning chasm at least five yards deep and about ten wide. We just stared in wonder and awe at the incredible obliteration.

Had we really done this and how could there be so much power in such small packages, were the thoughts that flashed through my mind.

We now believed and appreciated the lesson taught earlier that it wasn't so much the amount, as the type and accurate placement of the explosives that mattered. We had been taught that anything could be blown up if the charges were correctly chosen and properly laid. Finally, we looked at the sheets of paper and cans. The blast from the Claymores had dislodged some and they were lying on the ground, but the others were pierced by dozens of small, neat holes where the shrapnel had passed right through. An arc, radiating outwards from the spot where the mines had been placed, was mowed clear of grass by the shrapnel, as though a Victa had done the job.

I was quite perturbed by the destructive power I'd just witnessed and saw that my friends' minds were similarly heavy as we drove back to camp. We had just been given the knowledge, the ability, and the materiel, with which we could kill hundreds at one time. It was a disturbing discovery.

Happily, and for the first time, the Lieutenant didn't appear for our usual morning constitutional the next day.

We didn't mind at all.

Chapter 15

There being only a fortnight left before the end of Corps training, the emphasis shifted back again in favour of the basics. Marching, spit-polishing, kit and room inspections became more common as march-out day approached. There wasn't quite the same degree of urgency about it as there had been at Pucka, although Warrant Officer Polkinghorne kept us busy with the timing, the wheels, turns, and formations to ensure that all would go smoothly on the day. While 1200 had marched out at Pucka, only 160 were involved this time so, as a spectacle, the production would pale by comparison. To be sure, though, the Eastern Command Band was to play and personal invitations had been sent to families. There was also talk again of television coverage, so the belts, buckles, and keepers had to sparkle and the parade ground was manicured to perfection. But this time it felt different and the theatricals of the occasion, which had seemed so essential to us after basic training, were tiresome and we could hardly wait for it all to end. After almost twenty weeks, we could no longer be intimidated, cajoled, or even motivated sufficiently to make an hour parade become extraordinarily important in the larger scheme of things. That larger scheme and our obsessive preoccupation at that time were with postings subsequent to SME and corps training.

We still didn't know to which units we were going and it was already a week later than the promised date. After four and a half months of pressure, study, unnerving and constant supervision bordering on strict surveillance, unaccustomed physical demands, heat, constant hounding, and general bastardisation, the last thing we needed was this added uncertainty. We desperately wanted to know. Although I was no less concerned about it than anyone else, my circumstances as a single man, were comparatively easy. I sympathised with the married boys who had families or children on the way. They would have to make hurried arrangements for quarters and the transport of wives and children when and if the news finally arrived. We were, as always, at the mercy of the system. The reminder that we were almost one fifth of the way through those two bloody years was a helpful thought and was echoed by us more and more often. The whole situation, however, was not relieved in those weeks by the newspaper reports we began to read.

On the one hand, Nashos from the first intake of 1965 had just completed their two-year stint and were being discharged. It made us green with envy to see pictures of them walking out the front gates of Watsonia Army Barracks as free souls. We felt even more embattled and cloistered at SME to read of the plans these 'freedmen' had for their immediate civilian and normal lives. Many were talking about returning to former employers, some about taking trips around Australia and a few were embarking on business ventures. Whatever the plans, each of them sounded better than the purgatory that was still ahead of us in the next twenty months. During the final weeks of May 1967, I reached a personal low point in outlook and morale and felt as though the Gods were playing with me. Perhaps if I could have seen into the future and viewed the second half of 1968, I would have felt less sorrowful.

At the same time, news coming out of South Vietnam was even more depressing. Australian lives had been lost in a war for the first time since Korea. The overall US and Allied effort was largely at a stalemate and there was speculation about a massive North Vietnamese retaliation being planned for later that year. These developments, combined with our progressively more hostile attitude towards the tens of thousands who had missed National Service and were living the high life at our expense, made the latter part of Corps training a frustrating, angry, and unpleasant period. The training, however, continued. In our current state of mind, that was probably for the best, for it provided a focus, enforced though it was, away from our otherwise self-pitying, sorrowful outlook.

The second last week was spent on lessons involved with the operation of a variety of machines. We toyed with jackhammers and compressors, looked at bulldozers and graders at work, and drove some smaller tractors fitted with front-end scoops. The larger plant we dared not touch, since only qualified personnel could operate them. We did a cursory course in surveying and drove the army's new Mark V trucks, even though none of us was yet fully licensed to do so. The last two days were spent in the mock-up of a Vietnamese village on base. A dozen or so huts had been built, surrounding a centrally located well. Around the perimeter were some quite unconvincing rice paddies which, given the time of year, were actually flooded. The huts contained a collection of primitive tools and some farm equipment, which was strewn about on the earthen floors. There was some old furniture in the form of wooden tables and chairs and scattered bits of crockery to create a feeling of realism. Corporal Wash explained that, surrounded as it was by bush, the village was remarkably authentic to what a Vietnamese village actually looked like.

We spent a day devising different means whereby we could approach the village and attack and capture it if necessary. We practiced the obligatory screams as we rushed into the huts and pretended to imprison imaginary Viet Cong. We took turns at dressing in the black, pyjama-like garments often worn by the VC and got to know what it felt like to be dragged out of a hut at bayonet point, with arms and legs tied behind the body. Corporal Walsh got the better of us on one occasion. We knew that he had dressed in the black outfit and was hiding somewhere in the village, but for the life of us we couldn't find him. After a considerable time spent in fruitless searching, we suddenly saw him emerging from one of the huts we had just left. Bewildered, we asked the obvious question and it was then that we were shown the very clever and deviously camouflaged underground hiding places that traversed the whole village. Hidden by soil, there were entrances to both small and wider tunnels in most of the huts. Some were large enough to accommodate a single person, others as many as five. Huts were thus linked to each other and some of the tunnels had intricately designed offshoots from the main branch that ultimately lead to dead ends. One in particular – which had been deliberately flooded and running downhill quite sharply – could have claimed the life of an unwary intruder. Several tunnels had been booby-trapped with trip wires and deep trenches that gave way under a person's weight. At the bottom of the trench, sharpened bamboo stems had been embedded in the soil, which would have impaled anyone unfortunate enough to fall in. It was a very realistic exercise to crawl through these systems and to be shown the literal pitfalls. Knowing something about these systems and the tricks used in them, we were told, was essential if we ever served in Vietnam.

It was not a task for the fainthearted, or the claustrophobic. The tunnels were dark, damp, putrid, and narrow. It's often hard enough to crawl on one's belly on the surface, but in the confines of a narrow, unknown tunnel, the degree of difficulty increases sharply. I was five feet eleven inches tall and weighed just under twelve stone. There was ample room for me to fit through all the twists and turns, yet at one right-angled turn, I imagined that I had become stuck. A terror I had not experienced before gripped my being. I screamed for help, only to hear the reverberating echo of my own voice in reply. I began to struggle and thrash my arms and legs in the darkness and still felt firmly stuck. After what seemed like an eternity, I heard the sweet sounds of other life behind me in the form of Corporal Walsh.

'You're not stuck, Sapper Benko! You've stiffened up, that's all! Lie still and relax! Suck in your guts, twist to the right and move your arse forward!'

For perhaps the first time, I welcomed someone yelling at me like that. I shoved back my hips, rolled in the direction he indicated and crawled around the corner without any difficulty. I sucked in pure, delicious air when I got to the other end. The corporal was only a few seconds behind me.

'You know what they say about falling off a horse, don't you, Sapper Benko? You get right back in there and do that tunnel again!'

If he had given me the choice, I would have gladly run in the opposite direction. But I had no choice and, with several dozen pairs of eyes watching me, I marshalled what little courage I had left and dropped back into the tunnel. This time I was prepared for that blasted corner and got past it without incident. I clambered out the other end and a 'well done' comment from the corporal was very sweet indeed. I had never considered myself to be claustrophobic, nor am I one now, but I can readily sympathise with those who are terrified at the thought of being trapped in a closed place.

By four o'clock, we had explored what we believed to be all of the tunnels and had been shown the booby traps we could expect to find in them. As we were being assembled for what we thought would be the march back to the barracks, a hot shower and a feed, the lieutenant suddenly sprang into action, ran a few steps from us, and jumped into the well. We heard the splash of water and indeed had earlier seen that it was a genuine, water-filled well. Any moment we expected to see him climb back out, but as the moments ticked by there was no sound from, or sight of the Rabbit. A couple of minutes later, by which time we had crowded the well to see where the hell he'd gone, he appeared from one of the furthest huts looking positively shagged, with water and mud oozing from every pore. As reality dawned on us, there was evidently at least one more thing we all had to do that day.

As it was explained, there was an entrance to a tunnel under the surface of the water in the well. We had to jump in, locate that entrance, go in, and follow the tunnel to its end in the hut from which we had just seen the lieutenant emerge. The entrance was about a foot or so underwater and in crawling through it to the main branch of the tunnel, we would have to hold our breaths for about ten seconds. Upon hearing this, the only thought occupying my bewildered mind was what horrid things might happen if I got stuck again. Who would be there to talk me through it this time?

One by one, those lads who took such things in their stride vaulted the side of the well and disappeared under the murky surface. So as not to create a traffic jam in unknown and unseen territory, one of the corporals listened for the groans and grunts at the far end of the tunnel and when he heard the approaching squelch of one of us coming towards him, the signal was given for the next one to enter the well. I was about the tenth in line, which meant a wait of about a quarter of an hour. With each passing minute, the ugly spectre of imminent disaster grew in my mind. I was simply terrified and it was a relief when I finally jumped in. The water was freezing but I didn't mind. The opening was easy to find. I took a breath and dived under. I shoved my head through the entrance, pushed forward and was delighted to find that the water-filled section was only about three body lengths, after which it sloped upwards. I surfaced in the dark and took a welcome breath of stale air. Feeling around, I found another opening, so I hoisted myself into that and followed the available empty space ahead of me. Happily, there was only one simple right turn that I had to negotiate in the dark. I groped and grunted a little further, followed the natural rise of the tunnel and after that I literally saw the light at the end of the tunnel and heard the corporal's voice. I got out and found that the whole thing had only taken two minutes or so.

Many similar tunnels had been found in Vietnam and sometimes up to forty people had been found hiding inside them. I wondered what fears would have driven them to do such an unbelievable thing and live in such misery, but didn't dwell on that too long. Sappers had been killed searching through and clearing such tunnel systems. Hidden pressure mines had exploded, while some had jumped into wells as we had done and lost their legs as a consequence of landing on sharpened bamboo or wire spikes placed underwater. Based on what we had experienced that day, these were terrifying thoughts, and I wondered if I would have the courage to do for real what I had just done in practice. That imponderable and the taste of the filthy water in my mouth were soon dispelled by a warm shower and the good news that most of us received the next morning.

Chapter 16

With only a week left before march-out, our all-important postings had come through. I could hardly contain my joy upon discovering that my request for Southern Command had been successful and, further, that I had been given a clerical job at the Central Army Records Office in Albert Park, Melbourne. In one day, my situation went from total uncertainty, doubt, and indecision, to absolute assurance and finality about my immediate future. It was wonderful! In effect, the posting meant that I could spend the remaining twenty months in the relative comfort of a desk job, but – more importantly – that I could move back home again.

On an equally selfish level, I quickly realised that the Central Army Records Office, CARO, was hardly likely to be posted overseas as a unit and, as such, I had therefore evaded Vietnam as well. Terry was also smiles from ear to ear, for he had been posted to an Engineers' Squadron in Tasmania and although it wasn't Hobart, it was the next best thing. Only a half dozen got postings that didn't immediately appeal and only three got units that were already slated for overseas duty. Naturally we sympathised, but private joy was paramount.

Hurried interstate calls were made and we decided not to drive down to Melbourne that weekend as planned, but to make a real celebration of it in Sydney. After all, in less than two weeks, we would be home for good anyway.

6.6.67

You've already heard the good news when I called, so now you can read it too. The posting to Albert Park is from the 20th of the month, so I'll have four day's leave when I get home. I'll fill you in personally about what we've been doing in the past two weeks but suffice to say that it's been very busy. This might actually be the last letter I have to write to you! The only remaining thing now is the march-out on the 14th. I now owe you 29 shillings for the reverse phone calls I've been making. There won't be any further need for those from now on! Looking forward very much to seeing everyone again soon.

Kings Cross!
Ever since I can remember, the name had been synonymous with adventure, daring outings, the forbidden, and a degree of exciting escapism. During our first week in Sydney, it had drawn us to it like a moth is attracted to light. On this final weekend, we went there once more to treat ourselves to some more of this 'good life'.

Being from Melbourne, which was within the state named after a most conservative monarch and thus also behaviourally Victorian where such things would not be tolerated as seemly behaviour, the concentration of strip bars, flashing lights, massage parlours and available ladies made the Cross exciting and irresistible for us. Whether one did or did not partake of all the pleasures was irrelevant. What mattered was that by being there, we felt as though we were travelled, experienced men of the world, somehow more alive than others who were absent from the excitement of that vibrant place and scene.

We had a great evening. After seeing a strip show at the Pink Pussycat, we walked up and down the main street taking in the other sights and feeling ever so sophisticated as we turned down several inviting offers from the working girls. The very thought of it being actually offered was satisfaction enough in itself. After a massage, to which I had never before treated myself, we had a meal in a disgustingly expensive restaurant, drank much more than we should have, and returned to Liverpool in the early hours of the morning. The night was made doubly exciting because we met up with several American GIs in the restaurant who were on a period of 'Rest and Recreation' in Sydney. They were loud and somehow obnoxious to others around them, but treated us with some consideration and respect and spoke to us about a few, recent experiences in Vietnam. We were positively agog with everything they had to say.

As we suspected, the march-out from SME was less impressive than the one some months earlier. The entire format of the parade paled by comparison with Pucka. Nonetheless, we had again grown to respect our corporals and Rabbit to such an extent that we strove to do them full justice by performing the required drill to the best of our abilities. My parents could not afford the time to travel up to Sydney in response to the invitation that was sent from SME in much the same way as it had been done from Pucka and I think I even encouraged them not to bother. Afterwards, some forty very proud, fully-fledged sappers from 1 Troop celebrated the end of training in the common room.

Parting from mates at SME was easier that it had been at Pucka. Without realising it, we had been more frugal in the kinds of relationships we had formed there. For me, losing Barry's companionship some months earlier had been harder than I cared to admit. I missed him and I was not going to be that disappointed again. So the mateships I formed were more tenuous, less binding than those during basic training. Others had reacted similarly, I think.

It was with few regrets therefore, that on the 15th of June, I exited the SME front gates for what I believed would be the last time. A couple of hours later, with kit bag over my shoulder, I boarded the Intercapital Daylight for the trip home. Four-and-a-half months had gone, about nineteen and a bit were still left. I had beaten the system for I could easily sit out those months at CARO and that would be the end of it.

Part C

CARO: Central Army Records Office

JTC: Jungle Training Course

Chapter 17

The Central Army Records Office was situated a few hundred yards from Melbourne's Albert Park Lake. It was also, coincidentally, a similar distance from Fitzroy Street, where Barry and I had spent such a great Saturday night in April. The office complex was comprised of about fifteen large wooden buildings, most two stories high. Several hundred military and civilian personnel had the task here of keeping the army's records of all active and retired servicemen in order and up to date.

On my first day there, I was taken to one of those buildings near the main entrance, just off Aughtie Drive. I was introduced to my new boss, a Warrant Officer. To my surprise, he answered my fist-clenched by the side, straight-backed, loud 'Sir,' with an extended hand, which I shook. It was just momentarily disconcerting to find that not only was he willing to shake hands, but that there were only three fingers on the hand he offered to me. After being introduced to others and shown to my desk, recently vacated by another Nasho, the paperwork was explained.

If a serviceman enlisted, was promoted, was demoted, charged, fined, posted to a new unit, given a raise, married, divorced, given a commendation, required to undergo a physical examination, passed or failed a test, or had his or her service situation altered in the slightest degree, paperwork was involved and we did it. The pertinent entries had to be made on the soldier's records, after which this newly-gazetted information was forwarded to the unit's officer-in-charge. It was on receipt of this notification that action was taken by the unit's administration. The unit could have been anywhere in Australia, Malaysia or in Vietnam. As much as any bank, insurance company or other bureaucratic organisation such as the Postmaster General's Department for which I had worked prior to being drafted, the army had its own particular brand of paper warfare.

The green slips on my desk contained information 'incoming' from the units whose records I was to keep. The small white slips were for CARO's internal records. The large white sheets were for the compilation of the standing orders to be gazetted, while the five, very large folders contained the actual personnel records of the members of the units in question. As soon as the intra-office movement of this paperwork was explained – some slips to the man on my left, other slips filed, white sheets to the checker and relevant information entered in the folders – I felt at home. Having worked as a clerk in the frenetic madhouse known as the Telephone Accounts Section of the PMG, the relative peace and sanity of this office was not going to be too daunting a challenge. It was pedestrian by comparison and the work quite simple and straightforward.

In all, the records of about seven units fell into my care and, as it happened, a number of them were Engineer units and several were on active service in Vietnam. The names of three are still fresh in my memory: those being 55 Advanced

Engineers Stores Squadron, 17 Construction Squadron, and 1 Field Squadron. Thus over a period of the next few months, I was to become well-acquainted with the names and service situations of several hundred men as I would thumb through the alphabetical listings of the records in the folders on my desk. As new postings were made to these units, I got a sudden rush of adrenalin and a feeling of power and authority to know the names of those going overseas a day or two before even they knew of it. In similar fashion, I recorded details about promotions and raises in salary before the recipients were aware of them. Apart from that tiny, private satisfaction, however, the business handled at CARO offered no more special or greater thrill than clerical work would offer in any other office. It was basically repetitive, boring stuff. All of that notwithstanding, to be able to sit at a desk and to do work for which I felt suited was such a pleasure after the pressures of the previous five months, that I felt as happy as the veritable pig in shit. The remaining months, I assured myself, would literally fly and Nasho would be a forgotten memory.

At the same time, I was saving money for a car and arranged with the army paymaster to deduct a fortnightly allotment from my salary for that very purpose. I was still many hundreds of dollars short of the necessary funds and the car was just a distant dream. I had moved back into the family home and my father was fortunately quite generous with his pride and joy and I could have use of it on weekends when he didn't need it. On a social level, I quickly resumed past friendships and, after two or three short weeks, it began to seem as though the five months spent at Pucka and SME had hardly occurred. Often the uniform I wore was the sole reminder that I was still a part of something else, something other than being the normal civilian I had been before.

This growing comfort was further buoyed by the lack of military discipline at CARO. As long as we were appropriately and neatly dressed, punctual, and accurate in our work, life imposed few military intrusions and the days passed uneventfully. The only semblance of regimentation foisted on us was on Monday mornings when we assembled outside for a flag-raising ceremony. At these times, the officer-in-charge would glance at uniforms, suggest a haircut to someone if he thought that was needed, and perhaps ask if one of us had run out of shoe polish when the shine had worn off the toes. The place was so unexpectedly slack that in times of madness, I thought that a two-mile run for everyone would not be a bad idea and that I ought to scramble up a rope or two just to keep my hand in. These moments of lunacy were rare and passed as quickly as they sometimes occurred.

Saluting was out of the question because the place was awash in commissioned officers and we would have spent half of each day with hands to foreheads if that had been a strict requirement. Rather than being the feared superiors to whom we had become accustomed during training, these officers were happy to be treated as working partners who shared in our conversations and would tell or listen to a joke. Our hours of work were from 8.00 am until 5.00 pm, with a customary lunch hour and two short breaks for morning and afternoon teas. Lunchtimes were generally filled in with card games, 500 being the popular choice. Many left and right boughs were played amongst the green and white slips of paper covering the tabletops. Except for the nature of the paperwork in front of me and the uniform I wore, I might as well have been back at 441 Lonsdale Street, shuffling larger white sheets of perforated paper that had been the telephone accounts of the subscribers of the particular exchanges under my ledger's care.

I was one of many Nashos at CARO. We were a mixture from several Corps, the Engineers, and Signals, Armoured, Artillery, and even some from the Infantry. This was also true of the regular men and women at the place. In truth, it was an odd collection of types and individuals that worked there, with ages ranging from twenty to sixty. We were not an army unit in the real sense of the word. An infantry unit, for example, consisted of riflemen whose job was to fight. A signals unit was responsible for communications, while an armoured unit would have its tanks and armoured personnel carriers with which to play. A service unit would be responsible for transport, the caterers would cook, the engineers constructed, while the artillery units toyed with anti-aircraft guns and cannon. At CARO, our mutual bond and sole uniting factor was the paperwork in our care. There was a common purpose, of course, but little sense of unity because of the diverse Corps backgrounds, substantial age ranges and the unusual work responsibilities. Consequently, there was little social contact outside the hours of eight and five and after work we went our separate ways, as any office workforce would normally do. Somehow, to me, the situation felt immediately inappropriate and wrong. As ludicrous as it might sound considering my earlier fervent wish for an easy office job in Melbourne, within weeks I began to have the very uneasy feeling that I was a willing party to an unfortunate masquerade. I had seen nothing wrong with donning a three-piece suit for my office job as a civilian and working with dozens of others in similar attire. However, strutting around in the office in Albert Park, wearing a battledress and sitting behind a desk as a soldier, suddenly became an uncomfortable contradiction that began to fester at the back of my mind.

The more often I added names to the growing folders on

my desk, the names of those sappers, signalmen, and privates going overseas, the more bothered I felt for sitting behind my desk. For the first time I began to take the taunting barbs about me being just a paper-pusher seriously. Friends had thrown those at me quite casually in the past and I had never been too troubled by them, but the realisation of their possible relevance in my current situation was quite unpleasant. I was fit, healthy, young, and in the army, yet I was sitting behind a desk, wearing a uniform, with possible finger cramp and paper cut as my only sources of discomfort and compensating solace. While I had security, relief from physical pressure and comfort on my side, these were accompanied by a progressively diminishing peace of mind regarding the matter of my unusual situation. The bleak, winter months of Melbourne didn't assist the situation and thoughts of undeserved, warm hibernation, utter indolence, and consequent guilt began to dominate my thinking.

The names just kept coming in and I dutifully marked and stamped the service records as these postings were finalised.

Sergeant Marlfield, Sapper Waterford posted to 55 Advanced Engineers Stores Squadron, South Vietnam. ETD, 22 August 1967. Qantas Flight 01. Depart Sydney at 2230 hours.

Sappers Clift, Davenport, Tannon and Tidey posted to 17 Construction Company, South Vietnam. ETD, 29 August 1967. Qantas Flight 01. Depart Sydney at 2300 hours.

Lieutenant Clayton, Warrant Officer Ronald, Sappers Baimbridge, Benfield, Hutton, Moss, Parker, Tancred and Tunny posted to 1 Ordnance Field Park, South Vietnam. ETD, 3 September 1967. Qantas Flight 01. Depart Sydney at 2200 hours.

A growing sense of uselessness welled up inside and what made it worse was the notion, incorrect though it was, that my family might also harbour similarly negative thoughts about what I was doing. The emotion often reached its peak, however, when I came across the name of a friend who had been with me during basic training at Puckapunyal or whose name I recalled from SME.

It was at those times that my seemingly petty and menial contribution brought about the harshest pangs of a feeling that didn't actually equate to guilt or of conscience because I had no real reason to feel either of those, but it was a bothersome unease that settled at the back of my mind as an unwelcome guest. The posting to CARO was quickly souring and I began searching around for both an answer to my quandary and an alternative.

Chapter 18

I was a month short of my tenth birthday when I came to Australia in 1956. Not knowing a word of English, I found early life somewhat difficult in Grade 4 at Brighton Road State School. I had no trouble with the daily quota of mathematics that was dished up on the blackboard because maths is a universal language and I had received a good grounding in it, but in all other schoolwork, the language difficulty set a barrier which seemed at first insurmountable. There wasn't even another Hungarian child at the school with whom I could talk freely, so making friends was a trying task. My parents already spoke English and, with their encouragement and the special help of Mrs MacFarlane – my Grade 4 teacher – the language skills necessary for everyday conversation were learned quickly. By the last term of 1956, not only had I learned the peculiar rules governing the local brand of football and began to beat some of my classmates in spelling competitions, but had learned sufficient English to understand that in a game of cricket, the out team was trying to get the in team out, after which the out team would go in and be subsequently bowled out. By the time of my eleventh birthday, I had made enough friends to fill a room in our house on Brighton Road and I wore the funny hats, threw the streamers, burst the balloons and blew out the candles, all of which I understood were the required elements of an English and therefore an Australian party. Even at that age, I was encouraged to adapt to new situations and adopt some new ways and customs, while at the same time maintaining a respect for old traditions and values.

There was, however, in my parents' general attitude an undercurrent of isolationism, which didn't permit the complete acceptance of all things Australian. Undoubtedly, every immigrant who moves to a new country experiences a painful and difficult period of readjustment, and perhaps only those who have gone through the process of assimilating a new culture will understand how difficult that can be. For this reason, it's not uncommon to find that ethnic groups often choose to live together in particular urban or rural areas. There they have a ready access to their own clubs, shops, and restaurants and they can enjoy the proximity and security provided by friends from a common homeland. This was certainly the case in my home. At the time, we lived in Elwood, a suburb of Melbourne which was the chosen home for many Eastern European immigrants. Except for a few Australian families that my parents had befriended at work and who visited us on an irregular basis, we were completely immersed in a Hungarian lifestyle. We ate Hungarian food, spoke Hungarian in the family home, attended a Hungarian church, and played host to many Hungarian friends whom my parents had either met in Melbourne or knew from an earlier place that they all exclusively referred to as home.

I remember long parties and dinners with great affection and I used to sit spellbound with interest as friends related endless stories about their childhood, travels, courtships and memories of Hungary. There was often a hint of sadness at these parties when those gathered would invariably begin to sing songs of their youth, usually sad songs that made them reminisce even more profoundly about what they had left behind. Being so young, I hadn't yet formed the love for and the emotional attachments to a homeland that the adults were experiencing, and it always seemed strange to me as a child that these people had made the conscious decision to leave Hungary, yet pined for it so deeply. As the years passed and my parents and friends established successful lives in Australia, many of them planned and finally achieved their dream of a visit back home. My mother, father, and younger brother Greg made that trip some years prior to my call-up. After that, it became an accepted fact in the family that one day I would also make the pilgrimage to visit grandparents and aunts whom I could remember only faintly from before 1956.

My upbringing was, in every sense, European and strictly Hungarian. There were perhaps four unquestionable imperatives. It was frequently stressed that my behaviour was supposed to be better than that of my Australian friends, that the advice and counsel of parents and adults always needed to be heeded, that hard and honest work was expected at all times, and that learning and a good education were necessary elements for future success. While I had no difficulty in accepting, believing, and obeying the last two, the first couple were often a source of angst between my parents and I. As a young teenager, I questioned why I had to act superior to or try to behave better than my friends who I though were quite well-mannered anyway – and if they were somewhat unlike me in some aspects of their lives that was simply because of a different heritage which, I thought, ought not to have mattered. Along similar lines, my parents' belief in the sanctity of Hungarian parenting also made me question the necessity that their views were always to be respected and accepted. My conduct and attitude, which were at times contrary to these demands of theirs, were to be central to problems and misunderstandings that created conflict between my parents and their elder child.

Just the same, I respected them and often swallowed my pride, did my best to live within the parameters they had set and was, I think, a dutiful son. I worked hard, tried to be honest, asked for and nearly always followed their counsel and tried to behave as well as I could, even though the comparison of my conduct with that of others was, to me, of continuing irrelevance. It was in the arena of education and learning where I let myself and my parents down most disappointingly.

At the end of 1964, I failed in getting my matriculation at the end of Form 6. Having spent five years at Bentleigh High School and having obtained fairly good results to that stage, either conceit or an over-abundance of self-confidence made me choose a full science course for the sixth year. Of the six subjects that we had to study in order to matriculate, four of mine included physics, chemistry and two maths subjects, while the other two were French and the compulsory English. It was by far the most difficult range of subjects that students tended to choose. In my case, an inadequate prior knowledge of the sciences, combined with an unpredictable, almost slothful laziness and reluctance to work until it was too late in the year, resulted in eventual failure. I only passed three of the six subjects and even the escape clause that was built into the system called a compensatory pass was not granted, because the subjects I had passed were only bare passes and those that I failed, I had done so miserably. Repeating the year was not an option offered by the school, nor was it one that I wanted. At that stage, I yearned for some independence and some money, so I went to work.

The first clerical job with an insurance company lasted for all of six weeks before I resigned, but the second with the Postmaster General's Department was more enduring. I became one of several hundred clerks, tending the telephone accounts of all of Victoria's phone customers. The work was tedious and repetitive, basically paper-pushing office work and not entirely what I had hoped to do with my life, but the pay was fine and being based in the city, it was geographically convenient to University High School in Parkville, where I had enrolled to complete my matriculation on a nightly, part-time basis. The job, as such, was therefore satisfactory at the time. Four days each week, I would finish work and catch a tram to uni where, over a period of two years, I was finally able to get that important piece of paper which showed that I had completed high school and had matriculated. It was about halfway through that second year in 1966 that I received my call-up papers.

Some of my friends who had been more successful when leaving Bentleigh High had either gone on to a Teachers' College, to university, or took up apprenticeships. Many others like me who had failed Form 6 ended up doing jobs that involved manual labouring, or had followed their fathers into family businesses. I was naturally envious of the more successful ones, because the failure entailed some honest soul-searching on my part, prompting the realisation that they had achieved something which, but for my laziness, I could also have had. On the other hand, I felt a little smugness and a degree of superiority over those who had ended up digging ditches or had become labourers for a bricklayer or concreter. Wearing a suit to work and doing relatively easy tasks in an office was far better, I thought, than filling wheelbarrows with sand and rock outside in all sorts of weather. So, to me, shuffling papers and answering customers' queries over the telephone with the PMG felt altogether fine.

It wasn't until we would meet socially and I would discover that the bricklayer's labourer, the car salesman, the factory hand, or the boy who had become a hairdresser, all who had until recently been my schoolmates, already had cars, steady girlfriends and were earning just as much or more money than yours truly, that I suddenly questioned the whole notion of my grand station and significance in life. One of them had even joined friends from outside our immediate circle and become a member of a newly-formed rock band. The very thought of that was enough to set my mind racing and to ponder on all the wonderful things that I might be actually missing out on. To pour salt into the wound, some talked about the future possibility of purchasing land, perhaps starting to build and moving out of home, or embarking on overseas travel. Matters were not helped at all by the fact that, jokingly, they referred to me as the paper-pusher from the PMG, with the unspoken suggestion, it seemed, that I really could have been more than I was. They were good friends who didn't necessarily flaunt what they had, or who were making fun of me, but in my mind uncertainties had been awakened which festered and cast doubts on the wisdom of the choices I'd made and the situation in which I found myself.

Nonetheless, I was determined to finish the two years of part-time studies that had been commenced, not only to satisfy my parents' wishes but to complete my own unfinished business, and shelved the initial urge to chuck it all in to form a rock band of my own, or to invest in new tools in the shape of shovels, rakes and trowels in order to start working for a carpenter, gardener or plumber. Accordingly, the daily train trip from Moorabbin to the city, eight hours poring over telephone accounts at work, a tram ride from the city to Parkville, two to three hours of study at school and the tram and train trips back home each night became my daily fare and way of life until 1 February 1967.

Chapter 19

It would have been obvious, even to blind Freddie, that apart from my boss who had sacrificed two fingers in the service of his country, there were many others who had been posted or superannuated to CARO because of one disability or another. Among the regulars, several had distinctive speech impediments as a result of service-related accidents. Many others were there because of advanced age or because of the less perceptible, but equally debilitating effects of cardiac and respiratory ailments. There was also a group, Nashos included, who had obtained the posting for a variety of medical as well as for private, compassionate reasons. These included such things as wives who might have been prone to suicide if separated from a husband, or to an ill, widowed mother who might have relied completely on a son's presence and help. I included myself in the remaining largest group who were at CARO for no better reason than that we had either applied for the posting, or had been placed there because the army had found no more suitable a place for us. This realisation also worked on my conscience and hurt my pride somewhat.

My father worked in South Melbourne and as a rule drove past the Albert Park Barracks on his way to work. Even though he began work at half past seven each day, I was able to save a considerable amount of time and money by getting a ride in with him. Being so early, I was generally one of the first to arrive in the office. As such, I could read the morning paper in relative peace and quiet, waiting for the rest to arrive. The news from Vietnam became even more disturbing during the second half of 1967 than it had been during the two previous years. It was strikingly obvious that more and more reports from there began to appear on the front pages of newspapers, rather than being printed on pages four or five. The war was creeping ever so slowly, but intimately, into the national consciousness as the lists of dead and wounded Australians began to grow. The American commitment was intensifying, the nightly television coverage was both graphic and immediate, and there was renewed speculation about a massive North Vietnamese offensive that might come within months to coincide with 'Tet', the local New Year.

One particular morning as I entered the usually deserted office block with an unopened newspaper in hand, I noticed a colonel leafing through the folders on my desk. Without daring to ask what he was doing, I watched him open the arch file and remove the files of two men. He then moved to another table where he collected at least three more. There was really no need for questions or explanations. In fact, apart from my initial greeting to which he hadn't responded, we didn't exchange a single word during the several minutes that this whole process had taken. Our eyes met for an instant as he hurried out clutching the files. He looked very tired. I sat down, threw the newspaper on the table, and tried to visualise the events of the next few hours. A minimum of five hurried phone calls would be made to army offices around Australia, from where at least that number of officers would travel to each one's given address to inform the next of kin about a sad, sudden loss. As I sat in the silence of the still and empty room, I didn't have the wish to open the files in front of me and check the alphabetical listings of names I had against the remaining files in my folders.

I didn't want to know the names. I didn't feel I had the right to know them before wives, mothers and children of the dead had heard the awful news. So I pretended to read the paper which didn't yet contain the very sad news about which I already knew a few facts and made myself a cup of coffee. As others arrived for work, the word about our horrific loss of life during the previous night had spread around the office and became the topic of muted conversation. A minute or so after eight, I flung open the files, located the missing names, and scribbled them on a pad. They were familiar in that I had processed some paperwork on them, but thankfully no more familiar than that.

The files on two close friends, which I had dreaded not finding, were still there. A rather selfish wave of relief swept over me as the anonymity of the dead somehow lessened the blow. I settled back in the swivel chair, picked up a fresh sheaf of papers for the day's work and listened to the chesty, rasping cough coming from the man at the table behind me. The evening news service confirmed the detail that was common knowledge around the office that morning. The heavy loss was the result of an Allied push from the Australian base at Nui Dat in Phuoc Tuy Province. Two of the names from my files had belonged to sappers. One had stepped on a mine and the other was blown up by a delayed booby trap in a tunnel he had been clearing.

At about this time, I took another trip back to the Second Recruit Training Battalion in Puckapunyal. The ninth intake of Nashos had finished basic training and Andrew was marching out. I accompanied his parents and other friends on the journey to the well-remembered parade ground, suggested a spot from where I thought they would get a good view and took charge of Andrew's movie camera to film the event. The format of the manoeuvres had not changed since April and even then, some six months later, I could anticipate the commands and remembered the drill as the platoons went through their paces. The whole thing looked just as impressive from the outside as it had felt from within. The music, the practiced oneness of movement, and the measured crunch of boots on gravel were a delight to observe and, as spectators, we all reacted with genuine satisfaction and some wonder at what we were witnessing.

Afterwards, we visited Andrew in the huts, only to be told that his platoon had faulted in some way that morning and all the boys were due outside for a further inspection in thirty minutes. Visitors were expected to leave in twenty. There was the usual frantic air in the hut that I remembered well as boots were being buffed with soft cloth, belts were straightened, and rifles were getting yet another cleaning. Andrew was somewhat behind, so I offered to clean his rifle. I took the weapon to an empty table in a corner, cocked and broke it, removed the dust cover and lifted out the bolt in an almost single movement, having remembered exactly what to do. Just as I began to brush inside the bolt housing, two of the recruits who had seen me with the rifle sidled over to ask whether I had my own SLR and, if so, how did I, as a civilian, get one. Andrew and I quickly explained my situation. One question led to another, so that in the space of a few minutes I was able to give them a tip or two about my post-recruit experiences at SME. This was of particular interest to one of them since he, along with Andrew, had been posted to the Corps of Engineers. In that short time, cleaning the rifle and chatting to them, I relished the feeling of being the old soldier giving the younger troops the good oil, as old soldiers invariably do. Their last question concerning my current posting, however, made me hesitate before answering that I was at CARO in Melbourne and that I was a clerk. I think my reply was almost apologetic. It was probably not so, but I felt that their interest in what I had to say suddenly waned and they returned to their preparations for the inspection. I guess that if there was ever a single occasion, it was in that hut and in that moment that I finally admitted to myself the truth. I also finally recognised something that I had been trying not to do for quite some time. I was, rightly or wrongly, genuinely uneasy about being just a paper-pusher and suddenly wished with all my heart that I wasn't one. The old feelings of inadequacy awakened in me by schoolmates two years earlier resurfaced and I felt a tremendous need to alter my current situation quickly. The obvious alternative had always been at the back of my mind, but not till then did I consider and acknowledge it with any seriousness.

A day later, without telling the family of my intentions, I fronted the boss at CARO and advised him that I wanted to volunteer for overseas duty. He asked me why and I gave him an honest answer. He told me to put the request in writing and that he would forward it through the proper channels with his recommendation. I gave him my typed request the next day.

Perhaps this was an overreaction to the existing circumstances on my part. After all, I could have applied for a more active role with another unit in Melbourne, or even with one of the engineer units operating somewhere in Victoria. However, at the time, the decision, and the choice seemed correct and having finally made it I spent very little time worrying about its correctness or its possible consequences. I had been humbled by an inner sense of failure and to redress that perceived wrong, I volunteered for an experience that I had previously dreaded. Psychiatrists could, I thought at the time, read a multitude of sins into that kind of reaction. After submitting the application, I waited for the outcome, not knowing whether such things took a day, a week or even months to be processed. The entire prospect became shelved at the back of my mind.

In early September, I was given a week's grace from CARO. Along with half a dozen others, I was required to attend a bivouac in the hills east of Melbourne. This was part of the army's sensible programme of trying to maintain the fitness of those of us who had fairly sedentary desk jobs. We were joined by groups from Victoria Barracks and Watsonia, so about sixty in all were trucked out to bushland near present day Kinglake National Forest. Carrying tents, radios, sleeping bags, and water bottles – equipment I hadn't used since SME – we trekked along a narrow trail until we reached the camping site. Although it was the first month of spring, September is still quite cold in Victoria and the week we spent out was no exception. As sleep was out of the question on at least two of the six nights due to temperatures falling below zero, we sat around the fire, fuelling it all night to keep us from turning blue. No matter what anyone might say about the beauty and wonder of sleeping under the stars, I'm convinced that it's an experience impossible to enjoy if one is not warm and dry. During the day, we went on compass marches and fired a few practice rounds on a makeshift range. We had carried in all our food and the week of eating bully beef, powdered eggs, tinned beans, jaw-breaker biscuits, and an assortment of chocolate bars that the ration packs contained, was a unique experience. I enjoyed the outing despite the cold, for by making me suffer a little it acted as a salve, soothing my wounded and currently sensitive conscience. The camp ended as abruptly as it had started and, on the following Monday, I was back to the promotions, fines and estimated times of departures as I resumed the padded seat in the office in Albert Park.

As I had done often before, I picked up a new sheaf of slips bearing the names and details of about thirty men who were to receive orders very soon, moving them to units in Vietnam. I put the papers into unit and then alphabetical sequence, when the service number 3790533 leapt up at me from one of the sheets. It had an uncanny familiarity. It was no wonder that it did, because the number, the sheet, and the details on it were mine. My immediate reaction was disbelief – that I should actually find out I was going to a war in this most unusual way. After that came the high sensation of eagerness and anticipation, followed by the sinking feeling that this was no longer part of a future potential plan, but a sudden reality. For some minutes, I stared and I think grinned at the piece of paper I held. There was no doubt. There couldn't be two people with my name and my number.

> 3790533, Sapper Frank Thomas Benko. CARO to 55 Engineer Workshops and Park Squadron, South Vietnam. Posting as

Field Engineer. Posting dependent upon successful completion of Jungle Training Course. Departing from SME Sydney. Report to SME by 6 January 1968.

Being mid-November, I had to return to the familiar surroundings of SME in about seven week's time.

Chapter 20

The reaction of workmates in the office was perhaps predictable in that some were congratulatory and wished me well, while others gave the distinct impression that, after shaking my hand, they had just touched a damned fool. At home, the news was received in a similarly divided fashion. The immediate shock and disbelief was soon replaced by my parents' quiet resignation. The former response somehow kept me from telling them the truth that I had in fact volunteered for the thing. I finally decided not to tell them at all, since no worthwhile purpose would have been served. Some weeks later, however, the truth did emerge.

Andrew, by this time, was nearing the end of his Corps training. On a fairly regular basis, his parents and mine, together with some other acquaintances, would get together on Saturday nights and meet for dinners or outings. Not surprisingly, one of the main topics of conversation on these social occasions would be the fact that their two sons were in the army and both probably faced the undesirable prospect of Vietnam. Notes would also be exchanged on how the boys fared during their respective periods of training, what hardships they might be encountering and what a terrible misfortune had befallen both families to have both sons' birthdates chosen in the draft. It was as a result of one of these Saturday night dinners and subsequent conversations that truth from both sides eventually surfaced. Contrary to what we in the Benko family had thought, Andrew's birthdate being drawn for National Service was of no actual consequence, because he had been an earlier volunteer. Being clever with his hands, a jack of all trades and being between jobs, Andrew was not going to miss out on the opportunity of being involved in the adventure called military service. He hadn't confided this in me, but when his parents discovered the fact, they lost no time in telling mine. As I was lying on the carpet watching television the following Sunday, my mother blurted out the most unexpected question.

'Frank, did you volunteer for the army?'

Naturally I replied that I had not, wondering at the same time what had brought on this strange and sudden query.

'Did you volunteer for Vietnam, though?'

Having been asked that direct and straight question, I could not lie or evade the issue and replied that I had. This, of course, necessitated detailed explanations and justifications. When I explained my thinking and feelings on the matter, my parents accepted the decision, although I got the usual lecture about there being no need for one to look for trouble, since trouble had a way of finding one anyway. Despite that, maybe, just maybe, they felt a little pride about what I'd decided to do. I don't know, but whatever their final thoughts might have been, I did it solely and exclusively for me.

I continued working at CARO until Christmas, at which time the usual end of year holidays combined with a week's leave owed me, meant that it would be early January before

I had to return to work. This coincided with the impending return to SME.

As from 6 January, I knew that my fate was, again, literally in the army's hands. I began to worry about the dreaded three weeks I would have to spend at Canungra in Queensland on the Jungle Training Course. Prior to sending any serviceman abroad, the military requirement was that each soldier needed to pass a three-week course of jungle training, JTC, at the Canungra camp, a site used for that purpose since World War II. The most teasing rumour about the place was that no matter in which direction one left camp in the morning and no matter from which direction one chose to return at night, both trips, going and coming back, would have to be done by going uphill.

While we didn't automatically or unquestioningly accept this topographical impossibility as fact, it was sufficient to instil in us a healthy fear of what the place might really be like. To say that we expected a very tough course run by fierce and demanding instructors was undeniable fact. With this extra, self-imposed burden in mind, I reported once more to the Regional Traffic Officer in charge of military movement at Spencer Street Railway Station. It was the first week of 1968 and I had been in the army now for eleven months as I boarded the train for Sydney and good old SME.

11.1.68

Arrived safely back in Sydney some days ago. SME still looks the same. Believe it or not, since reporting here on the first day, I haven't lifted a little finger. About seventy of us are waiting for JTC, but after each morning's roll call, seventy of us head back to bed, to sit or to play cards. Very slack but who's complaining? The very good news is that about forty of us, including me, are going to do JTC at Pucka and not Canungra. That's fabulous and again none of the forty is complaining. We saw a James Bond film in town last night. I'll ring from Pucka as soon as we arrive. There are four familiar faces here from Corps Training. It's been great to have people around that I know from before.

During 1966, the American commitment to South Vietnam increased and it did so even more exponentially in 1967. This continued until it reached its maximum level at about 600 000 men and there were much smaller, but pro rata increases in the Australian contribution. Consequently, the jungle training facilities at Canungra had been stretched to their limits and could no longer prepare the required number of troops for overseas duty. As a result, two new JTC camps were established: one in Sydney and the other at our old torture ground of Puckapunyal. Unexpectedly, therefore, in mid-January, almost a year to the day that I had first laid eyes on the place, I returned to this hot, dry, dusty, and uncomfortable place just outside Seymour.

During the ten weeks of basic training we had marched, run or jogged and been trucked to many places around Pucka, but never to the Armoured Regiment's Barracks where we now went. One of the large, two-storey brick quarters occupied by the armoured personnel was now used as the billet for the JTC groups. The interior was quite plush and this did not surprise us at all, for we had heard that the armoured boys were catered for very well. We were housed three to a room and, thankfully, the building's solid brick construction ensured that it was bearably cool inside. The summer of 1968 was in full cry and days of above-century temperatures were quite common again.

As well as the forty of us from SME, almost two hundred made up the entire squad on our first day. If I ever thought that the crew at CARO was a mixed bunch, then this lot was even more so. With the exception of the infantry, who were still obliged to complete JTC at Canungra, this lot had a sprinkling from just about every Corps, even three cooks from Catering. Also included were about twenty officers from the rank of second lieutenant to major, who were to do the course with us. We thought this was terribly democratic of the army and looked forward to having them sweat and toil by our side. As we arrived, the smell of diesel fuel permeated the place and we watched in awe as several tanks rumbled past us to join those being serviced in the hangars. There was, however, little time for sightseeing, for as soon as we were unpacked and assembled, we were treated to the first of many five-mile jogs. Canungra might have had its endless hills and steep forest trails, but Pucka could boast ceaseless miles of both hilly and flat terrain and a sauna-like atmosphere to boot. During the next three weeks, we were treated to views of most of its entire area.

Jungle training was intended to be a refresher course in basic soldierly skills as well as a toughener of the body and mind. In the case of the former, drill was kept to a minimum, although we were made to run very long distances in formation, which was pretty much the same thing. The emphasis was on rifle skills with the SLR, the F1 sub-machine gun, and the M16 machine gun. Those going to Vietnam with postings as clerks or cooks wondered, perhaps justifiably, why they had to be able to strip and reassemble a weapon in a matter of seconds, but it had to be done by all. During running and shooting sessions, we took particular delight in seeing captains and majors being castigated and taunted by the training staff in exactly the same way as we had once been treated.

'With all respect, sir, you run like a flaming fairy! Get those bloody knees up!'

'You're meant to be firing at a target, sir, not spitting cherry seeds in the bloody officers' mess!'

One particularly rotund captain from the Service Corps seemed to come in for special attention as he tried, in vain, to run. This was an activity that his legs had long ago forgotten and against which his generous midriff rebelled.

'There's a three-inch thick pavlova waiting at the end of this run, sir! Now move!'

'Sir, if that guts of yours sways any more from side to side, you'll knock out the bloody man standing next to you!'

'You're doing push ups, sir, not embracing your wife! Get your gut and nose off the ground and bend those bloody elbows!'

It was wonderful stuff that we enjoyed immensely. They took it in their stride, as we all did, put up with the barbs that were sometimes totally unwarranted and often bordered on cruelty and, as always, everyone just offered the best that was within each one's physical capacity. We would have been stupid to do otherwise. The clear message on the first day had been that no one failed a JTC course. Those who didn't pass the first time would be invited back for seconds and thirds if necessary until a passing standard was finally secured. The pressure was therefore on us, as individuals, and even after day one we had seen enough to know that one period of three weeks was quite sufficient punishment. Repeating this course was only for the birds or those who might have had well-defined masochistic tendencies.

I paid close attention to every order, carried them out as

accurately as I could, and hoped to remain inconspicuous. An early reputation for slackness wouldn't endear one to the instructors and I didn't wish to be singled out as before. A determination to succeed is perhaps as important as skill, because I quickly regained what former expertise I had with the SLR and shot even better groupings than a year before. I crawled in mud with the best of them, battled my way through barbed wire, charged as fiercely and as loudly as I could with bayonet fixed and put on a brave face as live shells were fired some yards above my head. It only mattered to me that inwardly I trembled at the thought of all that hurtling lead whistling so close by. The outward show and front was what really counted. In what might loosely be termed the soldierly skills, I satisfied the requirements and surprised myself by performing better than many others did. In the more physically demanding aspects, trouble struck again. I suggested to mates that my immediately previous, sedentary work and lifestyle had something to do with that, but the actual truth was that I had never been a superman, and I knew it.

By the end of the second week, I finally ran the two miles within the required time although, along with others, I vomited quite shamelessly and publicly at the end. By that time, I had also satisfied myself and the instructors that I would never be able to climb to the top of their bloody rope and down again, not even if they built a fire at its base with me halfway to the top. That gave me a first black, failing mark. The second such mark was dished out in the swimming pool. I was a confident, if not a strong swimmer and I was able to swim about two hundred yards if I really had to. However, there was no way that I could cover that distance fully clothed in a given time. The pockets of my greens filled with water and pulled me down, my arms felt like lead weights and, after half that distance I couldn't raise a decent dog paddle, let alone a proper stroke. I was informed about the second black mark having been put against my name. I knew that a third demerit of any kind would almost guarantee me having to repeat the course. That third failure did, in fact, eventuate during the final week.

Under the leadership of the officers doing the course, we had to spend three days out in the bush on an exercise, which was to test our fitness and general bushcraft. All food and water was carried in and had to last the seventy-two hour duration of the mission. The objective was to reach a predetermined spot at the top of a nearby mountain by the afternoon of the second day. Once there, we had to set up an ambush for an enemy force of unknown size. At first glance, the task seemed reasonable and certainly achievable. Looking at the map, it only appeared to be a couple of inches from start to finish and having been dropped off at the starting point, we settled down for a good night's rest prior to leaving the following morning. If we had taken a closer, proper look at those two inches, however, the number and the close proximity of the contour lines would have suggested that the trek would be incredibly more difficult than we imagined and our sleep would have been less peaceful. The ground to be covered was, in fact, harsh in the extreme, both in its steepness and in the density of the undergrowth through which we had to cut a path.

There was an ominous stillness in the air when we broke camp at five the next morning. The preceding two days had been warm but this morning's heaviness and humidity hinted that another day in the nineties was in the offing. As we trudged quietly along the first ridge, we spotted the lights of Melbourne illuminating the distant horizon. It was a pleasing glimpse and a reassurance of those things that are synonymous with home. Then we plunged into another deep valley. At this early stage of the bivouac, we were laden with packs full of rations for three days, rifles, and sleeping gear. Several full water bottles were also suspended from our belts. This combined with boots and jungle greens meant that we each carried about forty pounds of load. As luck would have it, I was singled out for the dubious honour of carrying my group's radio as well and those added pounds, along with the uneven distribution of the load in my pack, made walking a real strain given the terrain we were covering. By the time we stopped for a short breakfast at eight, the temperature was already in the high eighties and our breathing was becoming distinctly laboured. Although there was an obvious need to conserve water given that there would be no fresh supply until we completed the ambush, it was equally important under the circumstances to drink fairly liberally to avoid dehydration. By this time, our shirts were soaked in perspiration. I decided to have a warm cup of tea for breakfast, which we were told was better than drinking cold water. I set up a small stove, which we all carried for cooking purposes and lit the hexamine tablet that provided the heat source. While the water was heating, I was summoned by the section commander who wanted to use the radio and inform base about our present position.

When I returned, I reached for the pot which was boiling, burnt my hand, and promptly spilled the lot. With that single, careless move, I had lost a precious cupful of water and developed a very sore hand that I began to favour. Since there was no time to heat another cupful, I took a quick swig of cold water, ate a biscuit and by then we had to leave. It was an unwise and hasty meal for which I was about to pay a high price. The horizontal distance to the top of the mountain as previously measured, was about seven miles, a ridiculously short walk to make in the two days allotted for the task. In reality, it turned out to be at least four times as far given the terrain we were covering. At times we spent as long as an hour and a half edging our way to the bottom of a single ravine and then clawing up the other side. The total horizontal distance covered in that time might have been as little as five hundred yards. The gradients we traversed were extremely steep. A careless foot or handhold could have resulted in one of us sliding thirty yards down the hill, after which that particular ascent would have had to be painfully repeated. I slipped and fell several times, as did others, and on each occasion a man went down the entire squad had to halt, assess the damage, and wait until all was in readiness again. It would have been next to impossible to locate a lost straggler in that bush. By midday, the heat had become unbearable. Tired frustration became commonplace and our progress had, if anything, slowed. Those in charge reasoned that we were falling behind schedule and made a monumentally bad decision.

Rest periods were shortened and by about one o'clock, almost conspicuous by their absence. The tactic was wrong and didn't work. We became more exhausted, made more errors through anger and impatience and instead of making up lost time we continued to fall further behind. A lunch break was finally called at two, by which time we had already walked for nine hours. The most disheartening aspect of the morning's effort, however, was that as we looked back during lunch in the direction from where we had come, it looked as though we were only spitting distance from it. We began to think that we were being led by idiots who either didn't know what they were doing, or who had gone out of their way to make our lives difficult by choosing the most tortuous route possible between the start and finish. Watching them sweat, toil and suffer along with the rest, reassured us about their sanity somewhat, albeit not totally.

There was a brief respite in the hour after lunch as we walked along a relatively level stretch of a fire trail skirting a ridge. The column we formed was quite spread and there would have been at least three hundred yards separating the leading man from the one bringing up the rear. No one spoke and hadn't for some while and the only sound we heard was the repetitive rattle of equipment and the scraping of boots on the rocky ground. Under different circumstances, we would have admired the wonderful scenery and the splendour of nature at its bright, picturesque best.

Suddenly, a painful-sounding, guttural scream pierced the silence. It had come from ahead. I picked up the pace and joined the converging throng. One of the cooks was lying on the ground groaning in agony. His face and hands were oddly contorted, fingers half-closed and arms and legs looking unnaturally stretched and rigid. My first thought was that he had fallen and broken some major bone. He had in fact succumbed to cramp, but to a degree I found hard to imagine. One limb can be easily affected, but in his case almost every major muscle group had suddenly tightened. One man forced salt tablets and water through his clenched teeth, while others massaged his limbs. All the while he continued screaming and the effect of this, echoing through the surrounding stillness of the hills, had quite a profound effect on us all. The whole situation was so much at odds with the serenity of the place that I felt like we were undesirable intruders. It was great to see that some minutes later the cook stood and, in spite of his somewhat shaky legs, assured us he was feeling better. Obviously he couldn't continue, nor could he be left, so a stretcher was hastily constructed from branches and spare greens. We took turns, four at a time, carrying and pulling him along, in the hope that by evening he would improve and be able to go on by himself. Although the ground we covered during the afternoon was undulating rather than hilly, he did impede our progress and there was further talk on the radio about schedules and timelines. The pace was foolishly increased again. The heat bore down unmercifully and took its continuing toll. More of us began to stumble and fall as exhaustion took over and concentration lapsed. Hands, faces and clothing were torn by the undergrowth, the gradients of the inclines increased again, and by early evening we were reaching the limit of patience, strength, and the will or ability to walk any further.

I had been labouring pretty hard all day and the extra weight of the radio wore me down. Film clips I'd seen of diggers trudging along the Kokoda Trail flashed before my eyes as waves of nausea swept over me. Around five o'clock, my legs caved in. One moment I had been walking a straight line following the man in front of me and, the next, I was lying on the ground unable to move. I stood up to walk on, but within moments my vision blurred and I could feel myself lurching from side to side as though I were drunk. Others offered to carry some of my gear, an offer I gratefully accepted. Even without the radio and pack, however, I knew I couldn't last much longer. We reached the top of another ridge by six and a fire road made the going somewhat easier again. Soon after, the order was given to halt for the day and we literally fell in our tracks. It was only momentarily embarrassing to find that tears of frustration and exhaustion streamed down my face. I need not have worried, for mine were not the only tears shed that day,

Since our current position was accessible to a Land Rover, a call was put through to base for someone to come and collect those of us who would not be able to resume the next morning. As darkness fell some hours later, I was one of about six to be taken out. It was an admission of failure, but in my state at the time, I couldn't have cared less. I was suffering from dehydration and a degree of nausea I don't wish on my worst enemy. Later, we learned that the official temperature in nearby towns that day had been 108 degrees. I now had three black marks against my name.

'I'm considering making you repeat the course, Sapper Benko. What do you say to that?'

I had been ordered to the OIC's office the day before we were due to leave for the return trip to SME.

'I'm not overly worried by the fact that you had trouble on the rope or that you didn't complete the swim. But you realise, don't you, that having to be brought in from a patrol the way you were, makes you a liability to the rest of the team and a source of danger to that team? I don't know if I can take the risk of passing you and perhaps allowing that to happen again under actual battle conditions. Convince me that you should pass.'

What he said made abundant sense and I realised that there was a real chance I might have to spend another three weeks repeating all the crap I had just endured. The thought was devastating. I also recognised that he was undecided and I was being given the opportunity to rationalise and perhaps talk my way out of that painful possibility. Marshalling whatever wits I had, I explained that the failure had not been the result of incompetence, but a consequence of the extreme conditions we had experienced that day and the added burden of having to carry the radio. I may even have mentioned the discomfort of my burnt hands. Having exhausted the truth, I then lied slightly by telling him that prior to enlistment, I had been a member of an athletics club and had competed in many long distance events, so that stamina was really not the problem. I had in truth run in many cross-country races and ran regularly as a teenager at school, but I thought the bit about the club membership might make my appeal more convincing. I babbled on a little more about the lack of water and insufficient rest periods on the day, but there was not much else that came to mind.

Later that day, we assembled as a squad for the final time and several names were read out – the names of those staying to repeat JTC. Mine was not amongst them. I caught sight of the forlorn misery and defeated resignation in the cook's eye as I walked past him some minutes later. He was staying behind. The next morning we boarded a fleet of buses, which took us to our various destinations.

Chapter 21

For all but two of the original forty to leave SME for JTC, that destination was Sydney and the Engineers' school yet again. The two had our deepest condolences for having to stay back at Pucka. For us, all that remained, we thought, was to be quickly processed for the earliest available flight to Saigon so that we would begin the adventure that was overseas service. We really shouldn't have been too surprised because, after all, this was the army.

The wait for that was to be much longer than we expected.

7.2.68

We got back to Sydney yesterday. You heard it from me on the phone, so I won't bore you with another recitation of how close I came to another three weeks at Pucka! As far as leaving here is concerned, I still need a series of nine injections over a period of some weeks, so it might not be till later this month. I'm now into the second year, over the hump, so they're using their time, not mine.

Great surprise on returning – many more familiar faces

from before, even Barry. Unfortunately, he's going to a different unit. He sends his regards and still remembers the good tucker he got at our place when he visited.

I guess Greg would have started his first day in Form 3 yesterday, because we saw hundreds of kids in fresh new uniforms on their way to school as we drove through town, so the same would have been happening in Melbourne, I guess.

15.2.68

Not much is happening. The count on injections is ten, not nine. Plague, cholera, tuberculosis, yellow fever and God knows what else, plus boosters for all. We've started taking the Paludrine tablets against malaria that we'll need to take every day in Vietnam.

Before we can take the week of pre-embarkation leave I told you about, everything else, that is X-rays, passports, photos and injections, have to be finalised. There are over a hundred of us waiting to go, doing little other than sitting around or sleeping. As I said before, it's their twelve months!

3.3.68

Almost a month now and still waiting! They finally found something for us to do! I just finished a stint in the kitchen and thankfully the needles are finished, so I'll see you soon. Andrew walked into the kitchen unexpectedly on Thursday night when I was up to my elbows in dishes. We're sharing a room at the moment. Barry has left for Vietnam. Andy is waiting to see which JTC camp he's being sent to. Indications are that it might be Canungra, the poor sod. It's been great to have two good mates to spend some time with in this otherwise great place that lately has become so dreary. To think that I actually liked it here ten months ago!

The most enduring memory of the six weeks spent back at SME prior to departure, apart from meeting up with Barry and Andy for a brief few days – which was wonderful – is that of sheer boredom. There was little to do in camp and I had little desire to leave it for the local sights. It also seemed that the week of pre-embarkation leave to which we were all entitled would never arrive, so on the second weekend of March, I went absent without leave for the first and only time.

On Friday night, not wishing to spend another two days of fruitless sleeping and watching television, I simply walked out the front gate in the full and certain knowledge that I wouldn't be back until the roll call on Monday. I walked into Liverpool, found a busy intersection, and began hitching down the Hume to Melbourne. I spent the two days at home and hitched back on Sunday night, only to discover on the Monday morning that I could have taken the whole week off, because my pre-embarkation leave had been granted. On Tuesday morning, therefore, I was back on the train heading south again. This time, however, the journey was legal.

This week's grace meant that my date of departure was now imminent. I visualised the ETD stamp being put on my service records at CARO and the order being gazetted and sent to SME. The time spent at home was a blinding whirl of visitors, more farewells, and many final meals with family and friends.

On returning to Sydney yet again, the date of 24 March was etched into my mind as the date of actual departure. A quick estimate meant that with the compulsory discharge date of 31 January the following year, I had a maximum of nine-and-a-half months to spend overseas. My parents drove up to Sydney some time before the 24th and we spent a few glorious days together taking in the sights which, without them, had seemed less interesting. On the evening of the 23rd, we were joined by another mate, Ron, whose parents had been unable to make the trip down from Alice Springs to see him off. We had a royal feast at the Gap Tavern in Watson's Bay, drank a bit too much again, and continued doing so for some of the next day in the motel in Cabramatta where we were staying. Having that time with the family was simply precious and indispensable, but by lunchtime I had to be back at SME.

That afternoon, a group of about twenty left the Engineers' school by bus for the airport. I remember little of that evening except that the goodbyes were very difficult. My mother reminded me of something that I had told her in Richmond on the day of enlistment. She chided me for having lied that day by saying that I was only going sixty miles away into the army and not halfway around the world.

The Qantas 707 took off and banked to show a brightly-lit Harbour Bridge. By this time, the alcohol had pretty much taken its toll and I fell asleep. When I awoke, the plane was in semi-darkness and most of the 230 men aboard were sleeping. I found out that an hour earlier we had taken off from Darwin and were now airborne again somewhere above Indonesia heading towards Singapore. I had been asleep for about seven or so hours and had completely missed the stop-over in Darwin.

We had left Australia.

Part D

Vung Tau, Vietnam

Chapter 22

The lectures, newspaper reports, television coverage, and training films had all been inadequate in preparing us for the sights, sounds, and smells of even the first day. The dawn landing in Singapore had been uneventful, except that for most of the Nashos, getting off the plane that day was the first step they had ever taken on foreign soil. Apart from a quick stroll around the airport transit lounge and the opportunity to mail a postcard home, there was little time for anything else and we departed. Shortly before midday, the pilot announced that we had entered restricted airspace around South Vietnam and would be landing shortly in Saigon.

The tension in the plane was palpable. The earlier, excited conversations became subdued and there developed an air of apprehension and uncertainty. Those nearest the windows were glued to them, while the rest craned their necks to see as much as was visible from 5000 feet. The very use of the words 'restricted airspace' conjured images in the mind of fighter planes that might, at any moment, swoop out of the midday sun and attack the defenceless Qantas bird. As no such attack eventuated from above, my eyes rested on the beauty of the flooded landscape below. There was so much water in all directions, I wondered if sufficient dry land existed in all of Vietnam for us to make a landing anywhere.

For the briefest moment, a lecture given by Mr Phillipson during a Form 4 geography lesson flashed through my mind. In that lesson at Bentleigh High School some six years earlier, he had talked about the Asian method of raising levees and then planting rice in the flooded area surrounded by the levee. I smiled inwardly in remembrance as I saw, for the first time, the practical application of his lesson, which had interested me quite intensely as a student. It was beautiful, for as far as the eye could see, the land had been subdivided into geometrically perfect squares, rectangles, and even triangles. These thousands of small plots shimmered, as the rays of the sun were reflected back from their watery surfaces. The embankments separating this myriad of lakes were accentuated by their Lincoln greenness and by the momentary loss of reflection as we flew over them. It was difficult, in this first instance, to reconcile the serenity of the picture I was viewing with the mental preconceptions I had formed about Vietnam. Surely this couldn't be the place I'd seen in the television reports! Mesmerised by the extent and brilliance of this aquatic display, I began to wonder if I would spend the next nine months knee-deep in paddy fields. As we descended, further evidence of civilisation became apparent. Roads and villages were suddenly discernible and I could pick out the occasional vehicle travelling along one or more of these routes. All too suddenly, the concentration of buildings increased and the outlying suburbs of Saigon were below. The scenery accelerated, individual structures could be seen, and several minutes later the thud of the wheels on the runway indicated that we were there.

For overseas travellers, one of the special thrills is always the moment when their feet first stand on the soil of a foreign country. For me, this was certainly the case. The walk down the steps and the setting of foot on the tarmac of Saigon afforded a special high, accentuated by the long mental preparation that had gone into the moment. We had, after all, just entered a war zone and none of us knew what to expect. The classical Hollywood, John Wayne version of laughing, confident, carefree GI's jumping out of transports ready to tackle the enemy didn't apply to us. Indeed, it probably never applied to any soldier, other than those on celluloid accompanying the said John Wayne. We were scared, hesitant, and totally submissive in those first few hours.

After assembling in an airport building, we were told that there would be a two-hour wait before military aircraft could fly us to Vung Tau. This we could manage easily, because if there was one thing the army had taught us extremely well, it was how to wait patiently. The pause of two hours fortunately gave us the opportunity of seeing some of the local sights at the airport. Far from giving the appearance of a war-ravaged, strife-torn place, there was an air of urgent normality as people, both military and civilian, prepared for flights that were taking off almost every minute. Having just moved through the two airports of Sydney and Singapore, which we thought were busy, this one in Saigon was positively feverish and the noise of aeroplanes quite deafening. Commercialism seemed rampant as dozens of vendors approached us, offering anything from cigarettes, drinks, wooden carvings, and prophylactics to one very optimistic fellow trying to flog off used bicycle chains. I was struck by the look of sadness and some desperation in his face as he held out an arm draped with heavily oiled, albeit rusty chains that had left greasy marks up to his elbow. A negative answer to one didn't deter five others from trying to show us their wares. They all knew sufficient English to assure us that local piastres wasn't necessary as payment and that they would be equally happy with Australian, or if we wished, American dollars. Since we hadn't yet been given the opportunity to exchange any money into local cash, some bought items with Aussie dollars. The true intent behind their generous offer to accept these other currencies became evident to us later, when we discovered that foreign currency was literally worth its weight in gold on the black as well as the open market. In reality, the least favoured form of payment the locals usually asked for was, in fact, their own money.

Apart from the various military uniforms that strutted past us as we waited, we remarked on the distinctive uniforms and garb worn by the Vietnamese locals. The vast majority of men wore loosely fitting trousers, a flattened, conical, straw hat, thongs, and shirt. The younger girls wore dresses made from a single length of cloth, almost exclusively white, and pinched in at the waist, giving them a very attractive, petite, and feminine look. The older women had similar dresses of darker cloth and, without exception, all wore the thongs and the inevitable straw hats.

Our own polyester shirts and trousers were becoming increasingly uncomfortable and ties were ripped off as the humidity and ninety plus degree temperature took its toll. The logic and suitability of the locally worn garb was immediately evident. It was light, loose, and airy while providing protection from the sun. Clothing in that climate needed to do little more. Being well after lunch, we bought some food at an American PX, which we learned stood for Postal Exchange, and marvelled at the excellent turkey sandwiches we got. For the next nine months we were to eat the same food as the American military and turkey soon became an increasingly less-admired staple.

The small transport shuddered as it took off from Tan Son Nhut Airport for the short hop southeast to Vung Tau. The pressurised Qantas jet had been almost inaudible compared to the loud shriek that this overworked, propeller-driven monster produced. The compensation was the wonderfully cooling air that rushed in on all sides. With a mountain of green and brown duffle bags down the centre aisle, we sat on seats on either side of the plane, wondering again about the next, new revelation. The landing, about half an hour later, was so loud we thought we'd landed in the middle of a metal junk pile. In a sense, we had. The small, relocatable, and portable runway at Vung Tau was made of sections of iron mesh of the type we'd used at SME for bridges. It was quite surprising to see this new application of a material with which we were familiar. Ushered onto several Mark V trucks and driven – we were delighted to see – by Aussies, we headed towards our final destination for that day.

That part of Vung Tau through which we were trucked looked dreary, poor, deserted, yet at the same time utterly fascinating. One straight stretch of road about half a mile long led from the airport, and after a left turn and another similar distance, we arrived at the heavily-guarded front entrance of the First Australian Logistical Support Group's camp, situated on a narrow strip of sand near the beach. 1ALSG was to be our home for the balance of 'time in-country'. On the way, I noted the smallness of the buildings and houses we passed, the flooded fields I had so admired from above, water buffalo squelching in mud up to their knees, peculiar three-wheeled taxis known as Lambrettas that belched smoke and made an awful din, a double-storied, whitewashed building from which colourfully dressed local girls gave us a cheery and welcoming wave and, above all, the uncomfortable, persistent and bothersome stench of decay. The odour permeated everything and was inescapable.

The entrance to camp was situated at the base of a substantial sand dune some twenty yards high so that one couldn't see inside. To the left, a narrow access road had been blocked off with barbed wire and this road, which originally skirted the dune, was overgrown with vegetation and had not seen any traffic for a long time. To the right, the second arm of this T-intersection was still in use and, as we pulled up at the gate, a large blue truck of American origin and markings, with a Vietnamese driver and attendant, drove past us from that direction and headed back towards town the way we had just come. The stench of that vehicle added even more to the generally unpleasant air of the place and, from its rear, we saw it to be a hydraulically-operated garbage truck. Judging from the way that it turned the corner, the waft of rotting rubbish, and the hollow rattling sounds that emanated from within, we reasoned that it was empty and had probably just unloaded its evil-smelling cargo. A comment from someone behind me in the truck summed it up.

'Bloody marvellous! So we're going to live next to a garbage dump?'

'Welcome to the funny country,' was the comment from the guard who climbed up the tailgate of the truck to see who was within. After reassuring himself that we were the genuine, newly-arrived goods from Australia, he waved the truck through. There was an incline of some thirty yards inside the gate that took us to the top of the dune and from that vantage point we got the first glimpse of 1ALSG with its stores, huts, tents, plant equipment, cleared spaces, and the blue sea for a backdrop. It was neither welcoming nor foreboding – simply army in its organised geometry. The truck verged to the right and descended. There was a chapel to the left of us with a distinctive and simple A-frame construction and its steeply-angled roof reached almost to the ground. The dirt road we were on skirted another dune, atop which were several buildings more elegant than the other prefabricated structures around and, having passed those, the whole camp came into view again. For hundreds of yards in all directions, we saw huge stockpiles of stores packed and stacked in neat rows, columns, and bundles. Large fenced paddocks were overflowing with bundles of barbed wire, others held lumber, and many were filled to capacity with tyres, and some with huge fuel bladders that served as the above ground equivalent of service station fuel tanks. These, given their size and shape, looked like and reminded me of helpless, beached whales. There were also large numbers of steel containers that could have held just about anything. As we weaved in and around these piled stores, the truck would occasionally stop at the orderly room of one or another unit and those posted to that unit would be ordered off, to report to their respective commanding officers. The four of us posted to 55 AESS, which was quite recently renamed 55 EWPS – 55 Engineer Workshop and Park Squadron – were the last to disembark as 55's office was located at the southernmost end of camp.

    A sergeant greeted us inside and he called the unit's CO, a captain, for the formal introductions. We saluted a friendly gentleman whom I guessed to be forty, and who was dressed in shorts and singlet, which no longer surprised us, for every Aussie we had seen in the previous hour had been similarly dressed. He took our movement papers, passports, and pay books. As these were being examined, we shook hands with those who worked in the office and others who had come in to check out the new arrivals. I was delighted to see more familiar faces from Corps Training a year earlier and at least two from JTC. Names just as much as faces sprang to mind as we were introduced to several whom I remembered from training at SME, and on whose postings I had worked at CARO. We were given an orientation by the captain as to what our duties would be. Ron and Kevin had been posted as clerks and they were shown the desks they'd occupy for their work in the orderly room. Gary, a tall, serious-looking fellow, was a motor mechanic, so he would be in the workshop. As a field engineer, I would be working outside, repairing and upgrading the camp's perimeter fence and new quarters that were being built for the members of 55. That being settled, the four of us were accompanied to our quarters by a growing number of lads who were eager to hear fresh news from home. They took us to a palatial tent situated on top of yet another sand dune that overlooked the orderly room.

We threw our luggage in the closest available vacant spot in the tent, set up the small cots we'd been given and flopped on them in utter exhaustion. Some eighteen hours earlier I had been in a motel room in Sydney and was now inside a tent, on top of a sand dune, on a hot, windy beach off the South China Sea – in a war zone. Not only was the trip itself tiring, but this sudden change in circumstance was quite difficult to absorb and handle. There was no jet lag as such, since the time difference between Australia and Vietnam was only two hours, but so much had changed in those eighteen hours that we felt disoriented and most definitely out of time and place.

The tent, I thought, was a miserable mess and it was the

first army habitat of any description I had seen, to which I could honestly apply that description. The afternoon wind had whipped up the sand and dust so that everything crunched as we moved about. I suddenly couldn't picture myself living under those conditions for the best part of a year and I felt like screaming and telling someone that surely a grave mistake had been made and that I had been taken to the wrong place. Our shoes had filled with sand from the climb up the dune and the monumentally unsuitable polyester shirts and long trousers for such weather having been drenched in perspiration were ripped off. We hunted through sausage bags to locate the boots and shorts that everyone wore. After that, we literally threw our spare clothing into a corner, adding to the already existing chaos of the tent. With a can of soft drink in hand, we did our best to answer questions about the trip and about home and were, of course, keen to ask many of our own questions. Yes, the flight had been fine and we had stopped off in Singapore and, yes, Sydney was still at its most beautiful sitting there on the shores of Botany Bay. Yes, there was a continuing hold-up of some sort at SME with about one hundred waiting for a flight and, yes, I had seen such and such, but no, had not sighted someone else. The conversation persisted along these lines, as we were gradually welcomed into the fold. Curiosities on both sides having been momentarily satisfied, I lay down, closed my eyes and tried, but failed to relax.

Basically, 1ALSG was what it appeared at first glance: a stores dump. From there, trucks and helicopters collected the materiel requisitioned by units at the other Australian base at Nui Dat and at times we also provided the Americans with stores they needed at bases like Bien Hoa. It was the job of many hundreds of soldiers at 1ALSG, as members of a dozen different units, to collect, store, catalogue, guard, transport and – in a variety of ways – disperse this materiel to other places as the need arose. Contained somewhere in the stockpiles was everything from the smallest nut or bolt, through items of clothing and food to complete generators, trucks and even tank parts and these were for our own, as well as for use by our front-line troops.

During the introductory patter of that afternoon, our other perhaps most pressing and immediate concern was also answered when we got the reassuring reply for which we had been hoping. No, we were not in any diabolical danger. There had not been a shot fired in anger at 1ALSG for a long time. Yes, everyone had to walk around with a rifle to which two taped magazines were attached, a sight that had scared me when we first entered camp. Only the visible one was loaded, the other inside the rifle being empty. Yes, this was a sensible precaution since we were at war, after all, and you never knew when you might need to shoot. Yes, the locals were friendly, on base at least, and scores of them worked inside the camp on a daily basis doing washing, some cooking, and other cleaning jobs. No, we needn't worry too much, things were pretty slack, and after a probationary fortnight, we would be given leave to go into town for the first time. Yes, we had to do guard duty about once a fortnight, but even that was slack, with some guys actually managing to sleep through it.

The predominant anxiety had been removed. The awful spectre of spending nine months, knee-deep in paddy fields was replaced by a contented euphoria which that magical of army expressions, *slack*, was able to create. If anything was ever described as being slack, then it was bearable, endurable, and perhaps even enjoyable. Why, there was even a nightly film shown in an outdoor area of a neighbouring unit, 17

Construction Squadron, up on top of the next dune! Needless to say, we were relieved by what we heard and it was with renewed vigour that we accompanied new mates for a quick stroll around the unit, before heading over to 17's mess for the evening meal. Apparently, 55 didn't yet have its own mess, but one was being planned. What rejuvenated our spirits even more was the news that in a few weeks, the unit would be moving out of the tents into the newly-built huts we had been shown above the existing unit's area on top of another dune. This explained the captain's earlier reference to my working on new quarters, which I hadn't really understood at the time, and also provided a vague, yet acceptable reason for the unaccustomed disorder in the tents. The boys, I reasoned, knowing that a shift was imminent, had become just a little careless with the manner in which they had folded and stacked their socks. That logic seemed all right and all of this reassured me that the army was, after all, still the army and that God must therefore still be in His heaven. As a consequence, I knew that all would be well.

In spite of our hunger, the meal was remarkably forgettable. The attractive pork rings, shaped in a manner that I have never before seen pork adopt, were tasteless, with or without the liberal application of salt that I poured on. In the same way, the potatoes and corn gave the distinct impression, both to the eye and to the tastebuds, of having been manufactured from plastic. But I was devouring something much more appealing – the uniqueness of the whole scene.

In particular, I was fascinated by the Vietnamese workers who hovered around the mess. I watched the small, stocky, and gaunt group going about its work and I immediately and incorrectly reasoned that it must have been more than twenty years of war, conflict, and deprivation that were responsible for their thin statures and the drawn, sunken features I was witnessing. Their mode of dress was the same I had noted in Saigon, right down to the plastic thongs they all had, revealing tough, calloused, weather-beaten, and small feet. What struck me most as I continued to stare at them through the open windows, was their apparent preference for working in a crouched, squatting position, with toes and heels both touching the ground simultaneously. In this position, their bent knees, looking grotesquely bony, came almost up to head height. It appeared to be an incredibly uncomfortable position and when I later tried to squat down in similar fashion, I either fell backwards very easily or found that my ankle muscles soon screamed in agony. Yet here they were half an hour after I had first noticed them and certain individuals hadn't shifted from their original positions, but still continued to scrape plates and to stack dishes. I remarked about this to a young lance corporal, Wayne, who only grinned and said that they always worked in that squat and usually stayed so for hours. Wayne was something of an expert, it seemed, for he had already been in-country for six weeks.

I also noted that they spoke very little while working, but the few words drifting through the windows made me ask whether they had spoken or were, in fact, singing to each other. Their words sounded quite accented with high-pitched consonants, giving them a musical, melodic lilt. Their straw hats were, as ever, either on their heads or very close by like treasured possessions. As we left the mess, plates had to be cleared of scraps which we scraped into plastic bins and then left them on top of a growing pile to be washed by the locals. As I deposited my plate, I couldn't shake the guilty feeling in my mind that my slaves were about to do something that I should really be doing myself. As we walked past a group of three, I happened to notice the foot of the first one was covered in bits of meat and corn that had fallen off some plates, some of which were wedged between his toes. My lofty, poetic, and picturesque ruminations of the previous half hour were suddenly shattered by this totally unsightly discovery.

After returning to the tents and rearranging our scattered clothing, we accompanied the others back to 17's boozer. Neither Gary nor I wanted to drink beer, so we were treated to soft drinks, which were given the rather quaint name of gofers. We looked enquiringly at the small, ten, twenty, fifty cent, and dollar notes that Wayne produced. They were Military Payment Certificates or MPC, supplied by the Americans for use by all allied servicemen as legal currency. We sat outside the boozer, drank the cold drinks, continued to sweat profusely, and listened to the various conversations around us. Being utterly tired and with attention spans to match, we walked back home which was all of one hundred yards across the dunes. It struck me as very odd to hear Wayne use the word home, but the reality of 55 being our home for the balance of that year had to be accepted as fact. On the way home, we saw a glorious, yellow to orange to partly red sunset, the type of which I had seldom seen before and the beauty of which still reminds me of the tropics whenever I see one that tries to imitate it. After taking the obligatory Paludrine tablets against malaria, I fell asleep and wouldn't even have stirred had I been lifted and carried away by the multitude of ravenous mosquitoes.

There was a lot to be thankful for at the end of that day. Things could have been much worse. I thought later about the truckload of boys who had gone from Saigon to Nui Dat that morning and wondered how they would have slept on the first night. We heard that the Dat was where the real war was playing.

27.3.68

Around the time I went to bed on the first night here, you would just have been getting home from Sydney. I hope you are well and thanks again for the last few days, they were fantastic. We are about sixty miles from Saigon, in this the 'funny country'. It's very hot, but luck puts us near a beach. We've been welcomed with friendship and the unity is great. There are several I know from before. The sand and dust will drive us nuts, eyes smart all the time. We are in tents, but new huts are being built. There is no fighting here, which was a relief to me as it will be to you. We even see nightly films. Tonight it's 'Bonny and Clyde'. After the film we will celebrate someone's 21st. Work itself will be pretty rough, but more about that later.

31.3.68
55 EWPS – AFPO 3
Sydney – GPO 2890

Unexpectedly, we moved into the huts this morning. The set-up is the same as at Pucka, with about 20 of us in one building. Well, the first week is gone, doesn't time fly! Hope you got my first letter. I'm told it takes four days for mail to reach home. During the week I did some concreting in the huts and cleaned them out ready for us to move in. The next job will be doing some extensions on the perimeter fence. I have already burned, peeled, and burned again, but it's so damned hot I can't work with a shirt on.

Although the four of us are not allowed into town for a fortnight, I got a ride in yesterday to pick up some laundry. I wasn't allowed to get out of the jeep at first, but did in the end. I'm fascinated by the locals, their appearance, customs, etc. Their food I will learn to live without however – it looks and smells horrid.

I'm smoking Rothmans now, would you believe a packet only costs $1.10! Things are very cheap. I'll be able to save. Out of curiosity, here are some of the notes we use; they're called MPC.

Would you please send my camera, if possible? There is so much to photograph here. Apparently anything under a weight of two pounds can be mailed here for twenty cents. There is a club down on the beach and on Sunday afternoons a local group comes in and plays western music. Their English accents are unbelievable we're told! There are two poker machines and regular broadcasts by the ABC of Melbourne and Sydney football matches on Saturday afternoons. It's not such a hard war really!

Everything with me is fine, please write soon. Incidentally, the AFPO in the address above stands for Australian Field Post Office.

Chapter 23

The entire unit assembled at half past seven on our second day. It was our first opportunity to see it as a whole. Apart from the captain, there was another commissioned officer, a Second Lieutenant, who conducted the parade. There were two warrant officers, two sergeants, about four corporals and a single lance corporal, Wayne. Sappers made up the rest of our number and in all, about fifty men formed the unit known as 55 EWPS. The second lieutenant, an F1 sub-machine gun hanging from his shoulder, and a warrant officer in tow, moved along the ranks, looking at those things which are normally checked at parades: length of hair, cleanliness of weapons, and tidiness of clothing. It was the strangest feeling to be inspected by an officer with a loaded F1 swinging like a pendulum under his arm. This was no longer the SME.

I felt somehow uneasy as a result and immediately understood the threatening effect that weapons in clear view would have on a potential enemy and why everyone carried one. Ron, Gary, Kevin and I having just arrived, had not yet been issued with an SLR, so we stood sheepishly and watched the practiced routine of the rest as they presented arms for inspection. The parade was short but necessarily military. By now, we had learned that our working hours were to be from half past seven until five on Mondays to Saturdays and from eight until one in the afternoon on Sundays. The one free afternoon on Sunday generally saw an exodus of troops from camp, as the majority went into town for the distractions and pleasures that Vung Tau had on offer.

On this morning, however, the four of us were ushered into the quartermaster's store to be issued with gear. First we got a rifle which was a greasy, oil-laden mess, having been stored like that purposely to avoid possible rusting in the humid climate. With it came four magazines and about one hundred rounds of 7.62mm ammunition. We also got an assortment of toiletries. The corporal who was the QM made some cryptic comment about the need for us to keep the rifles as clean as we needed to keep ourselves clean, but the deep significance of the message was lost on us at the time. I asked for another pair of GP, or general purpose boots, since mine had worn rather quickly at JTC. I happened not to mention to him that a lot of the wear and tear had occurred along the bitumen of the Hume Highway as well. I got a new pair. Kevin's question about the mail service between Vungers – as the place was generally called – and Australia got the rather curt and impatient reply that the mail was not his concern and we should ask about that in the orderly room. We didn't know what had got up his nose so suddenly, but didn't pursue the matter. After all, a corporal had just told us something and we were still sufficiently naïve to accept his words at face value without questioning it at all. I did wonder, though, why Kevin was so desperate to know about the mail, for this had been at least the third person that I'd heard him quiz about the matter. Before falling asleep, I saw him scrawl a lengthy letter to his wife the previous night, so I reasoned that he missed her or was already feeling homesick. We were not yet close enough for me to intrude and ask about further details.

Shouldering new rifles which had taken the best part of an hour to degrease and prepare, one of the corporals took us back along the road by which we had driven through camp the day before. Near the front gates of 1ALSG, we went into the area cashier's office. Here we received MPC to the value of $10, which was debited to our pay books. There was a suggestion from the corporal that if managed well, that sum ought to last us until the next regular payday. He then took us for a wander around. The imposing set of buildings I had noted on arrival turned out to be the officers' mess and clubrooms. We followed the road further, past mountains of stacked lumber and barbed wire and we arrived at the helipad just in time to see a Chinook helicopter coming in to land. It wasn't the first we'd heard in the last twelve hours, for they landed and took off regularly, but it was the first we had seen close up. These giants with twin propellers could lift loads weighing many tons and on this occasion we watched as forklifts assembled a load of steel girders, which the craft lifted with ease and carried away in a northerly direction.

From there we went to the club (later named after Peter Badcoe, VC) near the beach where the facilities available for our use on weekends came as a very unexpected – but welcome – surprise. Billiard tables, a jukebox, table tennis tables, and poker machines for my enjoyment were not items I had considered or had dared hope to have when I first knew that I was going to war. After returning to 55, we were given the rest of that day off to become further acclimatised and we spent it moving around the unit's area, finding out as much as we could about the people and our future work and responsibilities.

The physical area that 55 occupied was perhaps no more than three hundred yards in length and some fifty wide. Within this boundary we found the Q store, the orderly room and captain's offices, our tents, two large workshops and a steep, graded roadway next to the motor pool that led up to the area where the new huts were being built. There were four in all with more in the planning stages. Evidently, 55 was expanding and this was, in itself, commentary on Australia's future involvement in Vietnam. The Q store held the usual army paraphernalia of clothing, some non-perishable food items, and an assortment of weapons safeguarded inside a locked, steel cage. The orderly room was about an eight desk office, occupied by the current group of paper-pushers who kept the records of materiel moving in and out of the unit's stores as well as the progress reports on items of machinery being assembled or repaired in the workshops. As clerks, Kevin and Ron took particular interest in what was happening there. Behind the orderly room were two separate offices, belonging to the captain and his 2IC (second-in-command), respectively. A sergeant was in charge of vehicles and was responsible for the maintenance of jeeps and forklifts belonging to 55. He was a short, stocky man who gave the impression of being forever occupied, rushing constantly from one job to the next.

The hub of greatest activity was undoubtedly in and around the workshops. Here, a number of mechanics, plumbers, machinists, refrigeration mechanics, turners, fitters and carpenters, laboured over their respective tasks. They either built or repaired engines, jackhammers, outboard motors, refrigeration units, or a multitude of other building components that were needed elsewhere by some other army unit. Gary was of course interested in the goings-on there. The newly developing area on top of the hill was where I gravitated. The concrete floor in one of the four huts built with the help of local labour was not yet poured, while the surrounding area still required sandbagging and the spreading of screenings for walkways. That would be my job starting the next day. I made myself known to a moustached fellow who went by the nickname of Smokey and who was to be my boss. He was a physically strong guy and had an air of authority, even though he was my age and a sapper like me. We struck up a conversation quite readily and got to know each other's backgrounds almost immediately. As the son of an English army officer, Smokey had been born on the Isle of Wight and had spent his childhood on a succession of army camps both in Malaysia and later in Australia. It seemed that a life in the regular army had been predetermined for him. We discussed work, home, girls, food, drink, and more girls, so that by the end of the day, the connection was cemented.

We spent the rest of that day sweating profusely in the 95 degree heat, wondering for the first of many times just how much longer we would have to wait until the arrival of a cool change. It was perhaps fortunate on that second day in-country not to be aware of the fact that the wait would be about three months. I'm not sure we could have faced the immediate future as confidently if we had known. The dry season was at its height and the monsoon was not expected till mid-year. The constant weariness caused by the humidity and heat of that tropical climate was to be the reason for much of our angst, health problems, and discomfort in the coming months.

The next day we began earning our keep. I soon lost count of the number of shovelfuls of sand and screenings I loaded into wheelbarrows and mixers, but with the help of three Vietnamese workers, the floor in the hut progressed nicely. Inside, Smokey and two others spread and levelled the concrete. In some sense I was officially in charge of the three local men with me. However, since they knew a lot more about concreting than I did, and since they worked at a pace at least twice that of mine, there was little need for me to be a boss of any description. We worked as a team and I did my desperate best to keep up with them. After an hour, they were fresh and looking cool. I was already in a lather of sweat and panting like a racehorse. I could feel the blisters forming in my palms, but under the circumstances I could hardly slacken the tempo. Communication between us was rather limited and unnecessary since we were doing a simple and repetitive task, so hand signals sufficed. By mid-morning, the blisters had already broken. I asked Smokey if I could swap jobs with one of the men inside to give my hands a change of tool to hold, to which I first heard the reply, 'No sweat!' This somewhat vague, yet at the same time meaningful phrase was perhaps coined in Vietnam. Since sweating was an uncomfortable reality of everyday life, no sweat simply meant okay and was therefore considered to be a form of assent, meaning that things were good. I found that spreading and levelling the stuff inside was only marginally easier than shovelling the ingredients outside had been, but at least it required the use of different tools, so the blisters got a temporary respite. No sweat indeed!

At lunchtime, Smokey and I talked about the situation of the Vietnamese workers. They didn't eat with us in the mess, but stayed near the huts and ate a meal they brought from home. I caught a glimpse of the strange, salad-like contents of one plate, but the smell of the dish didn't do much for my appetite. On any given day, up to 200 local workers might have been doing a variety of jobs within 1ALSG. Although their jobs were often the dirtiest and most menial, there was still strong competition on the outside for the work. Not only was local unemployment high and hunger in Vung Tau common, the rate of pay offered by the military was much better than anyone could have hoped to earn in most local industries, with the possible exception of prostitution I was informed by Smokey. Their contact with foreigners, he pointed out, could also help those who might ultimately wish to leave Vietnam. Having successfully passed a security check, these people were therefore glad to wash dishes, clean toilets, empty grease traps, or mix concrete within the boundaries of the camp. Smokey went on to explain that the most sought after bonus, however, was the possibility that the workers might pick up a few extra dollars worth of MPC, which would afford them two other, very valuable opportunities.

Although MPC was legal tender for the military alone, its value on the black market was substantially more than any official rate it might be deemed to have. As such, it could be traded or swapped for local money very easily. Unsurprisingly, however, the majority didn't bother to exchange the MPC for the local Piastres. The MPC's greatest appeal was its purchasing power in the American PX stores, where piastres were not accepted. A huge range of foodstuffs and toiletries that the Vietnamese could never buy anywhere else was available in the PX. With MPC and an identification card that showed an association with the military, these products became accessible. In a country where soap, toothpaste, deodorant, and dairy products were considered luxuries, it wasn't surprising to find that jobs like collecting garbage and cleaning toilets were not viewed with disdain, but valued. Listening to this telling of the story, I couldn't help but feel that things hadn't really changed all that much since World War II. The ration cards and food shortages of that era, along with the special allowances, both financial and political given to supporters of the occupying forces in Europe, were identical practices being mirrored in the Vietnamese experience.

Smokey's explanation and story engendered an even greater respect for these people than the one I had first formulated the previous evening as I watched them wash the dishes. It wasn't difficult to put oneself in their position and readily admit that under similar circumstances which involved family responsibilities, I would act in exactly the same manner. I also took an immediate and particular dislike to the word Noggies, a condescending and thoroughly derogatory name by which almost everyone seemed to refer to them. I didn't know the meaning or origin of the word, nor did I care, but like the spiteful words *wog* and *dago* often applied to new Australians, it had racist connotations which I found distasteful. After lunch, I joined my three co-workers with a fresher and brighter view of our relationship. By five, we had completed half the floor in the hut, so we had another day's concreting still ahead of us. In spite of bleeding palms and an aching back, I thought I had done a good day's work and looked forward to another.

The soaked shorts, socks, and shirt were gladly removed after work. Had it been possible, a cold shower would have been a heavenly treat. There were two problems that hindered such bliss. Firstly, each unit's water supply was limited and trucked in on a daily basis, so conservation was an issue. Secondly, the water was never actually cold as we in Australia know cold tap water to be, but fell somewhere between tepid and lukewarm. Consequently, I had to be satisfied with a three-minute warmish rinse but felt relieved nonetheless. The quantity of water used for each shower was regulated by the size of a canvas bag suspended from crossbeams above the cubicles, into which the water had to be poured. Filled in this way, it looked very much like a cow's bursting udder prior to milking. A shower rose at the bottom of the bag allowed water to dribble out under the pull of gravity. We could regulate the rate at which the water poured out, which in turn determined the length of a shower. It was a totally sensible and satisfactory solution for a situation experiencing water shortage, but I must say we did miss those long, mains pressure showers to which we were accustomed at home.

If any of us had retained the slightest degree of shyness or modesty after the intimacy of basic and corps training, this soon disappeared in the showers and toilets of Vietnam. Both were very public in every sense of the word. The udders were hung in a row of six, only a few feet apart, and that was the number that usually showered together. There were no partitions that one might expect to separate the cubicles. We stood in plain view of each other and performed our ablutions, pretending not to notice the others' every move. The toilets had been designed for similar, communal use. A metal shed had been erected over a large pit about ten feet deep and twenty or so long. Inside was a wooden seat with six holes on it, each about two arms length apart. Thus, six of us could sit side by side to either contemplate our navels or read whatever we had on hand while we answered nature's daily call. It made for wonderful togetherness and mateship and removed all inhibitions we might have had. The place was exceptionally lively during the morning rush, or after a meal of curried sausages. Many thought, probably correctly, that some of our best work was often done inside this Lysaght-sided, aluminium erection.

I was less than thrilled to pick up the shovel and push the wheelbarrow the next morning. My hands were thoroughly blistered, worse than they had earlier appeared. It seemed that I was still only a lightweight paper-pusher. Smokey gave me a pair of gloves, which helped a little, and I wondered why I didn't have the sense to have used them the previous day. It was also heartening to get a cheery hello in English from my co-workers and I felt somewhat ashamed that I hadn't yet memorised a single Vietnamese word I could have used by way of reply. I had noticed, however, that when I put more sand or cement than necessary in the mixer, they had used the French word 'beaucoup' to indicate that it was too much. My reply to them that morning was a beaucoup hello, which they enjoyed tremendously and I believe appreciated. After a short period of moving more barrows full of sand, deliverance arrived in the form of the transport sergeant. He asked Smokey if I could be spared for a half-hour to go into town with him to pick up the unit's laundry. I think I might have killed Smokey if he had said no.

Although it had only been three days, the thought of being locked inside 1ALSG's perimeter fence was anathema. Given that just outside the wire was a war, an abundance of adventure and all sorts of uniqueness waiting to be discovered, the two-week period of restricted movement imposed on us felt like terribly unjust treatment, bordering almost on illegal imprisonment. The chance to go beyond the gate with the sergeant made my heart rate rise considerably and with rifle held between my knees, I rode shotgun out through the boom gates. My hands trembled as I fingered the weapon. Driving past vegetable carts, children on bicycles, pedestrians carrying household items and to all intents and purposes a host of innocent-looking people, the rifle in my hand seemed wrong and an unnecessary show of power. Where was the enemy against whose attack I carried that weapon? They were certainly nowhere that I could see on that road into Vung Tau! Images I had seen in films, of Nazis scaring and terrorising innocent civilians in France or Poland, suddenly came to mind. The comparison felt uncomfortable and was momentarily bothersome, for I had never before considered the serious possibility that my part in the Vietnamese involvement could be that of the villain or aggressor.

My expectations of this very brief outing far exceeded that which reality provided. Within five minutes, the sergeant had driven back towards the roundabout in the road, had turned left away from the airport and we had reached the laundry in town. He told me to stay in the jeep while he went inside. I was bitterly disappointed. I wanted to walk around, have a look, and sample the sights. In a moment, he returned with a number of young boys at his heels who were carrying piles of 55's freshly washed laundry. The sergeant yelled to me to run inside and fetch two more bundles. I did it gladly. I jumped out of the jeep and sprinted in, coming face to face with a bossy-looking gorgon of a woman who shrieked at me and pointed to the clothing I was to pick up. I carried them out and dumped them in the back of the jeep with the rest, taking my seat again next to the sergeant who had already started the motor. I wondered why the hell she had been mad at me, until I realised some time later that the voice I had taken to be her shriek, was simply hers and many others' normal manner of speaking.

'Why did you leave that rifle in the jeep, Frank?' That was the curt, but pointed question when we drove off. I suddenly realised what he was saying and then couldn't believe my own stupidity! I had actually left my rifle leaning against the gear lever when I had gone inside the laundry to fetch the clothing. I grabbed my head in disbelief, whitened substantially, apologised quite fervently, and hoped he was forgiving.

'Listen, Frank, these people will appear to be friendly. They'll shake your hands and smile sweetly and the majority will be genuine. But in this situation and this war, you'll never know who the real enemy is. The Noggy that smiles at you this morning might just as easily shove a knife in your guts tonight. Always be on your guard because you never know. The enemy isn't wearing an identifiable uniform in this place!'

Although I had heard much the same story from others and this had been the substance of several pre-embarkation lectures, the point was driven home with full effect for the first time. As I was digesting the consequences of what might have happened had anyone grabbed my SLR with its loaded magazine and run off with it, I was distracted by a stench coming from the back of the jeep. The piles of laundry, albeit freshly cleaned and pressed, stank unbelievably, and I wondered how many loads of washing had been put through the same water to produce that putrid odour.

```
                    AUSTRALIAN MILITARY FORCES

                                        B Company
                                        2 Recruit Training Battalion
                                        PUCKAPUNYAL, VIC

                                        Seymour   245
                                        Extension 571
Dear Mr. Benko.                         2 Feb 67

         Your    son    has arrived at 2 Recruit Training Battalion to
commence his two years' army service.

         During the next ten weeks he will be trained in basic military
skills. At the end of this period he will be transferred to a Corps
Training Unit for specified training.

         Whilst at this battalion he will be encouraged to write home
regularly to attend Church and to take part in sport.

         The change from civilian to service life is sometimes unsettling.
If this should prove to be the case, I would be grateful if you could use
your influence to assist him over this short period.

         The first visitors' day will be Sunday 19 February 1967 from
10 am to 5 pm when you are most welcome to visit.

         May I also take this opportunity to invite you to attend the
March - Out Parade, to be held on Sunday 9 April 1967


                                        Yours faithfully

                                        [signature]

                                        (Major L.J.P. Quinlivan)
                                        Officer Commanding
```

The letter sent to families advising them of their sons' safe arrivals in camp and the invitation for the seventh intake's March-Out from Puckapunyal.

The spit-polishing of boots.

The first photo after the haircut.

The sixteen strangers who became such close mates during the ten weeks at Puckapunyal.

Corporal Gowans: centre of front row.
Barry: Standing fourth from the left.
Frank: Seated third from the left

School of Military Engineering
Milpo, Liverpool
N.S.W.

MARCH-OUT PARADE

WEDNESDAY, 14th JUNE, 1967

    The Commanding Officer of the School of Military Engineering and the Officer Commanding and Men of Corps Training Squadron request the pleasure of your company at a March-out Parade for the Corps Training Squadron to be held at the School on Wednesday 14th June, 1967, at 10.00 a.m. The Commander, Liverpool Area, Colonel L.I. Hopton M.B.E., is to review the Parade.

    Following the Parade, morning tea will be served in the Peeler Club.

    The Reviewing Officer will arrive at 10.00 a.m. It would be appreciated if you could be seated at the Parade Ground by 9.50 a.m. It is not necessary to reply to this invitation.

The invitation sent to families for the march-out from SME.

*1 Troop: Prior to graduating from SME.
Ron: seated fourth from left.
Frank: seated extreme right.*

Frank wearing waiter's outfit used to serve WWI and WWII Diggers at SME on Anzac Day 1967.

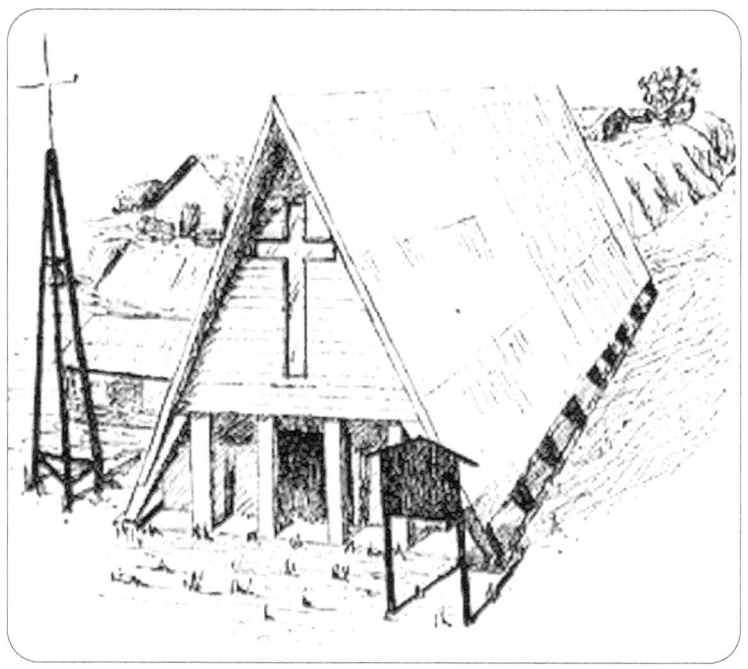

The Anzac Chapel is an all denominational church which was built by the Royal Australian Engineers of the 17th Construction Squadron. The first services were held in the Chapel on Good Friday, 1968, and it was dedicated on Sunday, 16th June, 1968.

The drawing on this card is the work of Sergeant K.J.O'Brien of the 1st Australian Field Hospital.

The Anzac Chapel located inside and near the front entrance to 1ALSG.

From left to right: Smokey, Gary and Andy near the front entrance to 1ALSG.

Ron, on a mission as he exits the Orderly Room.

Four close mates upon whom I relied so much.

Frank on the sandbags outside the huts.

The interior of the hut shown in all its drab glory.

Frank posing in battle gear outside huts.

Smiling faces of children accepting lollies in Vung Tau.

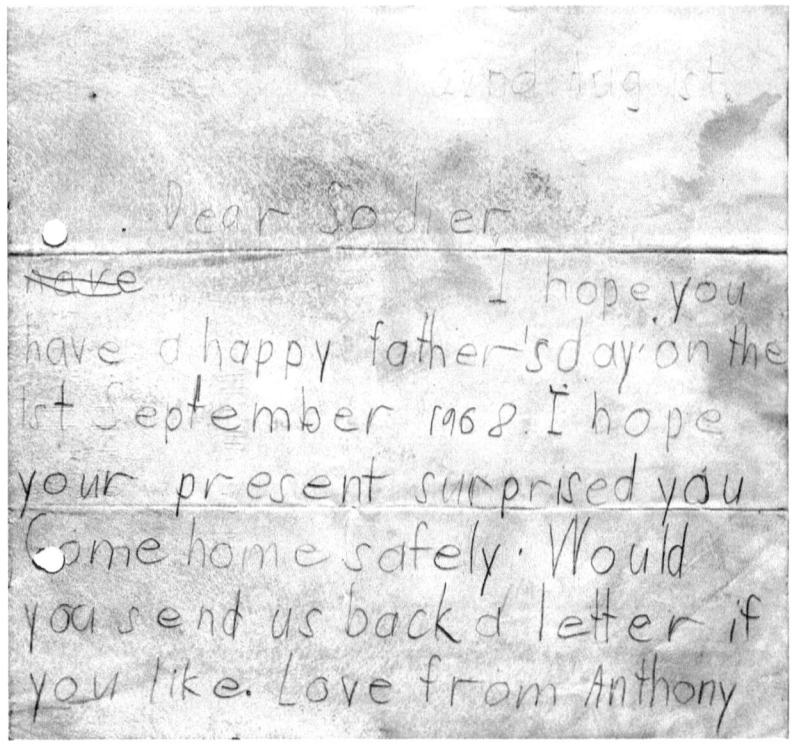

The somewhat faded, pencil-written letter from Anthony, which was just wonderful and thoroughly appreciated.

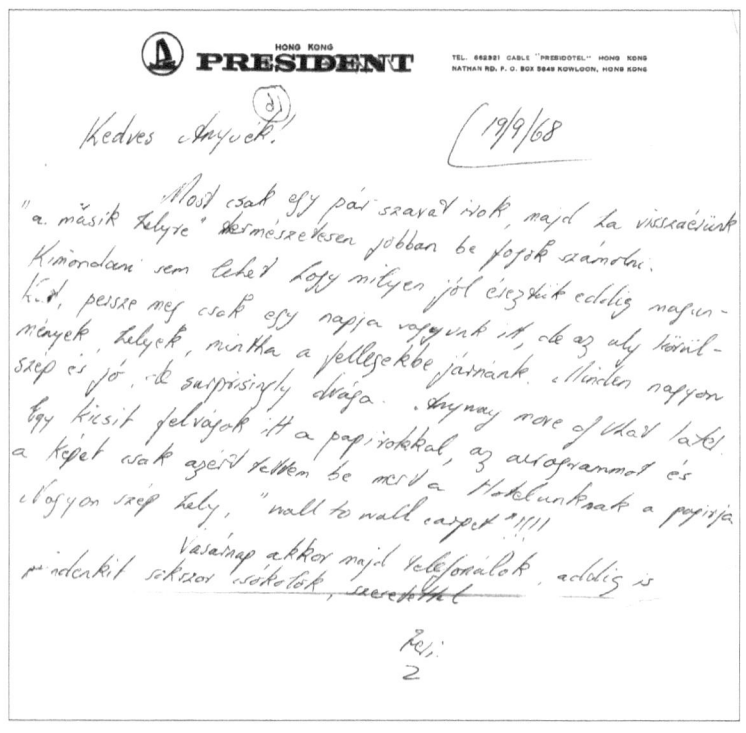

The letter written on hotel stationery from Hong Kong.

Translated: My dear parents. I'll only write a few words now. When we get back to the 'other place' I will write in more detail. I can't tell you how much we've enjoyed ourselves, even though we've only been here for one day, but the whole place makes us feel as though we're floating in the sky. Everything is wonderful but surprisingly expensive. Anyway more of that later. I'm showing off here with the paper and aerogramme letter from our hotel. It's a wonderful place and we have 'wall to wall carpet.' On Sunday I will call, until then my love to everyone, Frank.

```
PARLIAMENT OF AUSTRALIA            418 CENTRE ROAD,
HOUSE OF REPRESENTATIVES           BENTLEIGH, VIC.,
                                   TEL. 97 3158.

                                   3rd. December, 1968.

Mr.& Mrs.L.Benko,
  23 Rae Street,
  EAST BENTLEIGH.  3165.

Dear Mr.& Mrs.Benko,
          Thank you for your letter of 22nd.November.

          I have been very pleased to take up your
request with the Minister for the Army and have asked
him to examine your case urgently.

          I must say that after reading your letter,
I am in complete sympathy with you and hope that I can
do something for you.

          With best wishes,

                              Yours sincerely,

                              DON CHIPP, M.P.
                              Member for Higinbotham
```

Reply from our MHR Don Chipp to my parents' request for an investigation into my return to Australia.

The front bar of the 55 boozer, behind which I spent a considerable period of time as barman.

The back wall of the boozer featuring a very comfortable swagman in a relaxed pose.

At the Vietnam Memorial, Canberra. Members of 55 AESS/EWPS attending the reunion in Canberra on 30 September 2007. Seated: Captain Eddie Albrecht (retired). Standing behind Eddie: Three other commanding officers of 55 – Tony de Bont on left. Standing at rear: All others at reunion – Frank at right in light coloured top.

Chapter 24

7.4.68

What a great feeling it was yesterday to welcome two new guys to the unit! At last, we're not the virgins anymore around the place. I could see us a fortnight ago being just like them, a little unsure and scared. We've finished clearing and levelling the area near the huts, it's looking good. While working on the perimeter fence this afternoon, we watched a Buddhist funeral procession pass by. It was very colourful and the people didn't appear to be as sombre as many at our funerals often are.

    At long last, your first two letters have arrived. I was beginning to think that something might be wrong. Great to read the pages and pages of news, the more the better, I'll write loads as well. I wish everyone a happy Easter, the first one that I can remember spending away from home. I've also done some more concreting in the new shower block. The weather is, if anything, even hotter. Still no rains.

    What has been the reaction at home to Hanoi's peace offer? It's really been the main topic of conversation here as you can imagine! Hopefully, Dr King's assassination won't influence things at all!

I guess Andy must be finished in Canungra by now. When is he coming here and to which unit? Would you believe that Ron got out of bed this morning and announced that there were only 299 days left until our discharge date on 31 January next year! He shouldn't have been so surprised to find himself being pushed naked down a sand dune after his shower.

I'll be sending you a small Vietnamese doll soon, they're very nice, and everyone seems to be mailing them to their families back home.

There had indeed been overtures of peace from Hanoi, reported over the Armed Forces Vietnam Network, the AFVN. After so many years of stalemate, the news caused quite a stir in camp. Following the initial announcement, the more naïve among us – which included me – had visions of packing bags and heading home within weeks. For a brief moment and to my eternal discredit, I even voiced the disappointed thought that if we were to leave the country within the week, the four of us who had arrived together would not be eligible for a War Service Loan. The qualifying period for this was twenty-eight days in-country. I need not have embarrassed myself by saying such a thing or bemoaned the possible loss of the loan. Little did we know then and how could we have possibly imagined that even months later, the shape, and dimensions of the peace conference table in Paris would be the main item on the agenda at the talks. During those months and during many more thereafter, while Dr Kissinger (the American Secretary of State) and Le Duc Tho (the North Vietnamese envoy) became household names around the world and argued over protocols, thousands continued to be injured or killed on both sides.

After our initial period of settling in, a daily pattern established itself. We rose just before six and after the usual shit, shave, shower and shampoo, we went to breakfast. The alliteration of those four words really appealed to me at the time and our morning ablutions were rarely referred to in any other way. My earlier dismay about the persistently undercooked food was resolved. All the vegetables and meat we ate were dehydrated prior to shipment to Vietnam. Thus, just before cooking, the food was immersed in a pot full of water and it was magical to watch pork chops, turkey, chicken, carrots, pumpkin, and potatoes grow and reconstitute as the water was absorbed. After a gentle wringing or draining, the ingredients were ready for cooking. Although reasonably tasty if adequately seasoned, the vegetables in particular were always crusty and reminded us of the look and consistency of plastic chips. Unable to dehydrate eggs, the solution to their method of preservation was to inject a tiny quantity of ether through the shell and, in that way, they kept for months. The unmistakable hint of ether in the mess at half past six each morning soon put us off eggs, however, and the very thought of the taste prevented me from eating eggs for months.

A hasty tidying of our quarters usually followed breakfast and this included time spent on cleaning rifles. We then walked down for the parade at 7.30. After this daily, almost unnecessary gathering, at which the lieutenant played the mother hen role by checking boots, shirts, weapons and haircuts, we filed away to our various jobs. These were briefly interrupted at midday for lunch, after which we resumed work till 5.00. Then, we showered again, had an evening meal, and continued our ceaseless attempts to find a cool, shady spot where we might actually feel comfortable. This was usually followed by a session of drinking in the boozer, the writing of letters home or watching whatever film was being shown that night. Most often it was a combination of all three, so that we would keep ourselves occupied at all times. Periodically, we got the regularly-rostered shifts of guard duty, which would mean having to spend twelve hours in the orderly room from six at night until six the next morning, guarding whatever it was that we were supposed to be guarding. During the next nine months, we often wondered whether this duty was at all necessary or was imposed simply to keep us busy and under tight, army control.

These things made up a normal day. A Monday was a copy of a Wednesday or a Saturday. It soon became apparent that only a few ventured into town during the week, even though the opportunity to do so was available. For the four of us, Vietnam was still new and challenging as March became April, but even after only three weeks, we began to feel the monotony which was to make the nine months seem appreciably longer than that. Our lives were not physically hard or unreasonably demanding. The days simply became maddeningly boring carbon copies of each other.

The move into the new huts occurred surprisingly swiftly about a week after our arrival. We each got a bed and a decent pillow, which were great improvements on the folding cot. The first night spent on the mattress was true comfort. I had only slept on the cot for a short while and sympathised with those who had used them for months. Mosquito nets were strung above each bed. Tucked in properly, the nets kept out a variety of winged livestock, while I was especially pleased to have spiders and geckos finally excluded from between my sheets. These had already taken up residence in the rafters and the clicking sound of geckos in the hut was a nightly lullaby. Green nets, green sheets, green pillowcases, and scattered green clothing gave the place the obligatory army atmosphere. For weeks beforehand, the carpenters in the workshop had been assembling wooden lockers, but these were scarce and issued in order of one's arrival in-country. We were a long way down that list, so our clothing remained in suitcases and sausage bags. Kevin and I ended up as neighbours nearest the door of one hut, with Gary on the other side. Ron was put in a hut next door. Within a few days of the shift, the tents we had been in disappeared and the much-needed space on which they had stood was taken over by many containers stacked three high.

The month had also given the four of us time to become closely acquainted. We were all Nashos from the seventh intake. Ron was a quiet, reserved lad from Alice Springs whose peaceful home life had been shattered by the draft. He was more ill at ease in uniform than most others I ever came across and he desperately wanted the two years to be over. He could then return to the Alice, buy a Kingswood – which was his dream motor car – and resume the ordered existence he'd known before as a builder's assistant working for his father. He was genuinely counting the days and had a special calendar with days marked off until the end of 1968. Kevin was from Perth and had recently married. Just prior to leaving Australia, they had discovered that his wife was expecting their first child. The separation in Sydney had been painful and difficult for them. Without fail, Kevin would write a long letter home each night and would receive one just as regularly in return. He was, in every sense of the word, devastated that he might not be home, to be with his wife at the time of the birth.

Gary was from Melbourne and had lived with his father in Ivanhoe. In many ways, he was a very highly-principled bloke in that he didn't smoke, had never taken a drink in his life, and swear words simply never passed his lips. Indeed, he was a total anachronism in the sometimes debauched environment in which we found ourselves. I was more than a little sceptical when he first told us about the drinking and the swearing, but as the weeks became months, it became evident that Gary was a man of his word. He never swore, never drank, and certainly didn't smoke. He was a mechanic by trade and had travelled to several parts of the world as a ship's fifth engineer, tales about which he had aplenty. He was also very sports mad, a keen golfer, and had been an Australian Rules football umpire in provincial Victoria before the call-up. The fact that we both came from Melbourne helped cement a close friendship, which sustained us in Vietnam and provided a continuing solidity, without which I would have been quite lost.

The concreting was finished some days after my trip into town to pick up the laundry and was replaced by an even more palm-destroying chore: sandbagging. As lectures back in Australia had informed us, actual combat was not anticipated in Vungers. The 1ALSG area's standing orders, however, dictated that all buildings had to be protected and surrounded by a wall of sandbags at least five bags high. If the need ever arose and an attack – either by mortars or ground troops – was to eventuate, we could then take refuge behind the bags and be somewhat protected. This meant that several thousand bags had to be filled, placed, and hammered down for maximum stability. Blisters quickly turned to calluses and I became darker and more sunburnt than ever before in my life. Smokey was seemingly tireless and revelled in the physical exertion of the work. He made sure that he always took the toughest job and ensured that none of us in his gang did more than he was able to do himself. In that sense, he was an excellent leader and his eagerness was so contagious that one evening he even succeeded in motivating about twenty of us to play a game of volleyball on an area of sand behind the huts. A full day's work was over, everyone was worn out, and the evening heat was at its usually intolerable worst, yet we threw ourselves into the match, diving for low returns and chasing the ball around the sand. We had a great time and volleyball became a semi-regular evening activity. Smokey's leadership skills were evident to all and we knew he would go far as either a commissioned or as a non-com officer in the army. He got the opportunity to further his career soon after we completed work on some ditches near the perimeter fence.

The captain called the four field engineers into his office one morning. This was unusual in that all our work to date had been allocated by the lieutenant. We were apprehensive about the summons. The boss, Captain Albrecht, was a quiet man to whom we responded with the respect that his rank demanded. He generally kept to himself and was well-liked by everyone in 55. He ran a smooth and successful operation as captain of a stores unit. In the preceding month, none of my small group had tried to approach him about any specific matter, the lieutenant being the go-between in most dealings involving the troops and the unit's boss. We stood in awkward silence while he made the announcement. As much of the hackwork around the area had been finished, 55 no longer needed four field engineers, so the captain wanted two volunteers to transfer to a unit in Nui Dat. Smokey immediately stepped forward as we knew he would, but the rest of us remained very still and very silent. Weighing up the response, the captain gave us twenty-four hours to reconsider the question and said that if there was still no second taker at that time, he would nominate one of the three to fill the second spot. I did reconsider the matter overnight, but was still not prepared to step forward.

If ordered to, I would have had no choice. I reasoned, though, that having volunteered for Vietnam and having ended up in a reasonably safe place, I was not prepared to tempt the devil any further by volunteering for potentially deeper trouble. It was the sort of logic which I thought my parents would appreciate under the circumstances. Smokey and Gary agreed with me when I discussed it with them that evening. After a restless night, the three of us fronted the captain again. No one was willing to go, so he gave us the decision he had already made. Happily, I had not been his choice. Days later, we bid two good mates farewell as they rode shotgun on one the trucks running the daily convoy between Vungers and the Dat. My relief at staying was soured by the considerable regret that I had just lost Smokey's immediate friendship.

With Wayne acting as guide, the Sunday finally arrived when the four of us made it into town for a first social visit. The Lambretta, a smoke-billowing, three-wheeled, very loud local version of a taxi, chugged and coughed its way down narrow alleys, depositing us in a square in front of the market place. My one previous trip to pick up laundry had been limited in distance and now I saw that there was much more to Vung Tau than I had originally thought. Beyond the dull, airport side and to an extent the poorer, laundry part of town, the area nearer the beach was lively, affluent, and very attractive. Its planning and elegance bore testimony to the claim that Vung Tau had once been known as the Riviera of

Indo-China and the much sought-after rest and recreation resort of the French forces a decade earlier.

The large, white Grand Hotel near the foreshore looked out over a crescent-shaped bay, which was skirted on land by a wide, palm-edged boulevard – not too dissimilar to those found in Cannes or Nice. The view, in comparison to any other I'd seen in over a month, was quite breathtaking. The houses in this part of town were large, quite clean, and opulent by local standards, even though some bore the marks of war as evidenced by years of disrepair and neglect. A number of homes built into the sides of hills were almost palatial, showing that even in strife-torn Vietnam, among the misery and deprivation, wealth still held sway. We noticed other western influences as we ambled around. Many younger men had foregone the usual, black, pyjama outfits in favour of T-shirts and jeans. Remarkably, though, the thongs persisted. The music which blared from open doorways was American or English pop, while Marlboro and Kool brand cigarettes, as well as Coca-Cola signs, were abundant. It seemed that just about everyone was self-employed, for there were hundreds of street vendors pushing small carts and selling their wares just as we had seen at the airport in Saigon. There was in the air a competitive, market-like commercialism, and the vehemence with which sellers were spruiking exceeded any of the enthusiasm one might have witnessed from vendors at the Victoria Market in Melbourne. We knew that the main market days were held during the week, so this Sunday effort was aimed primarily at the hundreds of Australian, but especially American servicemen, wandering the streets. Green uniforms were visible everywhere and for the first time we got the opportunity to have a good look at our US counterparts.

First impressions can be misleading, and perhaps one shouldn't rely on them too much. Nonetheless, my opinion about and attitude towards the American GI was strongly influenced by this initial encounter. Many were aloof, unapproachable, at times arrogant, and always conceited and loud. In their defence, it might be argued that we just happened to come across those who were all on a five-day period of rest and convalescence and had just come from a harrowing frontline fight. As such, they might well have been within their rights to treat us and everyone else they met with disregard and disrespect. After all, they had just witnessed death, escaped its clutches, and were now simply behaving like tourists blowing off steam. One could say that, but one would be very generous to argue such a case. The dozens of pot-bellied, cigar-smoking, and tobacco-chewing types we saw driving around in jeeps didn't come from any frontline, or from a life-threatening fight. They were clerks, cooks, and drivers who adopted a manner that the lord of the manor might employ when dealing with underlings. On the streets, in the shops, and – in particular – the bars, they behaved as though they were lords and masters of all they surveyed. They drove vehicles through crowds at high speed, a group of four would sound like twenty, and their abrasive and rude language towards the Vietnamese was embarrassing – even to us as bystanders. We felt guilty by our association with them. As the afternoon wore on and we visited several bars, I noticed that the reception we got was decidedly cooler than those given the Yanks in spite of their attitude. The answer became evident when we saw the wads of notes they produced when ordering anything. We were the *Uc Dai Loi*, which loosely translated as people from the south. We were welcomed warmly as the southerners, but the Yanks had the full wallets and also the undivided attention of the barmen and the bargirls wherever they went.

There was a narrow street that led out of the square next to the market. Wayne took us down there and the reason for its adopted name, the street of bars, was evident. For a distance of some four hundred yards, there were up to sixty bars on either side of the street. In front of most stood the girls whose task it was to entice potential customers into their particular establishment. We didn't need too much enticement or encouragement. On entry, the girls inside would literally and bodily grab us, and their job was to ensure that we then parted with as much of our money as possible within the shortest given time. Their commission was determined by the number of drinks we had and the number we were prepared to buy them. The sting was that while a shot of whisky for us might cost fifty cents, their drinks could cost anything from one to five dollars. In a place like the Grand, a ten dollar drink for the bargirls was not unknown. The popularity of some girls no doubt also affected the size of this hostess charge. Sexual favours were of course an optional part of the deal and would depend on the number and cost of the drinks one was willing to buy. The Saigon teas which the girls drank were aptly called, being nothing more than extremely expensive, sugared cups of cold tea.

Being short of funds that afternoon, we didn't get too far with the girls. It was an education in opportunism to watch the smooth and practiced ease with which they changed allegiances from one of us to another as they discovered that we were either out of money or unprepared to spend any more. They weren't even shy about lifting wallets out of our back pockets and checking to see whether we were worth any more effort or time, or if they could do better by looking for fresh prospects elsewhere. I must say that in their cut-throat business of soliciting, they could be extremely persuasive. For young boys unaccustomed to such direct and forward behaviour, a pretty head resting on the shoulder and an exploring hand on the thigh a minute after being seated at a table proved to be powerful inducements towards swift and eager capitulations.

The other revelation about the sleazy aspects of life was what we saw around the brothels and so-called massage parlours that afternoon. Young boys of eight or nine cruised the streets and spoke just enough English to be able to advertise their respective houses and the services that were on offer.

'Soldier, you want young girl for suck-suck? I take you to pretty girl, come.'

In other places, young girls stood outside houses with the words 'Barber Shop, Steam Bath or Massage' emblazoned in red on front doors and windows. We got the same offer from them. Aged twelve but going on twenty, these unfortunate children were the real victims of what was happening in Vietnam.

The political and philosophical arguments paled into insignificance. Here was a nation whose children were prostituting themselves and twelve and thirteen-year-olds were being offered to us to perform oral sex in order to survive. We had been told about this and had mentally visualised such a scene, but the actual sight of those small, helpless children of 1968 filled me with sorrow and shame. Less than ten years earlier, I had been twelve and at that time my greatest problems and concerns in life had been whether my homework was completed on time or whether my mother would notice that the right-hand pocket of my blazer had a tear in it after it had caught on the saddle and ripped as I mounted my bicycle. Was I a guilty part of a system which created this awful consequence? To what extent was I personally blameworthy? Could I have done anything to alter the facts? I didn't, and we didn't have answers to these disturbing questions, but simply watched in amazement as some actually took advantage of what was offered. To our credit and I think everyone's relief, our small group wandered off and we looked for something else to see that afternoon.

Chapter 25

Kevin was becoming noticeably more restless and quite morose as the weeks passed. Being an orderly room clerk, he was our pipeline to that office and kept us informed about new standing orders that were in the offing, new postings, transfers in and out of the unit, and other useful information. As a rule, he had also been good for a steady stream of humour. While we had become used to his changing moods – which were generally determined by the type of letter he received from his wife – it was out of character for him to become so totally distant and to do it so suddenly. Something was obviously gnawing at him and after the film one night we broached the subject. His wife was indeed the source of his concern because the pregnancy was not going well. She was losing weight instead of gaining it, was unable to sleep, and the doctors had expressed concern for her welfare as well as that of the baby. Additionally, the enforced separation was creating emotional scars for which she had sought help. No small wonder then that Kevin's state of mind was also affected. The information about his wife had been relayed to him by a family member, as she hadn't wanted to worry him. Naturally, this heightened Kevin's uncertainty about what he should or should not write in the nightly letters he so carefully and lovingly composed.

We could offer no more constructive advice than to tell him to see the captain and ask what his options might be. Kevin at first baulked at this, not wanting to discuss private matters with too many people and not wishing to appear to be asking for any special favours or consideration. We disagreed, but left the decision to him. Some days later, a course of action was determined for him. A telegraph arrived, via the captain, telling Kevin that his wife had been admitted to hospital and that there were serious complications affecting both her and the child. That same day he submitted a compassionate application, requesting an immediate transfer to a unit back home in Perth. This was not only endorsed, but probably suggested by the captain and to its everlasting credit, the army's administrative machinery – which could be ponderously slow at times – processed the application quickly, and Kevin was slated for the earliest possible flight home. Within the week he returned to the person who needed him most. We received a letter from him a month or so later to say that while not fully recovered, his wife was improving and that ultimately all would be well. We read the letter with considerable joy.

Some days before he left, there had been a party in the boozer to farewell two others heading home. They had completed their twelve-month tour of duty and, as such, commanded the awe and respect of all. The drinking was heavy and serious right up to the close of the pub at ten o'clock and we watched these two 'short-timers' quaffing pot after pot of beer. This was the first of many such farewells we would attend and, on each occasion, we were desperately envious of those who were leaving. I began a mental countdown of how many more of these parties I would have to endure before my own departure was at hand. The number, around thirty, which was the best estimate I could make, was the frightening result. After only six weeks or so in-country, the desire to leave was already strong. However, it was easier to accept the inevitability of the thirty other departures before mine, than it was to accept Kevin's leaving. His was a special case.

We admitted that he had to go and deserved to go, but having been one of our group of four, it was difficult to view his departure totally objectively and quite so selflessly. I would be less than honest if I didn't admit to feelings of envy and downright jealousy at the time. Kevin was well and truly packed the night before, only the polyesters and shoes were left out to put on early in the morning. He was woken by the guard at four, and being attuned to noises around us, we also awoke. We had coffee while he shaved and dressed. We walked with him to the jeep that would take him to the airstrip in Vungers, from where a Caribou would continue the trip as far as Saigon. From there, of course, a Qantas 707 would complete the journey home. It was just on dawn, a peaceful and exceptionally quiet time of day. He had slept very little the night before and looked haggard.

'I'm sorry to leave, boys, but I've no choice!'

'We're not so happy about it either, you know, and we're as jealous as hell, mate, but you have a family to take care of and that's the main thing. Take care of yourself and give your wife a peck on the cheek from each one of us.'

'It's been good to know you, fellows, even if only for this short time!'

'See you, mate, and Godspeed!'

This might have been the exchange of words between us, if any of the four had been thinking clearly and sensibly that morning. As it was, very few words were said as the jeep drove away from the orderly room and out of view. For some reason that I couldn't fathom, I felt as helpless as a child for the rest of that day. Gary was similarly affected, while Ron mumbled something about another day having finally passed. Although we grieved about Kevin's leaving, the topic was taboo and was not discussed by any of us beyond that day. It was simpler to keep quiet and not voice the bitter disappointments, rather than to dwell on them. With Kevin gone, Wayne moved his gear into the vacated area near the door next to mine.

There was little left for us field engineers to do after Smokey moved to the Dat. The unit's surroundings were completely established and apart from some barbed wire extensions, the construction of some drains near the motor pool and general tidying of sites, work for the two of us was really scarce. We began to think that there might be further enforced postings north. We often smiled wryly whenever we recalled the weeks spent at SME on bridge building, mine-laying and demolitions. Those skills were certainly not needed at 55, but we feared that at the Dat, we might just have to brush up on our mine-lifting techniques and the thought was unpleasant. When work outside had dried up completely, we cleaned out the Q store, swept the orderly room, sorted nuts and bolts in the workshops and considered, with some disquiet, our less than magnificent contributions to the war effort. By the end of April, the novelty and shine of overseas duty had all but worn off. A daily monotony had set in and the passage of time slowed correspondingly. We began to understand why so many of our mates drank and why they did so to a serious excess.

I was by no means an expert, but it seemed that a very large number at 55 spent too much time and too much money on the one pastime that satisfied an urge, appeased the loneliness, and provided the succour in times of need by its smooth, innocuous dulling of the senses. Of all the products we consumed, beer was perhaps the only one we didn't purchase entirely from the Americans. Thousands of pallets of Fosters, Victoria Bitter, Fourex, Tooheys, and Cascade were transported to Vietnam aboard HMAS *Sydney* on a regular basis. This provided the troops with the ales they most preferred and the 'piss' was really cheap. Nearly every unit had its own boozer and members of those that didn't soon found one that did. Abundant cans of beer found an equal abundance of willing customers at dozens of convenient outlets. In the first weeks, I joined others milling around the bar of our neighbouring unit, 17 Construction Squadron, but never having been a heavy drinker, I did so more for company than because of a liking for the stuff. I always felt that one can of cold beer at the end of a long hot day was great, but a dozen was impossibly over the top, a bad habit, and nothing else. After a while, I didn't bother going at all, but joined Gary who never went. We wrote letters, went to the movie with cans of soft drink in our hands, or just sat outside on the sandbags and talked to fill in the empty hours. Sitting there, we would sometimes watch the swaggerers, pissed out of their minds, trying to find the right hut, the steps, or their beds. If we were fortunate, they threw up on the sand outside before entering. Otherwise, we either had to tolerate the stench or, both of us having beds right next to the door of the hut, clean it up ourselves. Not only did we feel somewhat sorry for their predicament and plight, but seeing some who were in that condition fairly regularly was sufficient encouragement to keep me off the booze pretty much most of the time. Gary had no such difficulty and in spite of his total distrust of alcohol, he was more tolerant and understanding than I when it came to picking up or putting to bed one of our paralytic mates.

Our abstinence didn't win us too many friends. Gary, Ron, Wayne, and I became a small, non-drinking clique and we copped plenty of criticism as a result. Pointed barbs were aimed at our exclusivity and, on one occasion, an inebriated neighbour even questioned our sexual preferences. The logic in his sozzled mind was of course that since we didn't drink, we simply had to be raging queers. What other possible answer could there have been? This was a very unfortunate development, because it affected our relationship with at least a dozen members of the unit and there was an icy divide between them and us that persisted for the entire nine months. Gary being a teetotaller came in for particularly nasty treatment. It was with considerable satisfaction that we watched our greatest critic make a complete arsehole of himself one night. For a bet, he had guzzled down the contents of a whole bottle of Johnny Walker. As we were returning from the movie, we found him sprawled near the entrance to the hut, paralytic and almost choking on his own vomit. He was very ill as a result, could have been hospitalised, and in all probability could well have died. His great drinking mates and buddies had apparently left him supine as he lay and had returned to their drinking binge. After that, as far as we were concerned, criticism of our behaviour could be as loud and as vehement as anyone wished to make it. We simply no longer cared.

For many, drink was an available source of solace and the only viable outlet. Between 7.30 in the morning and five o'clock at night we were occupied with work. But that left a large portion of the day in which there was little to do unless one made special efforts to find distractions. Many sat, talked, and played cards, but then why not do that with a can in hand?

One could go into town but, in truth, three visits there would satisfy one's curiosity completely and all the sights would have been sufficiently covered. Once in town, however, the bars beckoned and a quick drink was never more than a few steps away. Many read or listened to the radio, but again, why not with an ice cold can in the hand? One could write letters home, but many didn't write more than once a week and that only occupied twenty minutes. It was also possible to go down to the club for a swim if one didn't mind sharing the South China Sea with swarms of jellyfish, but at the club there was a bar, so why not walk along the beach instead with a can in hand? There were always the nightly films to watch, but the 17's boozer was only ten or so yards from the screen. So what could be more comfortable and convenient than sitting outside in the tropical, balmy, evening air, watching a film in the company of good mates with a few cans to quench a powerful thirst?

In truth, we spent much of our time absolutely bored out of our skulls and it wasn't surprising that huge quantities of booze were consumed. Encased as we were by the barbed wire surrounding 1ALSG, the only difference between our situation and that of other soldiers back in Australia was the geographic location. It was a maddening and frustrating conundrum. We were soldiers who had been taught and prepared for war, who had been transported to a war zone, and yet we spent our time in repetitive, monotonous, un-warlike labour, with far too much spare time and precious little with which to fill it. The war, the action, the adventure, but above all the families we missed constantly were all outside the camp, out of reach. For many, this was a source of substantial regret and ceaseless sorrow. Drink turned out to be a pleasant, time-consuming substitute for all that we didn't have and for all the things about which, as Nashos, we felt unfairly deprived. Those causes notwithstanding, far too many of us used far too much drink in an attempt to consume far too much time. Quite fortunately, other, harder drugs were not so readily available. I suspect those, too, might have found willing users and customers.

The business with the drinking fully strengthened my friendship with Wayne, Gary, and Ron. We usually sat together in the mess and generally kept each other company and occupied in our spare time. Ron was, by choice, a loner. Unlike the drinkers who worshipped the contents of the can, Ron was totally immersed in all things that continued to connect him to Australia. Homesickness was really hurting this gentle, pleasant, and quiet country boy. He hung a map of South East Asia above his bed and drew a thick red line on it, joining Vung Tau to Alice Springs. He spent hours poring over the Holden pamphlets he had picked up in Sydney which featured his beloved Kingswood. When we walked past his bed, we would often hear him muttering, 'When I go home, this'll do me just fine.' He also bought a tape recorder and, as well as the lengthy letters he wrote to his parents, he would record hours of private conversation to send to them. Tapes recorded by his parents were played repeatedly and when bed checks were made in the early mornings, we sometimes found that he had fallen asleep with the tape running and the plugs still in his ears. Time for Ron seemed to pass as slowly as it would have for any prisoner who had been jailed for a year.

By early May, even the occasional sweeping, sorting, and gardening jobs had been exhausted. For some time there had been talk about the need for increased security around the unit and finally a decision was made. A boom gate was to be erected across the roadway near the orderly room's front entrance, effectively blocking off access to the workshops and the upper storage areas where the tents had been located. A man would be needed to control this gate and keep a register of all trucks and stores movements in and out of 55. I was given the job and welcomed the news, for apart from avoiding an enforced move to Nui Dat, it gave me a specified task which was preferable to the daily uncertainty that had gone on for weeks. Even though the job was bound to be dull, I would at least wake in the mornings and know precisely what lay ahead that day.

The plumbers welded together a tubular steel frame that formed the boom and at one end attached a metal box filled with concrete to act as a counter-balance. By slow degrees and some trial and error, just the right quantity of concrete was added so that a minimum of effort would be required to raise and lower the boom. In the meantime, we poured a foundation of about sixteen square yards and the carpenters whipped up the framework for a small shed. This was placed on the concrete floor and in a few days, some corrugated sheeting completed the walls and roof. From inside that small structure, I could see down the road, waiting for transports to arrive. About a week after I was first told about the job, I took up residence in the 'security hut' and having located a table, a chair, and a thick exercise book for recording the details that were required, I became a paper pusher again.

It was a welcome change to be able to sit rather than to be digging post-holes or drains, and I was the butt of friendly ridicule in that I had scored such a cushy job. In truth, a trained monkey performing his tricks needed greater powers of concentration than I needed for the task. The boom had to be kept closed at all times. If a truck arrived, I had to check either the requisition form for a pick-up, or the delivery docket for stores being brought to 55. If the forms were correct, I would raise the boom, let the vehicle pass, and record its registration number and time of arrival in the book. Upon its leaving, I had to check the signature on the release form for stores, let the truck out, and tick off its number in my book to show that the vehicle had left the unit. I repeated this procedure about eighty times a day. It was neither challenging nor fulfilling stuff, but it gave me plenty of time to read and to write, both of which I did assiduously.

14.4.68–7.5.68

Well, there seems to have been a mix up with our letters at both ends, with some arriving out of sequence. I've learned that from here our mail first goes to Hawaii by Pan Am and is picked up from there by Qantas and taken to Sydney. This roundabout route is probably the cause of the problem, but in any case the important thing is that they all arrive. Your letters are very eagerly awaited, that's for sure.

I've started growing a moustache, a bit messy at the moment, but it'll thicken up. It might balance out the hair I'm losing on top, sweating as I always am under this jungle cap. Handfuls are falling out in the shower every day...

For the first time yesterday, we were within earshot of the fighting – several rockets were fired at the airbase in Vung Tau at four in the morning. No great damage though, we're told.

Please put away those matriculation papers you wrote about, they'll probably come in handy sometime...

I'm amazed at how cheap the PX is here! An automatic date watch is only $16, a large mix master with all the attachments goes for $29. What the hell is a mix master doing in a place like this, I hear you ask? I don't know, either. If there is anything you need let me know, I can get it cheaply. Funny war! I'm able to send you stuff! Wasn't it the other way round not so long ago in the last war? Thanks for the photos, I'll pin them up when I finally get a locker. One thing we just can't get here is chocolate, so if you could send a couple of bars of Nestles, that'd be great...

I got a locker at last and packed all my stuff in yesterday, but a mix up again, it was supposed to be given to someone else, so I unpacked again. I'm not stuffing it all back in the duffle bag, I've hung it up on a wire, and it can collect bloody dust up there until I get that blasted locker!

We saw Elke Sommer in 'Deadlier than the Male' last night, a great film. Tonight it's something with Raquel Welch. Our congratulations to the supplier of films, whoever that might be!

We got a ten-minute dribble of rain this afternoon; the monsoon could be earlier than anyone thought...

Congratulations, Greg, for the fencing results in Wagga, how about writing to me more often, let me know the VFL footy results? I had trouble sending you the doll I promised. I tried to mail it, but the captain hadn't signed the customs declaration, so it had to wait. Apparently, some idiotic desert-head sent a grenade home in the mail last year and since then officers have to inspect all packages prior to mailing.

There's so little variation in our lives, lots of guys drink an awful lot just to fill in time. No I haven't been to Nui Dat. We whine and complain about the sand here, but seeing the trucks and the blokes that arrive from there! They are all covered from head to foot in a fine red dust, in eyes, ears, and the works. They usually can't wait to have a shower or a swim in the sea, more testimony to just how lucky I am to be here instead.

I'm sending some more photos next letter to show you some of the American and our own installations. It's amazing how completely and permanently the Americans seem to be entrenched here! Judging by the size of the Yankee effort, losing this war appears to be impossibility!

Great to hear that Andy might be coming to Vungers! Which unit, though? Did he say? There was a dawn service for Anzac Day on the 25th. It was a beautiful early morning ceremony held on the helipad with the Last Post being played just as the sun was coming up! We wore our new Vietnam ribbons. The six and a half day working week is long and tiring, not so much because of the time or the work, but the incessant bloody heat which saps all our energy.

We saw 'The Sound Of Music' last night. Great songs, didn't care much for the story, though.

There's been more shelling at the airbase, so we have compulsory lights out at ten, a few Vietnamese have apparently been killed in this latest attack…

Great entertainment at the club yesterday, a group from Perth was here, with Ron Blaskett and Gerry Gee. Old Gerry used language I sure haven't heard him use on television, though! Wow! A few of us are developing heat rashes from the constant sweating. It's called 'prickly heat'. It's incredibly itchy and cold water on it is the best treatment. Another truck just went through the gate. It's eleven o'clock and I've had only fifteen go through. As I've said before, it's a hard war...

The rains fell a bit last night and would you believe even a few drops of hail? Yesterday it was boiling hot, now it's lunchtime and still raining. It's the very early part of the monsoon they say, sometimes this happens and then nothing for months afterwards. We lost a refrigerator yesterday. I was worried because it had gone through the gate, but when we checked, the paperwork was OK. We finally traced it to an American unit in town and they were already cooling the beer in it...

It's now been a few weeks and not much progress at the peace talks! Wish they'd hurry. Lots of people are dying here! Some days ago, a woman carrying a baby threw a homemade grenade into the back of one of our trucks in Nui Dat. Fortunately, it didn't go off! Eight could have been killed we're told!

I'm glad the doll I sent finally arrived. You ask about a name for it, so let's make it Sung. That's the name of the first girl I met here. The letter 'g' is silent and the word is pronounced like our word 'soon', although not quite with the same broad Australian 'oo'...

The unit's boozer is finished and it was christened with the first drinks served last night. The local soaks can now drink to their hearts' content much closer to home. It's been incredibly windy and hot recently, the rains of some days ago have gone, we're back to stifling humidity. Hope is still high for what might eventually happen in Paris. We will see.

Still no bloody locker, this is becoming a joke...

Chapter 26

On our first night in-country, Wayne had mentioned that there was a Vietnamese girl doing some light clerical work in the orderly room. The next day I met Sung. She smiled at the new group of four faces that approached her as we were returning from the helipad. I took an immediate liking to her, without knowing why that might be the case. She wasn't a beautiful girl in the general sense of the word and her image would not have been used on a travel brochure advertising the wondrous and mysterious Orient. To be truthful, she was a little short and slightly overweight, but there was a gentleness and openness in her face and manner which made her beautiful nonetheless. Lawrie apparently thought so. He was a Nasho from one of the earlier intakes and, by any reckoning, his two-year stint was well and truly over. Like a small number of others, though, Lawrie decided that his future was brighter in the army than it might be elsewhere and he signed up as a permanent member of the force for three more years. To us, this was anathema. More importantly, though, we discovered that his twelve-month period of service in-country had also expired, yet he was still there. We wondered why!

From the very first we found him to be a very quiet, private person, and the little we could glean from our infrequent conversations was that, unlike the vast majority of us, he actually seemed to enjoy overseas duty, or had some other attachment to the place. We were told that several people had suspected that there was something going on between Lawrie and a local girl, but we didn't know how close the two of them had become. They gave away few clues about the nature of their relationship, even though they worked fairly close to each other in the orderly room. As we learned afterwards, Lawrie's frequent weeknight visits into town should have been an indicator to all that he was visiting something or someone other than the bars or prostitutes of Vung Tau. He was not the type that would have drunk or womanised at all. Lawrie had, in fact, fallen for Sung's sister, and had in some senses adopted the family, providing for them with essentials of food and clothing from the PX. Being an immature and selfish twenty-one-year-old at the time, such apparent foolishness and nonsense amazed me. I couldn't understand that kind of attachment to the girl, or for that matter anything Vietnamese. My own singular and ardent desire, which grew daily, to complete my allotted time and leave the place as soon as possible, was so strong that Lawrie's attitude and choice seemed alien and totally incomprehensible. He was still at 55 when we left and was well into his second year. He was, I think, considering applying for a third tour, but there was a question about his chances of success. I hope that he was ultimately successful and that he found with this girl the peace and contentment in life which he so clearly sought.

By early May, I was utterly convinced that the standing order in relation to rifles was a farce. War zone or not, carrying one around in the guarded safety of camp seemed ludicrous when, dressed in civilian clothing on a Sunday afternoon, we moved freely around town without it. Did imminent danger from the enemy disappear at one o'clock on Sundays, or was there a mutually-accepted ceasefire at that time each week specifically so that we could spend several rifle-free hours away from camp? It felt at times that the rifle was even less necessary than certain other items of our compulsory uniforms. It felt like just another form of inconvenient bastardization that the army had concocted for our continuing discomfort. When in camp, in uniform, among several hundred of our own kind, the rifle had to be carried. Out of uniform, in town, as we mingled with the potential enemy, rifles could be left behind. The rationale behind this decision escaped me since, in or out of uniform, we stood out like dogs' balls in the Vietnamese crowd of Vungers, and anyone who wished could have easily challenged us once we stepped outside the perimeter fence. In spite of many arguments we had amongst ourselves, and with sergeants on the subject of moronic standing orders like this one concerning rifles, we were, after all, only sheep and had to obey the shepherd's command. We carried rifles to the mess, to work and even to the movies at night while we were inside our protected camp, but went unarmed in town whenever we visited there in civilian clothes. The logic was mindlessly 'army'.

The other concern with my particular rifle was that the blasted thing was rusty. As original issue, it had been covered in a thick layer of grease, but shortly after this was removed, a furry film of rust began to form on the barrel and dustcover. It was not a new rifle and had been owned by someone in the unit before me, so I could only presume that it had been previously neglected. Perhaps that person had allowed some rust to form and had then attacked the barrel with steel wool.

That would have removed the rust all right, but would have scraped away the outermost, metallic, protective layer of the surfaces in question.

As a result, I had a running battle with the rifle and this involved daily oiling that ought not to have been necessary and which was generally not recommended. All I achieved, however, was to camouflage the problem and the rust was persistently present in minute quantities so that I was conscious of the faint whiff of rusting metal whenever the barrel came close to my face. The Q store corporal wasn't interested in my pleadings and wouldn't issue me another, claiming that he had given me a clean, rust-free rifle and the problem was therefore mine. The temptation to wrap the bloody rusting barrel around his morose head was almost overpowering, but I had to settle for a less satisfactory solution. I simply left the Q store muttering incoherent Hungarian obscenities about him and about army regulations under my breath.

It was definitely a problem, especially prior to each Monday morning's parade. At these times, the lieutenant inspected weapons closely and individually and I had the weekly hassle of getting the rifle just right. If insufficient oil was applied the night before, the night's humidity would ensure a thin rusty coating by morning. If I put on too much, it would glisten in the sun and give the game away. So on Sunday nights, I put on an amount that had previously proven to be sufficient and carrying a rag for the specific purpose in my pocket, I quickly wiped off the excess a minute or two before the parade. I normally held back and, as we were lining up and standing behind the others, I waited for the officer to exit his office before I wiped the thing furiously. This would involve removing the two taped magazines, wiping the barrel, dust cover and around the trigger housing before replacing the magazines. One morning, however, in this frenzy of hurried deceit, I made the unforgivable error of shoving the loaded rather than unloaded magazine back into the rifle.

The drill for weapons inspection was unmistakably clear and something we had practiced hundreds of times during training. 'Cock the weapon, hold the cocking handle back with the left hand, and insert the right thumb into the empty bolt housing, while holding the weapon at a forty-five degree angle.' In this way, the reviewing officer could peer down the barrel from the front, light would reflect from the thumbnail, and the officer could see if the rifling inside the barrel had been pulled clean or not. After his inspection was over, the cocking handles were released, the bolts would jump forward back into their firing positions, and triggers would be fired and released to the accompaniment of hollow clicks as the firing pins hit thin air. Held at that angle, the barrels would be pointing slightly above the heads of the men in front.

On this eventful morning, I cocked the rifle, inserted my thumb, and held the barrel in the required manner. The lieutenant peered down the barrel and apparently satisfied with the cleanliness he saw passed on to the next man. Following a respectful step behind him was one of the warrant officers who glanced at my rifle and went noticeably pale. He motioned with his eyes towards my magazines and I followed his glare by looking into the bolt housing. I went just as pale as he had done for I saw what neither of us ought to have been able to see. Gleaming in the sunlight and in plain sight to both was the uppermost of the twenty, 7.62mm shells of the loaded magazine. He waited another moment until the lieutenant moved further down the line before hissing at me.

'You will remove that bloody magazine before releasing the cock won't you, Sapper Benko!'

It was not a question but the bluntest of commands and the icy emphasis on the last four words, combined with the look in his eye prompted a swift, affirmative reply.

'Bloody oath I will, sir!'

The immediate frankness of the reply and the terrified realisation he noticed in my face no doubt reassured him that, although I had committed a monumental error, it had been unintentional and would never, but never, be repeated. He even ignored my incorrect address of him as sir and when the command to release the cock was finally given, I whipped the magazines around quicker than I had ever done before.

Afterwards, I stood there and tried to picture the unimaginable consequences had the warrant officer not noticed my error. In releasing the cock, a shell would have been put up the spout without me realising it. Then, when the order to fire was given, instead of hearing the hollow click of a firing pin hitting air, my rifle would have fired a live round, hopefully above the head of the man in front of me. At such a close range, I can't imagine what physical damage might have been caused even if the round had gone off above his head, but it was a consequence I didn't dwell on at the time. But as the least harmful of outcomes, I'm not sure which one of us would have ended up with more heavily soiled underwear if anything like that had actually happened. In any case, I remain eternally grateful to that vigilant officer and if I needed any reminding, I got the very clear message from this experience, that a firearm should never be treated with anything less than total care and respect. Only a very few around me were aware of what had occurred and they were kind enough, I think, not to mention the incident to anyone, but it was slightly reassuring to learn afterwards that I hadn't been the only one at 55 or in other units to have committed a similar error.

The subject of this frightening and sobering episode usually leaned against the back wall of the security hut, behind my chair. I had been on the gate for some weeks and the boredom of sitting and waiting for the occasional truck to visit 55 was becoming frustrating. Equally difficult was the heat inside the hut, about which I had been right. The small space combined with the fact that only a door and a small window let in any air produced a sauna-like environment inside the corrugated iron box. It was often more bearable to sit outside in the sun than to stay in. So I got some white paint from the workshop and painted the roof, in the hope that the white would reflect some of the heat. This was only partly successful. Lining or insulating it was of course out of the question, as that would have been seen as a waste of materials. So I persevered with the hundred plus degrees of heat in my workplace, sweated profusely, and scratched my prickly heat ceaselessly. This unwelcome, itchy, and irritating skin condition was caused by a combination of the heat and excessive sweating that resulted in small red spots appearing on those parts of the body where sweat collected. Many of us were affected, particularly in the groin, armpits and around the neck. I also continued to lose weight magnificently. At a height of just under six feet and weighing eleven and a half stone, I watched as the pounds I could hardly afford to lose fell off my increasingly bony frame. I did attempt to decorate the interior of the hut, however, with a selection of photos of ladies who were definitely in unladylike poses and in varying stages of undress. The obligatory Playboy centrefolds took pride of place. Miss March of 1968, together with Miss September of

1967, ruled over the harem from their prominent positions above the door.

I knew the work was going to be the pits when I accepted the job, but I wasn't quite prepared for its monotony. As an indication of its total lack of appeal, I can truly say that the single highlight of the three months I spent in that dog box was the passage of the Right Honourable, the Prime Minister, and his wife through my gate. On what was laughingly called a fact-finding tour of South Vietnam, the PM called in on Australian units at both bases and 55 was included for a flying visit. For days prior to their arrival, obscenely unnecessary steps were taken in an effort to beautify 1ALSG. Vehicles that were generally clean had precious water wasted on them and got an extra wash while areas that were tidy had to be raked in case a cigarette butt was still in evidence. Haircuts suddenly became more important again, office files and workshop tools were sorted more than once, and clean bedding was issued the night before the big day in case the PM decided to see the lines and check out how the troops lived. It was this last measure that really irked us the most, being nothing more than a blatantly false show for a man who was ex-air force and would have seen through the sham in any case.

Since I was to be the first person to sight the official motorcade as it drove up the road towards 55, I was to fling the boom gates open and – without requesting the usual identifications – allow the vehicles to pass while I flashed the snappiest salute I could muster. I was so struck by the importance of this exalted task, that with childish naïveté I even asked the lieutenant whether I should salute the occupants of each car separately or give one salute from the start of the convoy to its end. He was of no help by way of order or advice. We knew that the half dozen or more vehicles accompanying the limousine would carry officers from the rank of major upwards so regulation salutes would be essential, but we didn't know how close together the vehicles would be travelling. He left this seemingly unimportant decision to me, but at the time I agonised over it and considered it to be of immense consequence.

I was still sitting in the security hut wondering what I would do when the time really came as, sometime after lunch, I spied the limousine followed by its snaking entourage of jeeps. I raised the boom, yelled into the orderly room as previously arranged to warn them, and long before the first car reached me I snapped the salute. I felt so high and pumped by the gravity of the moment that I adopted a most unnatural stiffening of the back which was accompanied by an upward gaze so steep that my line of sight was above the tops of the vehicles that passed a few feet in front of me. I dared not glance back down for fear that the Prime Minister would notice that I had moved. My ramrod-straight stance was so good that it probably outstripped that of the guards outside Buckingham Palace. Incredibly, in spite of all the nervousness, preparation, and needless concern, I ended up not seeing the man at all as he passed. By the time I dared look down, only the back of the rear vehicle was still visible.

In all, Mr Gorton spent about twenty minutes at 55 inspecting our refrigeration plant, stores, forklifts, and – our pièce de résistance' –the tank-testing of an outboard motor on which the mechanics had been working for some weeks. I took a sneaky look round the corner of the workshops just to satisfy myself that Mr Gorton was, in fact, there in person. There was no mistaking the craggy-faced gentleman in the white shirt. There he was looking intently as the contents of toolboxes were displayed and as he was shown how ice blocks formed inside metal, wedge-shaped containers that were immersed in a solution of highly concentrated brine. Sarcastically, I reckoned that he would have left Vietnam much better informed about the progress of the war as a result of this visit to 55! By late afternoon or early evening, things returned to normal and the rain pelted down as usual. By then, the great excitement of the Prime Ministerial visit had passed.

During these months of internment in the guard hut as it eventually became known, Gary and I formed an increasingly closer relationship. This was reinforced by two incidents that occurred towards the middle of May. Having been a keen golfer and a country football umpire prior to Nasho, physical fitness was important to Gary and he found the inactivity of his tasks in the workshop unsatisfying. He would often speak about the pleasures he had experienced from a season of football training and the fulfilment that provided. During the season, he would often catch a taxi at six on a Saturday morning, be driven to Swan Hill, Bairnsdale or Warrnambool, umpire the match that afternoon, return home by nine at night and still get up on the Sunday morning for an early morning run and a game of golf. He was proud of his fitness and thrived on competition. 1ALSG obviously didn't offer the sort of outlet for which Gary ached. For me, the idleness of hours sitting in the guard hut, eating, and smoking to excess, had also become a form of drudgery, so we decided to liven up what was an otherwise inactive lunch hour. As a rule, we played cards or just sat around in the sun after the midday meal, working on our already deep tans and killing time as we would wait to go back to work.

Gary and I convinced the cook to set aside two meals for us, which we would eat towards the end of the hour. In this way, we could spend about thirty minutes on the beach, making up for the exercise that was otherwise lacking. As soon as the lunch period began, we hurried down to the beach, left our rifles with the duty corporal in the club, stripped down to bathers, and commenced the estimated two-mile run that had been mutually agreed. Despite the heat, the physical exertion was welcome and we pounded through the sand, dodging the sideways-running crabs as we ran. Had we been racing, Gary could have left me standing after the first four hundred yards, but we agreed to treat the run simply as a training jog. That at least was the original plan. We ran side by side for the first mile-and-a-half, but as we entered the final stretch, we automatically picked up speed and began accelerating towards an imagined finishing tape. Somehow, I never got to reach that tape before him. After the run, we dove into the tepid, murky water of the South China Sea in a fruitless attempt to cool off, this time dodging the floating jelly fish that infested the shores around Vung Tau. We then grabbed our gear, ran back to 55 for a quick lunch, and still finished it in time to resume work. Initially, these sessions pulled the stuffing out of me, and even Gary admitted to being out of condition. This meant that he had slight muscle soreness, while I was in agony. But we persevered and, after a week, began to feel better within ourselves and more prepared to tackle afternoons on the job. As the weeks passed, we noticed more and more runners doing precisely what we had started and, on occasion, up to thirty might be either swimming or hoofing up and down the beach. I began to peg back the distance between the two of us at the finish and stayed with him almost to the end, but the final two hundred-yard sprint was always won by the thin streak who, quite effortlessly, left me far behind. We revelled with smug satisfaction in the knowledge that others had copied our brilliant idea. Some years earlier while in high school, I had been a keen cross country and middle distance runner and on this far away beach in Vietnam, I rediscovered the joy of that kind of physical exertion and activity.

The stretch of coastline where we swam was part of a large, crescent-shaped bay, at the southern tip of which was a half-sunken hulk that in its day might have been about eight thousand tons. It had run aground years earlier and now sat rusting under the tropical sun. To the north we could see the top of a range of mountains where, we were told, Australian lives had been lost in skirmishes against an enemy that we, in Vungers, were able to dispel completely from our minds. It was a quiet, peaceful stretch of beach, but one that scared the hell out of me during one particular lunchtime swim. We had finished running and had just entered the water when things began to feel wrong.

Uncharacteristically, the sky was already darkening and the wind blowing harder than usual. Knowing my limitations in the water, I rarely ventured far from shore but swam parallel to it some twenty yards out. On this day, I amazed myself by the speed with which I seemed to churn through the water. Glancing towards the shore I noticed with horror that I was drifting away from it and felt the current and undertow that was clearly responsible for my newly-acquired swimming prowess. As a rational surfer or lifesaver would know, the thing to do under these circumstances is to relax, go with the flow, continue to swim parallel to the shore and be content in the knowledge that the current would eventually take one back to shore, albeit hundreds of yards further down. Being neither a surfer nor a lifesaver and finding that I was anything but rational at the time, I did precisely the opposite. I struck out wildly for the beach and flailed my arms in an energy-sapping and useless attempt to reach it. I experienced a sickening and desperately sinking feeling in the pit of my stomach as water gushed up my nostrils, indicating that I was still in the grip of the tow, being pulled feet first away from the shore and sanctuary. I panicked in the very worst way.

By the time I waved my arms and screamed for help in the direction of the beach, others had noticed my predicament and within moments I saw Gary swimming towards me. I stopped flailing and was treading water by the time he reached me. Without coming closer than two or three yards, he coaxed me into following him using gently measured strokes. He had no trouble in convincing me to do so. Amazingly, the current soon released me and we swam back to the beach with ease. Indeed, there had never been a great danger except that which was created by my panic-driven initial response. If I hadn't fought the thing in the first place, there would have been no drama at all. I felt somewhat embarrassed when we got back to shore and very grateful to Gary who had put himself at some risk on my account.

The other incident, which bound us more closely, happened at around the same time and could well have been a direct consequence of the episode on the beach. The sergeant in charge of clerical matters for the unit put the unexpected question to the four of us after parade one Monday morning.

'Where do you boys want to go for R&R when it's your turn?'

It was surprising to be asked the question simply because of its earliness. The existing arrangement was that all ANZUS servicemen became eligible for a five-day period of R&R, rest and recreation, at the end of six months of service in-country. For us, this was still some four months distant. When we asked about the need for such urgency, the sergeant explained that arrangements with the Americans who provided air transport for most R&R flights had to be finalised months in advance. Basically, we had to make a choice, which we viewed as a simple one to be made between two options. Either we wanted to see our families for five days, in which case we chose Australia, or if we didn't, we could go to one of a number of Asian destinations. Among those were Hong Kong, Taipei, Tokyo, Singapore, and Bangkok. American soldiers had the further option of going to Hawaii, but that was not open to us. There wasn't much discussion about the subject that night. We had been given one more day to decide and since we desperately yearned to see our respective families, Australia was to be our R&R destination. Ron also chose to go home which we knew he would anyway, but we were amazed that Wayne, for all of his nineteen years, wanted to see Singapore rather than go home. We told the sergeant of our decision the next day, communicated the good news to those at home and began a mini-countdown until September when the trip back home was to be a reality.

About a fortnight later, the captain addressed our Monday parade. In essence, he gave fair warning that unless a substantial number of us were willing to take R&R in countries other than Australia, a balloting system would have to be introduced. There were too many wanting to go home and airlines were having difficulty handling the increased traffic on their regular flights from Saigon. Married men, the captain explained, would be given preference over the younger, single men. He also explained in his most reassuring and paternal manner that we would be missing out on many valuable and worthwhile experiences by not taking advantage of the opportunity of visiting an Asian city while we had the chance. Having been given this ultimatum, we were forced to rethink the matter. Ron remained unshakable in his resolve to go home to Alice Springs and said that if he couldn't go there, he would rather forego the leave altogether. Gary and I were less resolute about the matter and changed our minds. Upon reconsidering the decision, the pivotal point that finally convinced me was not that I would miss a wonderful Asian opportunity by going home, but the disquieting thought of actually going home in September and then having to leave again after only five days. We reasoned, correctly I think, that it would be simpler for everyone if we saw out the year away from home, without a second, uncomfortable, and unnecessary parting midway. The sergeant was quite pleased to hear from us when we told him that we had changed our minds and would like to go to Hong Kong instead. He said that he would try to arrange for us to go together. We hoped it would be so. Having made a final decision, I listened even more intently to Gary's stories about his travels on ships that had visited mysterious ports like Hamburg and Rotterdam. We questioned others, who were going to, or had already been to Hong Kong and other cities in Asia, and in general prepared ourselves mentally and financially for a five-day sojourn in what was described by many as 'beautiful Hongers'.

Chapter 27

9.5.68-4.6.68.

I have guard duty tonight so not much sleep, but at least it means a day off tomorrow. Greg, best of luck for your Intermediate exams, hope you're successful. You asked again about Barry! Yes, he's here, but up in Nui Dat. Isn't it a major irony that he didn't ever want to come to Vietnam and he's up there in some danger, while I volunteered and I'm sitting here on a security gate in relative safety?

So Andy is really coming to 1ALSG and of all the units to 17? Only a few yards separate our two units! Now that's an incredible coincidence, don't you think? Two families leave Hungary for a better life elsewhere and twenty years later their two sons end up fighting for Australia in two army units so close together in Vietnam! What are the odds, eh?

You misunderstood what I wrote last time about Kevin going home and please don't reproach me for being 'here'! Of course I thought he was lucky to be going home and of course I wished it were me! But if it comes down to a choice between me going home and back to Albert Park or staying here – a choice which is no longer available incidentally – I would *now* choose to stay.

Yes, the troubles in Saigon are big news here too, but only on the radio. This 'Tet' thing has really stirred the pot and there is some heavy duty American retaliation. None of us here has seen a Viet Cong or are likely to do so. Then again if we did, I don't think we would recognise one anyway...

Thanks for the chocolates, etc. Please don't send anything else, I have plenty. I see Collingwood finally won a game, will wonders never cease...?

You write again about the fighting. All I can say is that it's not here! At times we hear the rumble of rocket fire in the distance and we definitely hear a lot about the war on the radio, but nothing in Vung Tau or the camp itself. Last week we saw what we thought to be a flight of B52's heading north. They're incredible machines that can bomb from a height of 40 000 feet. I guess a miscalculation of a few seconds from that height can make a great deal of difference to where the bombs actually fall! Unfortunately, it has happened, as we all know...!

It's Sunday morning and so much rain has fallen in half an hour that the whole camp is afloat, so we've been given the day off. More time in which there is little to do except sit, write or drink. A few really hit the grog last night. Most have welcomed the news about the day off and many have gone back to bed. First sleep-in that I can remember since coming here!

Thanks for the offer of books, but we get a lot of reading material sent to us, even some newspapers, although they're days old by the time we get them.

It's stinking hot again, prickly heat weather, many

are suffering. We have rashes of all description on every conceivable part of our bodies.

The peace talks in Paris appear to be more and more of a political joke. Sure doesn't seem as though a result will ever come from there! What's the feeling about it at home...?

Into the tenth week, time's crawling by, I'm still fine. HMAS Sydney arrived yesterday on its regular run; we're on shiftwork processing that part of its load meant for 55.

I've studied the travel brochures you sent. As far as the boat is concerned, let's make it the Fairstar and the booking to Lisbon. I'll travel from there to Hungary and then to England. Is that OK with you...?

For the first time in seventy or so days, we feel comfortably cool and not sweaty. The rain, bless its little heart, has been falling almost the whole day.

Interesting account you give of the ending of the 'Fugitive' on television. Poor long-suffering David Janssen can now finally rest in peace...!

We all received a gift from home yesterday. The 'Australian Forces Overseas Appeal' organisation sent us a small package containing lollies, tinned food, a book, socks, handkerchiefs, cigars, cans of rum and cola and so on. It's difficult to know whom to thank. We really appreciated the stuff!

I finally went up to Nui Dat yesterday. There's a lot to see in that short distance of about twenty miles without even mentioning the dirt, poverty, filth and smell along the way. Unbelievable! Dogs chewed on the carcasses of dead water buffalo by the side of the road, not far from where three locals were squatting, having a shit. Nui Dat is larger than 1ALSG, red dirt not sand, out in the sticks and of course at great risk all the time. They walk around there with loaded rifles and are expected to patrol outside the perimeter. It was with quite some relief that I returned last night...

My visit to Nui Dat was the first of only two trips I took outside the relative safety of 1ALSG and Vung Tau itself. Volunteers were always needed to ride shotgun on the daily convoys of trucks that carried supplies and men between the two bases. After passing up two prior opportunities for the trip, I reasoned that the third time would be lucky and went along. Although attacks and ambushes along that stretch of road were not regular, there had been isolated instances of trouble and it became the usual practice to travel to the Dat with loaded weapons, one shell up the spout and safety catches on.

This situation mirrored the ludicrous and at the same time hopeless position in which the ANZUS forces found themselves in Vietnam. We were prepared and armed to fight, but nine times out of ten could only do so in retaliation to an offensive move by the other side. Throughout South Vietnam, for much of the latter part of the 60s, our side conducted a defensive, reactive war in which the initiative always seemed to be with the enemy. So, while rifles were at the ready on the road from Vungers to the Dat, they would only be used in case of a direct assault on the convoy. The nature of an attack, if any, would be determined by the Viet Cong. The place, the timing, and severity of the contact would be dictated and determined by the enemy. If the attack was to be by men on foot, by a more distant mortar barrage or the booby trapping of the road itself, then that too would be determined by them. Only then and in response to an action by the enemy could we respond in kind. Of the hundreds of Vietnamese we passed on the road that day, half might have been Viet Cong sympathisers, but we would not have known. On this day, happily there was no incident, but on some other occasion, they might have lobbed a grenade into a truck, or shot at us from a distance. That unknown factor was the reason for our readiness, just in case. In spite of the total lack of testosterone-filled Audie Murphy-type bravado or action, for me the trip was action-packed nonetheless. The possibility, no matter how remote, that I might have to fire my rifle in anger made the experiences of that day more memorable and vivid in their intensity.

Once we left the outskirts of the city, I saw again the great expanses of paddy fields that I had noticed from 5000 feet earlier. Away from the freshening sea breeze, the pervasive smell that is the tropics was even more pungent and nauseating. Images of lions tearing into carcasses in the jungle came to mind as we glimpsed emaciated dogs gnawing on the rigid bodies of dead water buffalo. We drove past men and women relieving themselves by the side of the road, not even bothering to look up as the vehicles rolled by. Their indifference to our presence was not the result of surprised embarrassment, but simply the natural order of things. As an outsider, I felt pity for the victims of such lowly standards of living and of such poverty. But there was also an uncomfortable and growing sense of distrust and distaste in me towards these people. The feeling had been festering for weeks and was strengthened by the events of this day. Apart from the fact that any of those I saw might have been my enemy, and would have been therefore overjoyed to see me blown to bits, men I had known and boys whose paths had crossed mine had died in that bloody place. Yet the alleged recipients of that largesse, sacrifice and that selfless gift were now baring their arses and crapping as we drove by! That single act struck a cord and I found it to be so repulsive, that the temptation to shoot my rifle at the ground, between their opened cheeks, right in the growing pile of faeces, was overwhelming. I didn't expect respect or even thanks, for after all I didn't feel I was doing that much anyway, but the disturbing symbolism of the image bothered me greatly in the months that followed and remained with me for a long time.

Similar squalor was evident in all the hamlets through which we passed. It seemed that the entire rural population of the region had little else to do other than sit in front of dwellings and stare vacantly into an empty unknown. Yet these were people of the soil and, as any worker of the land will testify, there is always something on a farm that needs doing and needs attention. Not so for the farmers of Phuoc Tuy Province, South Vietnam, during the early monsoon of 1968. Small huts that were the homes of eight or ten seemed on the brink of collapse. Building materials seemed plentiful, yet they squatted on the ground inactively, passively, uselessly. Stinking, rotting garbage was piled high, animal manure lay in heaps in front of doorways, naked children crawled on the ground with snot-caked dirt hanging out of their nostrils, yet their elders sat, smoking, staring into space. The picture was desolate, despondent, and even surreal in its sad intensity. For the first time I understood, if not totally agreed with the generally-held belief among many Australians that we were dealing with and fighting for a mob of Noggies who really didn't deserve the effort or the time that was expended on them. I communicated some of these darker thoughts to my parents at the time and they scolded me for being so shallow and thoughtless. They cautioned patience and understanding and an acceptance of the fact that the negative effects of war;

real suffering, the pain of enforced dispossession, and the cumulative misery of generations-long sacrifice such as these people had suffered, can result in a debilitating effect on one's lack of desire to strive or forge ahead.

It was relieving to reach the ordered and comparatively sane environment of our base at Nui Dat. The entire area presented a temporary air. One could imagine that if necessary, every sign of human habitation could have been picked up and transported elsewhere within twenty-four hours. Although just as large and probably home to more personnel than 1ALSG, housing was exclusively in tents. Absolutely everything was coated in the fine, red dust of the region, a feature we had noticed on the vehicles and men visiting Vungers. Even on this calm day, the dust was clearly visible and was stirred into motion by the slightest movement of man or machine. I made a quick, silent vow never to complain again about the sand-related problems that we had being near the beach. It was amazing how speedily that vow was forgotten though once I returned!

After helping to unload the stores we had brought, I still had some four hours before the return trip and I spent the larger part of that time in an unsuccessful search for Smokey and Barry. I had no trouble in finding Smokey's unit, but was told that he had left the previous night on a three-day patrol. I could picture the reddish moustache quivering under an intent gaze as he wound his way through the bush. I didn't envy him. The quest for Barry was longer and even less fruitful, for not knowing his unit, I had to make the rounds of all the engineer orderly rooms in search of information. None of them was able to help me about a Sapper Trowse and, for a moment, I feared the worst. I learned much later that he had gone home some weeks earlier on a compassionate transfer. I became concerned and not knowing the details bothered me even more.

In my walk, however, I came across a group of tents which housed members of a SAS unit, the elite troops of the Australian Army. These Special Air Service men named after their British counterparts were easily recognisable by their distinctive berets. I scurried past the tents in almost reverential awe. We all held the exploits of these super men in the highest esteem. It was said that a patrol of five SAS men could achieve more behind enemy lines than a group of twenty grunts sent on a similar mission. What gave the claim a great deal of credibility was that the grunts were the first to admit its truthfulness. The rigorous and exacting selection procedures to identify suitable candidates, followed by a similarly demanding training regimen, produced extremely fit and successful fighting soldiers. Their kill rate, survival rate, and intelligence-gathering capabilities were legendary, even if most of what they did was confidential and classified. We were, however, privy to many stories of personal heroism as far as our SAS troops were concerned. I don't know how many medals or honours were earned by them in Vietnam, but each and every one of those would have been fully deserved and would have involved substantial effort and personal as well as collective sacrifice.

The tension in the camp was palpable. Even though several thousand were billeted in those few acres, only a small number was visible wandering the dirt tracks that crisscrossed one another. The men were in their tents and bunks, sitting at tables and movement outside appeared to be kept to a minimum. There was an air of expectant readiness about the place that was unknown to us in the freer atmosphere of 1ALSG. Here, a mortar could be lobbed into camp at any moment and everyone seemed ready, at a moment's notice, to run and dive into one of the many sandbag-protected shelters dug into the red earth. Those men I saw all had loaded rifles, wore long trousers and steel helmets, and not the casual cloth caps and shorts to which I was accustomed. In short, the place was quiet, reserved, yet very prepared for eventualities that might result from an action originating from outside the perimeter fence. What I interpreted as boredom in Nui Dat was probably an inner contentment felt by everyone, that all was uneventful and silent. Danger, after all, was imminent and not that distant. I felt like an intruder, an outsider with my suntanned legs hidden underneath the long greens that suddenly felt uncomfortable after months of disuse.

I found my way back to the marshalling point for the return trip to what I now regarded as home. The old adage that the grass is always greener on the other side of the hill certainly applied. I passionately despised the situation in which I found myself at 55, had seriously begun the countdown to Christmas, and couldn't wait to leave Vietnam, yet Nui Dat had felt infinitely more foreign, foreboding, and distasteful. I was actually pleased to see the huts, workshops, and gatehouse when we got back. This sudden, new warmth for the joint lasted about a day before the monotony of old cooled it again.

I must have been very hard to please. Vungers was boring, Nui Dat threatening and most places in between quite intolerable. It was just as well that the same situation applied to the majority of my comrades. We found an endless variety of things about which we could complain. This, of course, helped fuel our extremely self-indulgent sorrows. As much as any other factor, though, it might have been the single most unifying and satisfying feature of our meagre existence.

Indeed, I wonder what we would have done if we hadn't spent as much time in whining and bitching about things. Since we all did it equally well, it was an accepted form of regular communication. The weather was too hot, the rain too constant or too scarce as the case might be, the food stank, the cook's skills definitely stank, guard duty was a shit of a job, the mail service sucked, the beer was too warm, the sand unbearable, the mosquitoes were bastards, as was the government, the wind too gusty, the women too flat-chested, the films as boring as hell, the days too long, and the nights just bloody endless. God only knows how many facets of life we criticised and perhaps only He knows how much mind-numbing, idle time was successfully filled with our moaning. It was a wonderful outlet for suppressed anger and frustration, and one we all used with a remarkably practiced finesse.

We were eating dinner one night when I spied my heavyset little mate through the mess window. Andrew had always had a weight problem and he was the first to admit that he carried too much midriff for his scant five foot five. He was, however, very powerful in the arms, chest and wrist, and he had often beaten all comers in a friendly game of Indian wrestling, or in an unfriendly version of the real thing. As we shook hands and embraced, I noticed that he was sweating profusely. The heat of the tropics was evidently not going to be easy for Andrew.

It had been six months since we'd seen each other and there was much to talk about. He had seen my family only days earlier, so I was eager for fresh, personal news. Conversely, he had many questions about his role at 17. His posting as a field engineer meant that his tasks would be somewhat similar to mine, given the variations that existed from unit to unit. After being kitted out with bedding and helping him find his way around at 17, we went to the boozer and spent the remainder of the evening downing a couple of cool ones for old and for new times' sake. He passed on the news that I was most eager to hear in that he'd recently seen my parents and brother during his pre-embarkation leave and everything and everyone at home was fine. His parents were also well, except for the fact that their son had just left to go to a war. Those matters being settled, we relaxed and were happy in the knowledge that this was to be the first of many pleasant evenings that we would spend together, with me foregoing to an extent, my earlier commitment to drink as little as possible.

He was better prepared for Vietnam than I had been in that he had made firm decisions prior to arrival, whereas I had allowed external situations to control my destiny. High on his list of firsts was a desire to get his truck licence while in-country. He was also determined to spend some time in Nui Dat. Little that any of us said by way of discouragement had an effect on him regarding the second matter. Andy was smitten by the notion that he would be less than a man if by coming to Vietnam he didn't partake of a full measure of the experiences on offer. For Andy, this included some involvement in combat. He wanted to be able to say to his grandchildren one day that he had been to war and had fought the enemy, literally. I felt sure that after a few weeks the reality of the situation would force him to change his mind. For the time being, however, it was with quite a degree of selfishness that I looked forward to having an old friend close by.

Jungle training at Canungra had nearly been his undoing. According to Andy, the story about the hills was perfectly true and the forced marches along with the daily doses of calisthenics had almost killed him. While stocky and powerful, his physique was not suited to prolonged periods on the hoof and his situation at the end of the three weeks was not too dissimilar to what mine had been. He was also told that he might have to repeat as a result of poor performances. Never being short for words, Andy told the powers to be that if he was failed, he would be the most ornery, difficult, and unmanageable bastard with whom they had ever dealt. I doubt seriously whether this threat of his had anything to do with the eventual outcome, but he passed the course anyway. Now, as we drank another can, we did what the majority of semi-plastered drinkers often do, and began to exaggerate the stories we told each other and simply enjoyed each other's companionship. For the first time ever, though, I outlasted Andy in a drinking session and I helped an exhausted old mate to his barracks, took off his boots, and put him to bed.

One of the more disquieting pieces of news that had been filtering through to us by way of letters and old newspapers was now confirmed by Andrew. There were political and social problems brewing at home. There was indeed a rapid, recent growth in the anti-Vietnam movement. In essence it had always existed, but was apparently gaining momentum. Tens of thousands had marched in Melbourne in an anti-Vietnam moratorium march and the mood, according to Andy, had been ugly.

Historically, three years had passed since the government had committed Australian troops to the war. During that time, the national attitude to and perception of the war had changed radically. Originally, only a few warrant officers and ranks above that had been posted to Vietnam, and those purely in an advisory capacity, forming what became known as the AATTV, the Australian Army Training Team Vietnam. They had quickly gained the respect and admiration of the

South Vietnamese troops for the training and expertise they provided. These advisors were later followed by members of a battalion of the RAR, to match similar increases in combat involvement by our ally, the USA. The passage of time saw the inclusion of draftees like us among the numbers sent.

The early Australian emphasis in Vietnam had been on the creation and subsequent consolidation of our own defences. That having been established, attention was focused on our main aim of providing support and assistance to the overall war effort by the maintenance of peace and order in Phuoc Tuy Province. We were in effect trying to curb the spread of communist influences in that one province of the country. At home, in 1965, this had been acceptable to the majority of people as a reasonable national contribution, given the ANZUS treaty to which we were signatories. For some on the left side of politics, though, even the slightest involvement was unacceptable, treated with suspicion and considered to be 'brown nosing' of the Americans on the part of our political leaders. Such political sentiments spawned the Save Our Sons movement and the anti-conscription demonstrations of 1967 and 1968.

The deaths of Australian soldiers in battle, but in particular the deaths of young Nashos who were seen as sacrificial lambs, began to turn the tide of popular opinion. This was accelerated by the immediacy of the electronic coverage of the fighting that was compulsory viewing on nightly television. The broken and maimed bodies of the morning's battles became the evening's fare to accompany the family meal. As the severity of the fighting and bombings increased and, as horrid mistakes were made on both sides, the western world continued to question the veracity of the origin, as well as the wisdom of the continuation of the Vietnam conflict.

There being no universal nemeses such as Nazism, or the threat of the Japanese domination of the Pacific which helped create and maintain tight alliances in WWII, public support for Vietnam was beginning to wane and the substance of what Andy now told us was that even bigger and more violent protests were being organised and to be held at home, opposing all of that which had already been done and what we were currently doing.

For us in Vietnam in the middle of 1968, however, these new revelations became extremely painful realities to accept. The realisation that our efforts were viewed with hostility, that eighty thousand people had walked behind red and North Vietnamese flags in a Vietnam Moratorium March, that we were branded as child-killers, that we were seen as murderers and napalm bombers and that those of us returning home were spat upon, was demoralising and heartbreaking stuff to hear. Our honest feelings about what was happening were uncomplicated. As far as we were concerned, our Government had responded to a request by the South Vietnamese and American Governments for military aid. This aid was to help halt the unprovoked incursions by communists from the north into the democratically-controlled south. Some would have called these naïve and ill-informed conclusions, but that was nonetheless our view and our currently available information about the situation. We felt betrayed, ostracised and therefore utterly devoid of any warm sentiment towards those who were agitating against us. We had answered our country's call and we found ourselves being ridiculed and pilloried by the very people we were representing!

We were dumbfounded by this turn of events and our reaction was entirely predictable. The general consensus was that the politicians had failed us and that decision-making was now obviously in the hands of a multitude of snotty-nosed, mini-skirted teenagers, college students, and left wing, uninformed pseudo-intellectuals, who were apparently able to bring sufficient pressure to bear on the government for such absurdities as the marches to be allowed to happen. To see pictures of marchers in Melbourne preceded by red and huge banners of Ho Chi Minh! I don't possess sufficient venom with which to express adequately how much that hurt us and what a stab in the back that felt like!

Chapter 28

Andrew, Smokey, and I sat in the slightly cooling breeze outside the 55 boozer, munching happily on Hungarian salami and drinking gin and orange. My parents had sent the food, while the drink was a creation of ours which we found particularly refreshing. I had never drunk that concoction before, but its effect in the tropical heat was quite pleasant. The sunset was another glorious, burnt red. Smokey had returned from the Dat and we were getting reacquainted. Gary made up our foursome. He never ventured anywhere near the boozer, but on this occasion joined us to celebrate the return of the moustached little Englishman. He played nervously with the can of orange drink he had bought and was evidently uncomfortable being in the vicinity of the boozer. While I enjoyed and craved Andy's company and was content to be with him for the occasional 'booze-up', I realised that to be fair to my other mates, especially Gary, I would have to control and limit my drinking.

The four of us had spent the afternoon of that Sunday hunting for bargains in the American PX, followed by similar forays into our own ASCO store. The Australian Services

Canteens Organisation had a store near 1ALSG selling many Australian-made items of food, drinks, and electrical goods. It could not compete with the PX, which was huge by comparison and stocked a much greater variety of all consumables. Smokey was now regaling us with some well-chosen accounts of his time in the bush. He had returned whole and healthy and was pleased to point out that not once was he required to shoot at anyone while on his three outings patrolling outside the wire. Each of these missions had been for the purpose of reconnoitring north of the base, in search of suspicious movements in and out of neighbouring hamlets. It was often under the cover of darkness that the Viet Cong's sympathisers would sneak into peaceful villages, steal food or other useful supplies, and deliver those to the guerrilla standover merchants hiding in the bush. Should the demanded delivery not be made on time, those who had defaulted, or perhaps an entire village which had refused, would be taught a very serious lesson about who was really in charge. If we could detect such movements, identify them as sinister, and follow those concerned to their destinations, the enemy might then be more easily located. The theory was fine, but our success rate was abysmal. Smokey's group had no such contacts, but he wisely considered that to be a success in itself.

Only one painful chore fell his way and that involved an early morning search of a village suspected of sheltering VC. Smokey was remorseful about training a loaded rifle on a group of villagers who had been hounded out of bed at five in the morning, particularly since no evidence of VC was found anywhere in the entire area. Two nights later, however, another patrol investigated a small explosion that had been heard in the same village and found that two of the locals had died. They had blown themselves up while making grenades, using empty Coke cans and stolen explosives as the raw materials. A thorough search revealed a complex of tunnels that contained a variety of live shells, an F1 sub-machine gun which was embarrassingly an Australian issue, a quantity of gelignite, and – of all things – a carton of tyre valves. Naturally, all the villagers had feigned ignorance about the source of the goods and even pretended to be surprised by the existence of the tunnels. The engineers blew the tunnel complex and the hamlet was left to its own devices again. No doubt a new tunnel and a new cache of booty were in place within the week. A month later this, too, might have been found and destroyed once more. The cat and mouse game kept both sides busy and active, but we never really had the upper hand. We had the mightier weapons, the tanks, the cannon, and bombers. The opposition had time to delay, thwart, and undermine any forward steps we might make. These were weapons against which ours were no match. The longer the enemy could maintain an uneventful stalemate, the more assured it became of ultimate victory. Our illustrious political and military leaders probably knew or suspected this as early as the Tet offensive of 1968, yet the war was allowed to continue.

Apart from the many hours of watch or piquet that he stood, which Smokey found both fascinating and terrifying in the eerie night-time tropical clime, he recounted one further tale. Having heard it, we wished he had kept it to himself. It concerned the capture of a South Vietnamese regular by the Cong. This unfortunate soul had been shot while on patrol and had been left or forgotten by his unit. The latter was the more likely. Two days later he was found, close to death, having been dumped a few hundred yards from the perimeter wire. His lips had been sewn together and he was choking on something inside his mouth. When his sad story was finally unravelled, he told about being captured and tortured with sharpened bamboo sticks being pushed through his palms. When he was unwilling to give the VC the information they sought, spikes were pushed through his feet, ankles and calves as well. Still silent, they cut out his tongue, cauterized the wound so he wouldn't bleed to death and cut off his genitals, sewing it into his empty mouth cavity. He was then taken back and dumped like garbage near his unit. The significance of this sordid story sank in only partly, as the effects of the gin had by now taken a strong hold. Having heard it, we took a breath of air for relief as though we had just been cleansed of an evil, swallowed another swig of drink, thanked God for his kindness to us, and steered the conversation back to the events of that day.

To us, the PX in Vung Tau seemed enormous. At that time, supermarkets in Australia were still in their infancy and we were unaccustomed to these large, self-service stores. We spent several hours that afternoon walking up and down the aisles, inspecting the rows and shelves of goods on display. Things were quite cheap. A carton of cigarettes or a bottle of Johnny Walker sold for about $1.20, while a host of usually expensive tinned foods like crab and oyster could be bought for sixty cents each. Seiko watches went for $20, and electrical appliances and brand-name cameras were selling for $30. We spent some time ogling the centrefolds in a dozen different magazines that would surely have been seized by the police at home, and we watched in fascination as many Yanks broke off chunks of chewing tobacco, and stuffed it into mouths that were never closed and reeked of the smell of the weed from yards away. We also marvelled at the audacity of the place in that it had at least a dozen different kinds of letters for sale, in plain view of all the customers. At a time when the object was only ever referred to, in hushed tones, as a French letter, we read the labels on these wondrous items quite furtively and naturally pretended not to be doing so whenever a female customer walked by. Having previously only ever purchased one letter in my life, under circumstances that I still recall with embarrassment because of the puritanical, Victorian attitudes that existed, we were shocked by their easy availability in the PX. These were things that one only bought secretly from a chemist that stocked them under the counter. To discover that they actually came in regular, super, and extra large was a major revelation in itself, and the source of much discussion and wonderment as we tried to imagine how large one would have to be in order to purchase one that was extra large. There was, of course, a serious touch of the ludicrous about our surprised reaction to the letters being sold in a place where the local women might have shopped alongside us. Strangely that afternoon, we were just as shocked by their easy availability as we were by Smokey's awful story later that day. We were weirdly conditioned to equate the war and the death that raged around us, with the discovery that some individuals would openly and fearlessly select and buy a prophylactic in a shop and thereby publicly and openly declare that they were intending to use it.

We were really only young boys, totally out of our depth in an upside-down world that had highly questionable priorities and principles. We left the PX and I clutched a small, wooden cigarette box inlaid with mother-of-pearl. This was a local product hidden in a far corner of the store, but one that I liked and soon after mailed home to the family. The motif on the lid depicted a fisherman standing under a palm tree, wearing the ever-present conical straw hat and casting a net into the sea. On the way back to 1ALSG, we stopped off at the ASCO store, stocked up on some valuable home-grown stuff like Kia-Ora cordial, cans of baked beans, spaghetti, and some Aussie cards that we wanted to send home to our respective families which both Andy and I would sign.

6.6.68-4.7.68

I spoke to the boss today about a transfer off the gate. He told me he was surprised that I hadn't asked for it sooner. He walks past the guard hut several times a day, so he sees just what a boring, tedious job it is. He'll decide as soon as the stock take we're doing is finished.

Recent rains have meant that there is a lot of drainage work to be done, I'll probably get that. Andrew got his truck licence and drove up to Nui Dat on one of the convoys some days ago to check out the place...

The booking for the Fairstar sounds great, thanks for arranging it. Today, we turned the corner around the 200-day mark! Only 199 days to go till discharge date...

Had my first meal outside camp today at the Grand Hotel. The name is quite apt; the interior is luxuriously furnished, while the steak and onion rings were delicious after the dehydrated junk we normally eat.

Kennedy's death was big news here too, of course! For weeks now, the Armed Forces Radio has been on about the Californian Primaries and Kennedy's vow to leave politics if he didn't win. Well, he won! Incredibly unfortunate family, isn't it...?

I've just been thinking. If I go to Europe next year as planned, I will have been through five consecutive summers. The one at home prior to coming here, the one now, the one back home in January next year, the northern summer in Europe and the fifth will be the summer of '69 back home again! Many people might think that's a great outcome, but sitting in this sweatbox at the moment, the thought doesn't have much appeal...

Our planned trip into town this weekend has been cancelled, a number of us have extra guard duty. I hope my package has arrived and thanks for the cans of fruit you sent. I've put them in the boozer's fridge for a feast later tonight...

Stock take finishes this week, looks like I'll be out of the guard hut and back to the old job. I'm sending some photos that have been developed at last – meet some of my friends and a much thinner me! In these past three months, a lot has happened, so if you're keeping all my letters as you say, then they might make interesting reading in years to come.

Fantastic news about Greg's result in fencing and it's great that the sport is finally getting some coverage in the papers. The Robert Kennedy thing is still an issue here. We met a couple of Yank sailors last week and their conversation centred entirely around whether their countrymen could manage to keep their Presidents and presidential hopefuls alive long enough for any of them to make a difference. Political assassinations and terrorism seem to be the coming thing for anarchists...

Very short letter today, I'm sending some photos of camp, the days are passing slowly, back to the old job on July 1...

Taxation time here, too. In my top drawer, you'll find the cheque butt from last year's return. On it is my file number, please send it. I'm happy Greg liked the radio I sent. More rocket attacks on the airbase last night, the beds shook a bit, but that was all...

We had a meal at the RAAF base last night. What they say about the senior service is entirely true. Tables with tablecloths, two large pieces of steak with real potatoes, lemon meringue pie with ice cream and a milk shake to finish! That is their usual fare! We're considering joining the RAAF...

100 days have gone today, only 175 or so left. You say that it's very cold at home, well I'll gladly swap. Three of us are rotating the job on the gate at the moment, two weeks on and four off. I'm putting up shelves in the workshops, it's a pleasant change. Showed Ron the photos you sent taken at Sydney airport on that last night, he was thrilled to see them and asked about you. Actually, we're quite worried about Ron. He's starting to act even more strangely, homesickness is really hurting him. It's late. I'll have to finish now...

Ron was definitely becoming more morose, introverted, angrier and – at times – even unintelligible. For everyone else, the initial anger and despondency about being in Vietnam had worn off long ago, but Ron was unable to reconcile his personal situation. We all had moments – or even days – of depression and anger occasioned by what we felt was the unfair treatment life had dealt. We were, after all, marking time in a foreign country, while the majority of those our age at home were continuing their lives uninterrupted. The draft had either favoured or damned individuals and it often hurt immensely to be one of the damned. These periods of depression were becoming less frequent and the emotions less debilitating with the passage of time. Each day, however, Ron acted and looked as though it was still his first in-country. His job as clerk kept him busy during the day, but he could find no satisfactory way of shifting his attention and obsessive focus away from home other than during those working hours. He would lie on his bed for long periods poring over letters, looking at photographs, and listening to the audiotapes sent by his parents. No matter how hard we tried, no one could prize him away from those treasured mementos and we would feel childishly helpless when, walking past his bed, we would find him supine, earphones around his head and tears streaming down his cheeks. For a while, he had tried to hide the tears, but now he didn't care who saw them. He was poised on a very fine edge, playing a delicate act between realities – his and the rest of the world's. We spoke to the lieutenant and, subsequently, the captain, and Ron, I think, saw the medicos. He never told us any details about this visit and we dared not press him on the matter in case it was the totally wrong thing to do. To us pseudo-psychologists, however, it seemed logical and right to try to channel his attention away from the photos and the tapes. Once or twice, we succeeded in dragging him down to the beach for a lunchtime run and, on very rare occasions, he was even conned into a game of cards. Once a fortnight or so he wandered across to 17 with us to see a film and, on special days like farewells, joined us for a quick drink in the boozer. Apart from these infrequent social contacts, he lived a quiet, hermit-like existence, pretending to be a Robinson Crusoe who, although shipwrecked on an inhabited island, had foundered on an island not to his liking or to his choosing. In this way, he tried to ignore everything unpalatable around him and attempted to survive inside a shell of silence and denial which we found hard to penetrate.

Finally, in desperation, and as a result of repeated failures to make contact with our former mate hiding within, we began to think of him as one of those who, having gone troppo, could not handle the pressures and should be sent home. During one very early morning chat, I momentarily broke through his cocoon of silence and was privy to the thoughts and feelings of a very angry, frustrated, desperate, but totally rational and lucid Ron skulking below the surface.

Guard duty at 55 was a pain in the arse and universally despised. It came around about every two and a half weeks and involved two sappers and one non-commissioned officer. In general terms, it meant that between the hours of six at night and eight in the morning, the three men had to be either in the orderly room or somewhere in the compound, patrolling and ensuring the safety of all that was part of the unit. This would mean walking through the stores areas, the workshops, unit lines, administration buildings, and motor pool. What made the task more unbearable than it otherwise might have been was the accepted fact that there was no existing threat which necessitated such a constant and tiresome vigil. As far as we knew, the outside perimeter was patrolled by Military Police and 1ALSG was secure, so this extra guard within an already guarded area seemed superfluous and a needless imposition on top of our long working week. We were still thinking like the union members we might have been before the army, except that there was no shop steward curious about our job satisfaction and working conditions in Vietnam. Perhaps we should have been made more aware about isolated Vietnamese hamlets hiding boxes of stolen explosives and tyre valves in secret tunnels? Then, we might have realised that items of little value and consequence to us were highly prized by the enemy. We might then have been more assiduous in guarding and caring for the tons and millions of dollars worth of equipment that formed 55's inventory.

For another strange and inexplicable reason when on guard, we were expected to wear long trousers for the night's vigil and this made the fourteen-hour shift more uncomfortable. We would usually have an early evening meal and at six o'clock take up residence in the orderly room. We would answer the phone if it ever rang, deliver or file messages as appropriate, and take turns to reconnoitre the unit's immediate vicinity. Since much of the fourteen hours was spent sitting down, we were armed to the teeth with newspapers, magazines, books and letter writing materials with which to fill the quiet hours. Since one can only read and write for a limited period, we would be feeling quite worn, useless, and generally stuffed by midnight. At such times, it was always refreshing to lie outside on the sandbags to enjoy the cooler night air and watch the exquisite star constellations that can only be seen in the northern sky. It was an insult to all that is perfect and wonderful that such an ugly conflict like Vietnam raged below such incredible beauty.

It was on such a starry and quiet night that Ron and I crossed paths outside the orderly room, having been rostered for guard duty together. The NCO in charge was firmly entrenched in the comfortable swivel chair inside, feet up on a desk and newspaper in hand. I had just finished checking the beds, had scared off a few rodents lurking behind the workshops and returned to find Ron lying on the bags. I sat next to him in the darkness, slightly away from the light spilling out through the open door. I lit what must have been my tenth cigarette since the start of guard.

'God, I hate everything about this blighted place,' he said unexpectedly.

'I know what you mean,' I joined in, never being short for words when it came to complaining. 'The heat's bloody unbearable, I itch all day, the food stinks, the air stinks, and most of the time I don't know what the bloody hell we're doing or achieving here.'

'That's just the point,' he said. 'Sure it's hot and the food is bad and it stinks and we're thousands of miles from home, but you can get used to the heat. Don't forget, I come from the Alice so I know all about hot weather! You can eat the food if you're hungry enough and even ignore the smell. You can also pretend that a few thousand miles is only a few inches if you look at a map, but I'll chuck your own question back at you. What the hell are we doing here? Shit, not once in a single day have I ever felt that I was doing anything that mattered or was worthwhile. I shuffle damned papers, some of which list the numbers of sheets and bloody pillowcases we use. Is that worthwhile? We stuff around with nuts, bolts, screws, and refrigerators! Is that worthwhile? At home, I was a builder working for my father. When we started a job, we knew that in a few months we would build a house. We knew we'd achieve something! But here in this place? Day in, day out, the same pointless, meaningless garbage! We're going nowhere and we're moving towards it at a snail's pace! I hate this shit of a place and the shit of a situation I've been put in and the shitty way it all makes me feel!'

This was at least twice as much as I had ever heard Ron speak at the one time and both the quantity and the absolute truthfulness of all he said took me by surprise. I was so accustomed to his silent, uncommunicative manner that my response was slow in coming. Naturally, I agreed with him, for these had been the very concerns I had felt and had written about to my parents. Seeing an opening for some real communication, I pressed him further and asked questions about the type of work he'd done at home for his father. We spoke in general terms for a while, but he had already volunteered as much about his inner thoughts and self as he was prepared to do on that one occasion, and he cut proceedings short by flinging his feet off the sandbags and disappearing inside. This short exchange provided a few minutes of intimacy between us and was the closest that the two of us ever got. His moods persisted and we continued to tread warily around him.

The situation may have deteriorated even further for Ron during the remaining five months, but the news that we all received about a week after our talk changed him temporarily for the better. The R&R applications had gone through official channels and the necessary clearances had been obtained. In September, he was to get his wish and would be able to spend five days with his family back in the Alice. For quite a while afterwards, we got the chance to see a new, rejuvenated, positive, and – at times – even smiling mate about which we were delighted. We were happy for ourselves as well. Gary and I had been slated to travel together and were on our way to what we hoped would be a fantastic five days in the mysterious and alluring city of Hong Kong. Even though the trip was still many weeks away, we began to plan the costs, the itinerary we'd follow, the things we would buy – all the ingredients of this much-awaited and badly needed break.

Chapter 29

I read and wrote a lot while imprisoned in the guard hut. The regular letters home were the first priority, followed by a reading of the myriad of magazines, books, newspapers, and pamphlets that happened to be available. The brochures my parents had sent about European destinations and ships' sailing schedules – including that of the *Fairstar*, the ship on which my planned trip to Hungary would hopefully start – also took pride of place on the desk in the hut. In those, I searched for information and pictures about London, Paris, Berlin, Munich, Innsbruck, Salzburg, Vienna, and Budapest, being the cities that I thought I'd see and travel through by train on my way to the little town of Nyiregyháza where I was born and where my grandparents still lived. That exercise filled many pleasant and fruitful hours that would have been otherwise utterly wasted. Apart from the letters I wrote to my parents every second day, a few were also written and forwarded to my grandparents, although I wondered what the communist, Hungarian authorities might make of letters being sent to that country from South Vietnam. The tensions between the east and west were at their height, the Iron Curtain was a persistent reality, and politically and ideologically, the communist state of Hungary supported any enemy of America, and as a consequence would have supported North Vietnam. The family received these letters all right, even replied via my parents, so I reasoned that there was no real problem with my correspondence to that part of the world. Naturally, the letters had to be written in Hungarian. To please my parents and keep them reassured that I wouldn't lose my skills in that language, every letter I wrote to them was also in my mother tongue.

The other outlet to fill the hours was a small transistor radio. I usually had that turned on low and listened to whatever music and news happened to come over the air waves. There was really only one station of any consequence: the AFVN. Apart from the well-known European cities whose names currently occupied my mind, other placenames which had become unexpectedly familiar came repeatedly over my transistor from this source – the American Forces Vietnam Network. The names of Saigon, Tan Son Nhut, Nah Trang, Kon Tum, DMZ, Da Nang, Hué, Plei Ku, Bien Hoa and Quang Tri, were regularly mentioned. The AFVN became our eyes and ears on Vietnam and on the hidden, rest of the world. From the safety of our hermetically-sealed camp on that beach in South East Asia, we heard of a battle, a conflict, and a war that was there, after all. It must have been happening because we heard and knew that people were dying. We heard about individual and collective heroism, as well as shame. There were riots, captures, surrenders, attacks, withdrawals, airlifts, and ambushes. There were also births, murders, anniversaries, celebrations, drug overdoses, adoptions, assassinations, and sporting miracles. We were kept informed by radio about those things that occurred in our so-called outside world. For a very large group of young boys barely out of school who had left the comforts of quiet suburban homes and travelled overseas to fight in a war, paradoxically our world had shrunk rather than widened, sandwiched as we were between the wire and the sea on that beach in Vietnam. Except for the occasional foray into Vung Tau, our home and our world had become the hundred or so acres of 1ALSG. Outside it, however, the torment raged. Heavy fighting was often reported from the Central Highlands, while the airbases at Da Nang, and Bien Hoa were frequently shelled. The daily litany of those killed kept coming over the ether via the AFVN.

The names and places we heard about recorded the sacrifices of individuals from innumerable units, companies, battalions, and regiments. They bore testimony to the maddening acceleration of the war in the second half of 1968 – perhaps as a US reaction to the disastrous setbacks that had occurred earlier in the year with the north's surprise Tet offensive in February. With mounting discontent at home and increasing pressure for a speedy end to the fighting, the American President escalated operations against the guerrillas in the south and began bombing targets in the north. LBJ attempted several knockout punches that might have worked two years earlier, but did not in 1968.

'This is the AFVN. The time is 1500 hours.

'In the Central Highlands, an incendiary device was accidentally dropped on a Montagnard village this morning. Heavy casualties were reported and four Huey helicopter gunships transported the injured to the hospital at Qui Nhon.

'In the Panhandle, a Ranger regiment has killed twenty-three of the enemy after a brief contact. Army Sergeant Steve

Forrestier reports that several dozen AK 47 Russian-built assault rifles were found after the operation.

'A Chinook helicopter crashed and exploded in flames at Da Nang airbase yesterday afternoon. All but one of the five occupants was killed. The cause of the explosion is being investigated. There were reports of enemy activity north of that base last night and heavy fighting still continues just south of Saigon.

'This is the AFVN. We bring you the news from the Delta to the DMZ.'

6.7.68-9.8.68

Back on the gate again, life is as boring as ever. Two bits of really exciting news today, though. I went to the RAP (doctor) to get a wart cut off my finger. It appeared recently and hurt every time I closed my fist, which is often these days I might add. The other is that I got a haircut and had my moustache trimmed. The fellow in town who did it rubbed perfumed water into my scalp afterwards. As we said to each other on the way back, we don't know how much longer we can put up with the terrible inconveniences of this war.

Reading the article from the Hungarian newspaper you sent was interesting! The reporter who wrote the story presents a very one-sided view of things here and what he doesn't point out is that being allowed to spend three weeks with the VC probably meant that he was only shown those things that served Charlie's purpose for him to see. Sure, there are many damaged and upturned American armoured personnel carriers by the side of roads! Is that some sort of definitive statement about the conduct and course of the war? Does he mention that lives were lost on both sides when those vehicles were damaged, or that the battle that caused the damage might have been the result of an attempt by the Americans to chase or catch murderous VC? Words carefully chosen can either convey or deliberately hide truths and facts! He is right in one respect, though. The Americans are not winning! It would seem for the moment, anyway, that neither is the other side...

I'm into the seventeenth week. Time is not flying, however, nearly halfway through this wondrous nine-month holiday.

I got the tax papers, thanks. Listen to this for a comparison between my army pay and the previous pay from the PMG. A quick calculation shows that I earned $200 more in nine months in the PMG than during twelve months in the army! What is their advertising slogan? A man's career with a man's opportunities and a man's pay! Oh Yeah!

Onto more important matters, Collingwood's winning run will end next week because they play the Saints. Need I say more? Last night we saw a film called 'Who's Afraid of Virginia Woolf'. Lots of wonderful dialogue but little action in the film...

Yesterday, we farewelled the tenth guy to return home since we've been here. With each departure we're becoming more senior members of the unit and our own departure date comes that much closer. Guard duty again tonight, I'll finish this letter then, because I'll certainly have lots of time...

I went for a drive just a short distance out of town, to the top of a hill here called Viet Cong Hill, but only in name.

On it is the Northern Hemisphere's largest radar station. It's quite impressive in size as you can imagine. Next to it is our own radio station and it's a shack by comparison. Everything the Americans have here is big! It was lovely driving up there through the green trees, reminded me of the Dandenong Ranges, except that the eucalypt smell was missing. The other news is about the visit here of an Australian entertainment group, among them our own Patricia Carroll. I finally got my speedboat licence, so we might be hiring the boats on Sundays if they're ever free.

We've got our own mess at 55 at last. The first meals have been better than at 17. Today completes my fourth month here...

I've been helping lately on what is rudely called the Noggy run. This entails transporting the local people back into town each night after work. It's a welcome change in routine, although we got absolutely drenched during a monsoonal downpour some days ago. Always the extremes, it seems. First hot, windy and dusty, and now everything constantly soggy and mildewed. We're wondering if we'll ever be able to return to inner spring mattresses and wall to wall carpets, not to mention sleeping without a mosquito net strung above the bed...

The constant rain is shifting sand by the tons, so I'll probably spend next week shovelling the stuff from behind buildings. Did I ever say that I envied Lawrence of Arabia and wanted to live in the desert? I do not! I have judo tonight. Andrew hurt his wrist. No worries, though; he'll be back on the truck soon. For the moment he's babysitting the generators again. Thanks for the food, the cheeses, the chocolate and the cabbage rolls, they were great...

I counted again today, only 149 to go. In fact, I tell a lie, I didn't count today, but have been counting seriously for weeks now. I'll be painting a fence around the officers' mess for a while, I'm sure it will aid the war effort. Crazy! The total Australian contribution is so tiny compared to the Yanks. We do these shitty little jobs without even questioning them any more...

Payday today, just as well, I'm short. Money situation overall is good, though. I've saved $720 since arriving. I'm achieving that much at least...

Sorry for the delay in writing, we've spent a lot of time lately mending fences, literally. Somebody stole a lot of stuff some days ago and it seems to have been an inside job. What I've heard about the black market is astounding. Anything can be flogged easily. Still no word on the final date for our R&R...

There's been an earthquake in the Philippines that's created a tidal wave that was expected to reach us earlier today. Within a quarter of an hour, the whole lower beach area was evacuated, hospital, patients and all. The army can really act quickly in a time of crisis. An operation on a guy was apparently completed on a table in the sergeants' mess. In any case, the wave didn't reach us, but it sure created a commotion...

I thought you might enjoy reading a song being sung by the locals about us Aussies here. It's sung to the tune of 'This Old Man', repeating after each two lines. P is Piastres, the local money, Uc Dai Loi refers to us Australians in Vietnamese.

Uc Dai Loi, cheap Charlie, he no buy me Saigon Tea,
Saigon tea costs many, many P, Uc Dai Loi he cheap Charlie.

> *Uc Dai Loi, cheap Charlie, he no give me MPC*
> *MPC costs many, many P, Uc Dai Loi he cheap Charlie.*
> *Uc Dai Loi, cheap Charlie, he no go to bed with me,*
> *Go to bed costs many, many P, Uc Dai Loi he cheap Charlie.*
> *Uc Dai Loi, cheap Charlie, make me give him one for free,*
> *Mama San go crook at me, Uc Dai Loi he cheap Charlie.*
> *Uc Dai Loi, cheap Charlie, he give baby San to me,*
> *Baby San costs many, many P, Uc Dai Loi he cheap Charlie.*
> *Uc Dai Loi, cheap Charlie, he go home across the sea,*
> *He leave baby San with me, Uc Dai Loi he cheap Charlie.*

While it was true that in our small corner of the world, Vung Tau, the proprietors of the local establishments preferred Australian to American customers, the Yanks were undeniably more profitable. We perhaps acted in a more civilised manner and were more reliable, but one could not argue with the Yankee dollar. They not only had much more of the folding stuff than we did, but they flaunted that fact by often producing wads of dollars or MPC. In that comparison, therefore, we did enjoy the rather dubious reputation of being Cheap Charlies.

Apart from the Americans, I have yet to meet another people so fixated on money, as were the Vietnamese. Amassing as much of it as possible seemed to be the national pastime. Years of shortages and deprivation, no doubt, contributed to peoples' compulsive need to amass money by the fistful in case lean times were again just around the corner. For many, it probably represented the means whereby they could ultimately leave the country if that became necessary. To us it seemed, however, that many Vietnamese were more concerned with having pockets bulging with notes than they were with having well-clothed, properly fed children. The chase for MPC, but in particular the US dollar, was so intense that everyone was in on a deal, about to be in on a deal, or about to hatch a brand new deal in which everyone might be offered a share. The black market was an actively flourishing enterprise and some members of the military, from both sides, were willing and successful participants in it.

There were three main currencies most often in use in Vietnam. As seems to be the case in every part of the world, the American dollar was king, but its availability was determined by the rate at which the Yank soldiers were prepared to part with it. Needless to say, the locals would bend over backwards, literally, to obtain some of Uncle Sam's bucks. The second most useful and therefore desirable currency was the military scrip we used. The one with the least purchasing power was the Vietnamese currency itself, the piastre.

We were periodically warned, advised, and sometimes ordered to ensure that we exchanged our MPC for piastres if we were to spend money in places other than the PX or at ASCO. This was done so that there would be a limited quantity of MPC in general circulation. The order, however, was more observed in the breach than in the observance. At any time, there must have been countless millions of dollars worth of MPC doing a brisk trade throughout both Vietnams. In all honesty, we rarely bothered to exchange our military scrip and spent it regularly wherever we went. The local merchants were more than delighted to sell us their wares in exchange for that currency at the current rate of exchange. Indeed, the service and quality of the merchandise were invariably better when we used it. It was the job of the military police to stop trafficking in money, but to my knowledge no soldier was ever apprehended or even questioned by them for using MPC. That was probably a very good thing too, for just about every serviceman would have been behind bars for breaking the law. The merchants, in turn, used the scrip they obtained from us to purchase scarce goods, knowing fully well that piastres could never buy the more valuable items they sought.

Without any warning, a parade was called at the unaccustomed time of nine o'clock one morning. The captain strode to the front and announced that we had a further five minutes in which to return to our lines if necessary to collect every cent of MPC we owned. Some of the older hands might have known what this meant, but most of us were nonplussed by this strange order. Having reassembled, the captain explained that throughout the country at that time, similar parades were being held at all military bases for the express purpose of collecting all available MPC in the current series. He assured us that we would be issued with new money in a like amount from a new series. We dutifully handed over the money we had and received an equivalent amount in new shades of green, red, and orange. The whole exercise took about twenty minutes.

For us, little had changed except the colour and look of the notes. For hundreds of thousands, perhaps millions of Vietnamese, however, the moment would have been catastrophic. In a single instant, every cent of the millions of dollars they had squirreled away became worthless Monopoly money which could purchase absolutely nothing. There being an enormous quantity of usable money fuelling the black market, it was hoped that a surprise changeover of currency in a single day would thwart the activities of the shady marketeers. How successful the operation proved to be was never announced or detailed to us, but one would have to suspect that many large, illegal fortunes went up in smoke and dealings would have slowed considerably for a while.

They were certainly not halted. We were not too popular in town for weeks afterwards, but within a short time the new notes became just as acceptable as the old ones had ever been and business continued unabated and unchanged.

The purveyors of one particular commodity were never too concerned about the name or the colour of the payment they received. Indeed, their advertising material went to great lengths to point out that dollars of several denominations, marks, piastres, dong, yen, francs, or pounds sterling were all equally acceptable. I received an air mail letter from England one day, addressed to me personally, with my correct service number and unit clearly marked on the envelope. I knew no one in the UK so the letter was a complete surprise. I tore open the envelope and a photograph tumbled to the floor. I was more than a little amazed to find that it was the photo of a half-naked, well-bosomed young girl I had never seen before. After giving the picture more than just one scant glance, I read the explanatory letter accompanying it. Penny, it appeared, was a young English rose studying for a degree in one of England's foremost universities, who also did some modelling and photography on the side. She was gifted, the note went on to explain, with a particular facility for accommodating men, women, animals, or any combination of the three, in what was described as titillating photographs. As an introductory offer to a hardworking young soldier in Her Majesty's Service, I was therefore being given the opportunity of purchasing, at half price, photos, or 8mm film of Penny hard at her work. This would not only provide me with the diversion that I probably needed, but would also help Penny complete her studies. Postal notes or any of a dozen different currencies could accompany the order form which was enclosed for my convenience. The photo of Penny in the envelope was a gift, I was told, for which I didn't have to pay. She joined the harem on the walls of the security hut.

What intrigued me most was how my name, unit, and personal details had become known to someone in London. I suspected a prank or some madness on a mate's part, but questioning the guys proved fruitless and they all swore ignorance and innocence about the matter. It really didn't matter, but the mystery was partly solved a few weeks later as others also received similar material either from Singapore, Hong Kong, or Hamburg. We presumed that there was either a monster prankster in our midst who was operating very cunningly, or the pornographers somehow had access to lists of names of soldiers serving in Vietnam. Anything was possible.

Apart from this type of personalised correspondence, we were awash in a sea of pornographic pamphlets, magazines, newspapers, books, and films. Some of it – like Penny – arrived unexpectedly, but a lot was dumped in Vietnam and sold very cheaply by publishers who saw the half million force of isolated, sex-starved servicemen as a fertile market for their publications. A lot of it was of course purchased quite avidly, because we were, after all, dirty-minded, horny little bastards who enjoyed looking. If nothing else, the magazines and photographs provided a few contented hours of reading during guard duty. I never did get to see Penny hard at her work, however! Once or twice, I nearly filled in and mailed the order form, but only because I wanted to help her finish the university course, of course!

Locally, the back beach in Vung Tau was the usual marketplace for such films and photographs. Photos depicting action on absolutely any subject, however debauched, were readily available, and there was a busy local trade in that particular commodity – to which the Australian military contributed handsomely.

With the onset of very heavy rain, the temperature dropped eight to ten degrees and, for the first time, living became bearable. But the rains brought new, unexpected problems. When as much as three inches of rain falls in one hour on sand that is already waterlogged, the sand has a natural tendency to shift. It shifted! Whole sand hills moved covering roadways, crept in next to and under doorways, and piled up against the sides of buildings in such amounts that they were sometimes in danger of imminent collapse. This was particularly true of the Q store. With Smokey's return, we again had a full complement of three field engineers and we spent several weeks in July and August shovelling sand from one place to another. The actual labour we did in a week could have been done by a front-end loader in an hour, but we didn't have one. I was glad to be out of the guard hut doing something more active and, under Smokey's directions, we installed more ditches and corrugated iron drains where water flow was the heaviest. My calluses returned again, bearing testimony to the performance of honest labour.

At this time, though, I would have been content with almost any work, for Gary and I were within thirty days of R&R. Hong Kong became the focal point of all our thinking. We'd made shopping lists, had decided upon the exact amount of money we'd take, made plans about the places we would see and we had prepared and put aside the civvies we possessed weeks before in readiness for the big day. My short-sleeved blue shirt and grey trousers were washed and a brown pair of shoes polished to a mirror sheen. The very sight of civilian clothing made our hearts beat faster. Like children preparing for their first night's sleepover at a friend's place, we were ready and eager to be away. I doted on the moment when the plane would finally take off and I could say that I had left Vietnam.

To fill in the empty hours remaining during that month prior to R&R, there were three extracurricular activities in which I became deliberately involved. One was the new-found freedom of a speedboat, the second was the judo lessons with which, to my amazement, I actually persevered, and the last was the nightly Noggy run.

The unit's opportunity to get a boat for leisure activity came about quite by accident. For practice, the mechanics had been reconditioning an old outboard they'd come upon by either fair means or foul, from an abandoned wreck located miles down the beach. One thing led to another and the idea of using some spare time to rebuild the whole boat seemed appealing to them. We chipped in, bought some fibreglass from the Yanks and, with more luck than perhaps skill, they managed to make the tub seaworthy. When the two completed parts were married, its creators were amazed to find that the thing actually floated, steered, and handled satisfactorily. Having a boat was one thing, but having the necessary wherewithal to run, keep, and manage it was another. Unable to store and transport it from the unit down to the beach every time it was wanted, we gave it to the 1ALSG club for use by all. The club administrators then undertook to safeguard and maintain it. They also found a qualified instructor to teach, test, and license any prospective users.

One Sunday afternoon, Gary, Andy and I sat through the thirty-minute lesson, passed the test which entailed manoeuvring the boat around for about five minutes, and from then, three more commodores became licensed to pilot our new toy. We joined an increasingly long line of like-minded pleasure seekers, so that as the weeks passed, the opportunities to actually get the boat for ourselves were becoming more limited. I can only remember two occasions on which my turn came up, but the boat provided a lot of enjoyment for many, even for those who only sat on the sand watching others motoring back and forth about a hundred yards out to sea. A few supreme optimists even tried to water ski behind it using makeshift skis, but with little success. In the main, enjoyment was derived from the speed, the noise, the spray, and the imagined success of having escaped from camp, if only for an hour and if only for a few hundred yards.

Andy, who had done a bit of judo at home, was the one who talked me into joining the judo club. One moment, I was tugging at his collar with my left hand and searching for greater leverage with my right. The next, I felt the curiously relaxing sensation of floating through the air before crashing heavily to the mat. In a vain attempt to regain some of my lost dignity, I repeated this futile exercise twice more, only to be thrown again each time. Having finished using me as an object lesson for the others gathered around, our brown-belted instructor released me and I thankfully crept back to the safety of the group.

We had spent the first four lessons practicing break falls. We had fallen backwards, forwards, thrown ourselves sideways, slapping at the mats to the left and to the right until our hands seemed to hurt even more than our backs. It had been fun and an education to discover that I could fall from a considerable height and not be injured if the fall was executed properly. We had then thrown each other. A quick twist of the waist, accompanied by a pull on the opponent's jacket had him off balance and so his body went sailing over our own to land with a thud. Those falls had not hurt. After this particular throw by the instructor, however, even though my lower leg had been fully extended and I had performed the obligatory slap of the palm on the mat at the moment of contact, it felt as though my spine and pelvis had parted company. He had dumped me really hard and I was nursing more than just a bruised ego. It was some consolation, though, that I was only the first of four sacrificial lambs he treated in the same way, and I had the pleasure of watching three others suffer a similar wounding of pride.

There were about twenty rag dolls like me who had taken advantage of an offer to learn judo. This was made possible through the good graces of the YMCA. The mats and uniforms were provided by the Y, while our nemesis, the brown-belted executioner and teacher was a regular army man who had volunteered his services for the duration of the course. In all, I attended about ten lessons on a fortnightly basis, and while I started and finished as a white-belted beginner of low rank and very limited skills, the effort proved worthwhile. Like the boat, the judo helped fill the interminably long and boring hours between five and midnight, a time that, like Ron, I was beginning to fill with too much brooding, introspection and private thought.

Gary and I rode with a succession of drivers on the Noggy run, including Andy, who had recovered from his sprained wrist and was back in the saddle. The so-called Nogi run was the disparaging name we had given to the nightly transportation of the local workers home to Vung Tau after work. Around six, the Vietnamese would leave the units in which they were based and gather near the front gate. Several Mark V trucks would be there and the people would board the designated truck travelling in their particular direction. The vehicles would then complete the run, depositing their human cargoes at predetermined spots in town. It was generally a fun ride in the cooler part of the evening and we would joke with the older workers who had been with us for a long time, and tease the girls by deliberately hitting every pothole in the road, or by taking curves more sharply than was necessary. Mostly, it was yet another chance to depart the sand, the huts, stores, and faces that were beginning to haunt us with their monotonous regularity. It was at Lawrie's suggestion that we visited the RAAF mess near the airbase one night after dropping off the last of our passengers. Truly, the Air Force boys were catered for very nicely. Delicious food was available in more attractive surroundings than those we had and having access to speedy and regular deliveries of any item that was needed, they ate real rather than dehydrated food. The taste of fresh potatoes, tomatoes, carrots, beans, and meat was a culinary delight after the plastic fare of the previous five months. Subsequently, we made a point of eating there once a fortnight following the Noggy run.

In the meantime, my two separate countdowns progressed slowly and ponderously. Hong Kong was now twenty, while home was still about a hundred-and-forty days away.

At times, both seemed too distant, almost unattainable.

11.8.68-14.9.68

After all the ditch digging and sand shifting, I've been entrusted with another responsibility of monumental proportions. Every day, a local contractor comes into camp with his four helpers to collect the worst kind of refuse we generate – the oily leftover foodstuffs from the kitchens.

I have to ride in his truck and conduct them around from unit to unit. The need for a guard is apparently because they would pick up more than just rubbish if given the chance! The stench of the truck is quite unbearable and I feel like a fool riding shotgun on a garbage van, but there you have it, that's the job and my current contribution to the war effort.

Saw Marlon Brando in 'The Wild Ones' again last night and enjoyed it again…

We've had a few recent stirrings here about the possibility of another offensive by the VC similar to Tet of last February. They're calling it the Third Offensive. We've been put on ready alert with – wait for it – extra bullets! Reasoning here is that this might be their last big effort before they get down to serious talks in Paris. That'll be the day! Secretly, some here are hoping an incident does occur just to break the blasted monotony… Very heavy rain last night! You should have seen how much sand's shifted!

Andy is giving me a few secret lessons on the Mark V truck. We use the back roads after the Noggy run. I crunch the gears a bit, but then so does he sometimes. I notice you're counting the days, too. Not more fervently than me! Don't take any one date for granted, but I'm certainly not coming home in November and while I'm hopeful about Christmas, that's not a sure thing either. I could be here till sometime in January if they choose to give me pay in lieu of days off. I'm sending my driver's licence home, would you please take money out of my account and renew it. I'll send photos again soon.

127 days till Christmas…!

Smokey finishes his tour towards the end of January and since he'll be spending some time in Melbourne, I've invited him to the house for a few days, hope that's all right...

Each day we get up, dress, eat breakfast, work, eat lunch, more work, eat tea, see a film or write, drink, and go to bed. For this, the army gives me $104 a fortnight. Christ, I've had enough of this! Give Greg my best – by the time I see him, he might be shaving...

I've been here five months today. Big celebrations as a result I hear you ask? Well I'll probably get dressed in a tuxedo, go to the opera, then to the Chevron for late night champagne and I'll spend the night on a circular bed with Brigitte Bardot. If any of that doesn't happen, I'll wear my best green shorts, watch tonight's film, drink a gin and orange, and curl up with the mosquito net. I'm forever faced by these difficult choices.

Some of our plans for Hong Kong include the usual sightseeing, a round of golf which is Gary's choice, swimming in a freshwater pool, a hot bath, and some purchases. About the phone call from there, let's make this the final date and time: Sunday, 22 September. I'll call at 8 pm and since you're two hours behind, that'll make it 6 pm at home.

Incredible situation in Czechoslovakia! Seems like a repetition of what the bastards did in Hungary in 1956! Thanks again for the latest package of food, it's always wolfed down. There is a possibility that all seventh intake Nashos might be going home in December, which could therefore be the 3rd, 10th, 17th, 24th, or the 31st. I hope, though, that it's not one of the last two dates, as I would then spend either Christmas Eve or New Year's Eve on the plane. But then, even that would be fine just to get out of here...

Four guys from the sixth intake went home today. Our time is really approaching...

Here are some more photos I promised. One of them was taken on the Noggy-run which Andy and I are doing more regularly now. We have three or four regular stops where we give out lollies to the children who are now used to us and are waiting each night. Just look at their faces, how glad they seem to be for a few lousy sweets. It's better than winning the war. Maybe it is winning the war...!

I'm including a letter I got from a young child in NSW. It seems that the teacher of a grade 2 class got her children to write to us here for Fathers' Day.

22nd August.

Dear Soldier
I hope you have a happy father's day on the 1st September 1968. I hope your present surprised you. Come home safely.
Would you send us back a letter if you like.
Love from Anthony.

Isn't it marvellous?

They had a series of fundraising activities in their class and sent us lollies and cigarettes with the proceeds. I was given a letter from a little boy called Anthony. We read all the letters and in one of them a little girl wrote, *'Dear soldier. I hope you don't get shot. I hope that you win the war because I'm on your side.'*

Naturally I'll write to young Anthony Jeffs as soon as I can. These letters were really a great pick-me-up.

Washed and ironed the clothing for Hong Kong, we're

ready. No, don't send the licence back. It's hardly going to be of any use to me here but thanks for arranging it...

I'm back on the gate again. The countdown to Hong Kong is in single figures...

You'll hear about it on tonight's news I'm sure, the little hamlet of Ba Ria near Nui Dat, was overrun by VC last night. Their tactics are to burn and loot for some hours, terrorise, plunder, and be gone by morning. They're bastards, but a clever enemy. An action such as this ruins six months of effort on our part. Regaining the confidence of those people in Ba Ria will be very difficult now. So little progress is being made in this bloody place! I reckon, and I'm no real expert, that unless the Yanks make a radical change in the current course of action, we will still be at this stalemate five years from now. There doesn't seem to be a genuine desire for victory, but just pissing around! Perhaps Dad was right when he said that the Americans' main objective was to keep half a million troops on China's doorsteps rather than to be trying to win in Vietnam.

Yes, Ron is heading home for R&R, about a week after we go to Hong Kong. It should help him. Departure for us is at six am on the 18th and I'll speak to you soon on the phone from Hong Kong, my love always...

Chapter 30

Almost six months to the day that the shuddering RAAF plane had dumped us at the Vung Tau airbase, another that could have been its twin sister picked us up for the return trip to Saigon. Conversation being out of the question, we stared gleefully into the eyes of those sitting opposite during the flight and revelled in the first gush of truly cold air we had felt for half a year. Farewells at 55 had been brief, for Gary and I had risen, dressed, and departed before most were even thinking of getting up.

We knew, of course, that our movements had woken quite a few of those nearest our beds, but we had been deliberately ignored while they feigned sleep. We hadn't taken this as an insult, nor was it intended as such. The unspoken rule had been observed. Since it was pretty damned difficult to pretend happiness about someone else's departure on R&R, the generally accepted practice had always been not to make a big deal out of anyone leaving, but simply pretend not to notice the fact at all. Secondly, since it was only R&R and not the true, definitive, final departure, an event that was truly celebrated for all by all, everyone knew that in an altogether speedy five days there would be an inescapable, inevitable return. Not much of a production was therefore made of anyone going on R&R. At Tan Son Nhut airport, we passed through the already crowded terminal that had been our introduction to the funny country six months earlier. The sudden sight of the blue and white Pan Am 707, our conveyance to freedom, was a true delight which was only surpassed by the sensation of joy as the wheels lifted off the runway.

It was a raucous, at times unruly flight to Hong Kong. The Australian slouch hat was outnumbered twenty to one by an assortment of American berets, but regardless of uniforms, tongues were loosened and friendships formed for no other reason than that we were all heading away from that place. It was certainly not a topic of conversation and no one dared even ask, but as recently as a day or so earlier, many on board could have been in the firing line, flying helicopters, making bombing runs or, like me, on a security gate. Whatever the situation, an outpouring of emotion attended the take-off for each of us on board. The air hostesses came in for more than their fair share of attention and they did their best to serve meals to the two hundred passengers, while artfully dodging the unwanted advances of at least half that number. The specially printed menus welcomed us aboard the Pan Am R&R flight, pointing out that the hostesses had been volunteers for this trip from Saigon. By comparison, we were aware that Qantas didn't allow its hostesses into Vietnam, deeming the task unacceptably dangerous. The two-inch thick steaks served with fresh rolls and butter was a culinary delight which we devoured, removing the taste of etherized eggs still in our mouths from breakfast.

Our treatment in Hong Kong upon arrival was less than regal, however. The local constabulary was out in full force and looked intently into every crevice of our sparse luggage. Our reputations preceded us. We were each asked if we carried any firearms or had drugs in our possession and, in spite of successive answers in the negative, skilled hands frisked us to make sure. The packet of Rothmans in my pocket was emptied and individual cigarettes were examined and sniffed to ensure that they were the legal article. Alsatians on leashes eyed us warily as we moved along an inspection line. Those with something to hide must have sweated through this ordeal, but for most this wait simply meant the loss of a few precious minutes from an all too short five days. We then boarded a fleet of buses which took us to an American military base for more wasted hours of briefing. We already knew about the three classes of hotels that were available. We knew about the dangers of venereal disease and the current rate for female companionship. We knew about the official and unofficial exchange rates for US dollars, as well as the best tourist spots and shopping areas. Finally, we also knew that we were compelled to return to the airport at 0800 hours on the 23rd of the month. We had heard all of this many times over from others in the unit who had previously been to Hong Kong.

It was already mid-afternoon when, along with about thirty Yanks, Gary and I got off a bus outside the Hong Kong President on Nathan Road. We registered at the front desk, left our money in the hotel safe, caught the lift to the fifth floor, and finally entered our own, private rooms. Within minutes, as I sat there without a shirt, drinking from the complimentary bottle of lemonade and enjoying the air conditioner, I realised that this was the first time I had been totally alone in a room since leaving home to go to SME about ten months earlier. The long-awaited holiday known as R&R had begun.

While it is not uncommon for people to fly, eat juicy steak, sit in a comfortable chair, ride a bus, or catch the lift in a hotel to the fifth floor, for us at the time, each of these things was an experience so uniquely refreshing to the spirit, that they were savoured and enjoyed. We rediscovered old pleasures that we had taken so easily for granted in the past. Sitting in the padded seats of the 707, eating the tender meat that had been served by a very attractive woman was exhilarating. The wooden seats and the cook at 55 could hardly compete! We remarked upon just how quiet the engine of the coach taking us to the President had been. In truth, we'd simply become too used to hearing the whine of the thrashed engines of jeeps and trucks and this had made the bus seem quiet. We had become so accustomed to the crunch of boots on sand and gravel that now, as we rode upstairs in the carpeted lift, the feel and sounds below our shoes were magical. We had spent six long months sweating in the humidity of the tropics and now I thought I was in heaven as the cooling breeze of the air conditioner caressed me lovingly. The changes were extreme, sudden, and totally refreshing, as were all of the events of the five memorable days that followed.

Privacy! How sweet it was! Since the departure from Melbourne those months ago, I hadn't had the opportunity to experience it. I looked around the room, surveyed my personal kingdom, tested each of the two beds and making a choice threw my gear in the wardrobe. I ran the bath, stripped off and wallowed in the decadence of the warm water. Gary and I had chosen one of the medium-priced hotels and while the furnishings were not as opulent as the Park or the Imperial, to me they were perfect nonetheless. After all, they were mine. All mine to sit in, lie down on, or mess up as I wished. Spending the best part of an hour in the warm bath, symbolically scrubbing every remnant of Vietnam from my pores, I returned naked to a very cold room and actually shivered for the first time in ages. As if to make a point even I didn't understand, I turned the air conditioner to a much lower setting and I lie there, shivering some more before getting dressed.

Gary's room was only about twenty yards down the corridor, but instead of walking there, I used one of the disgustingly extravagant items for which I was paying a substantial amount of my hard-earned money. I phoned him. He was also dressed and ready, having performed much the same rites as I had just done. We met downstairs, withdrew some of our money from the safe, and were about to walk out the front door, when we were literally grabbed by a pair of excited hands and ushered into one of the clothing stores in the hotel lobby. Even though we probably needed them, never in our wildest dreams had we previously considered spending money on such clothing. Yet, within half an hour, we had been talked into ordering two, hand-sewn suits, which we were assured, would be ready in three days. In those thirty minutes, we had been convinced of our desperate need for new suits, had been measured by the Indian tailor, had chosen the cloth, and had been relieved of the necessary funds to pay for the goods. It was the first, but not the last financially-draining encounter that Hong Kong thrust in our faces. We almost ran out the front door in case either the jeweller or another cloth merchant who were both sniffing around nabbed us.

To be sure, we had come to Hong Kong with two or three definite things planned, but for the most part we wanted a carefree, *we'll-do-it-if-we-like*-time. The financial arrangement at the President included bed and breakfast, but all other meals had to be paid for separately, so on this first night we walked the streets of an unknown Kowloon in order to get to know the place, as well as to find something to eat.

We didn't succeed in either of these objectives, for we ended up in the inviting atmosphere of the New Piccolo Nightclub, where food and local geography became matters of secondary importance. For the first time in a long time, we sat down, talked with, and enjoyed the company of two attractive girls whose English vocabulary, along with many other of their exceedingly desirable qualities, kept us suitably enthralled. I felt as though I had emerged from a time warp, and there really was normality existing in life after all.

I've often heard it said that the main ingredient needed for a good holiday was to be doing something that is diametrically opposed to one's normal routine. If that statement contains any truth at all, then we had an outstanding holiday. All that we saw, ate, drank, touched, and smelled over the next five days was so different to the accustomed norm of the previous six months that we soaked up each day and lived each experience to the full.

For two guys on such a short leave, perhaps the most unusual activity we ended up doing was to play a game of golf at the Royal Hong Kong course in Fanling. I had never been bitten by the golfing bug and had never played the game before, so I knew almost nothing about woods, irons, tees, and divots. But since Gary and I had a gentlemen's agreement to do most things together, I went with him so he could enjoy a round of his most favourite game. I was prepared to give it my best shot. That best, however, turned out to be less than satisfactory.

Gary made all the arrangements in the pro shop, which he assured me, had no connection whatsoever with the many ladies of the night we had seen in Kowloon the night before. Armed to the teeth, as they were, with bags, clubs, hats and umbrellas, I looked at the two young boys who were going to act as our caddies or pack mules for the occasion and immediately decided that they would get a huge tip afterwards. We followed them to the first tee. I watched earnestly as Gary positioned the ball, placed his feet carefully in line, took his back swing, and belted the thing down the fairway. The execution looked simple enough, so I followed his example. By the time I'd wound up, I had forgotten which elbow Gary had told me to keep locked and which way I was supposed to look. I just swung at the ball and hoped for the best. I felt contact with the ball, so I was momentarily happy. A split second later, my caddie, who was standing about fifteen paces away at right angles to the intended flight of the ball, made a groaning sound and fell to the ground. The ball had hit the poor bugger right in the stomach. We rushed over, but he was up in no time and was fine to continue. I felt so bloody foolish that I decided not to go for any more long shots in case I killed someone. Consequently, I walked around the eighteen holes and putted out each green from wherever I happened to drop the ball while my woods, irons, and wedges stayed safely in the bag which was dutifully carried for me by my slightly wounded caddie. I recompensed the young boy handsomely at the end. Gary, on the other hand, played a fabulous round, or so he told me, getting such a high that he immediately bought a complete set of clubs at the pro shop, which he arranged to be shipped back to his father in Australia. My disaster at the 300 yard, par 4, first hole, 'The Meadow' at the Royal Hong Kong Golf Club, was a misadventure I promised myself I would never reveal to anyone.

 I took $400 with me for R&R, which I considered to be quite extravagant. Gary, I think, took a little more. The airfare was of course paid for by the Australian Government or, more accurately, the Australian taxpayer, but we were responsible for accommodation, food, entertainment, and whatever purchases we made. The rooms at the President cost $8.50 a night, so we paid out $45 upon booking in. I had absolutely no trouble in disposing of the remaining $350 of the small fortune I had with me at the start. In fact, by the last evening, as we were taking a final stroll along Chatham Road, we were both so broke, yet still wanting to see and do more, that instead of accepting the offered ride from a rickshaw driver, we jokingly offered to run him up to Victoria Peak if only he would pay us. Unfortunately, he declined the offer, smiled, and politely left muttering Chinese obscenities about moronic tourists. Wherever we turned, attractive and tempting goods of an endless variety were readily available. Apart from the suit, I bought some camera gear, a set of stereo headphones I'd promised Andy, two watches, some light clothing to replace those I had brought with me, a cigarette lighter, a transistor, and an assortment of gifts for the family including a length of Thai silk cloth for my mother. If I had taken $1000 with me that, too, would have been spent, I'm sure.

    We did eat well, though! We deliberately shied away from the foodstuffs sold on the streets, ordered the best, and paid the highest prices for restaurant meals and at the President where we ate each evening. We would have paid an astonishing $20 each on the fourth night when, resplendent in new suits, we strode to our usual table and instructed the waiter to spoil us. We couldn't resist a disbelieving, wry smile as he gave us a scented towel with which to wash our hands prior to starting the first course. Seventy-two hours earlier, we had entered the mess at 55, covered in mud and sweat to the eyeballs and had eaten a meal of dehydrated pork chops. Now, we smelt rosy and dined on oysters, lobster, roast duck, and a fabulous selection of chocolate cakes washed down with chilled apple and orange juice. We faced a number of severe culture shocks in those few days, but they were altogether welcome and in every respect good for the soul. I respected Gary's wishes and didn't drink alcohol while we were there, which not only saved me a considerable sum, but no doubt also gave my liver the slight respite it needed.

Both of us noticed and spoke about how clean everything appeared to be. In spite of the millions of humans who were cramped into such a small space, the buildings, streets, and harbour were generally spotless and even the tidiness of the people themselves was evident. On the streets of Kowloon, or on one of our frequent crossings to the island on the Star Ferry, there was no sign of the refuse, jetsam, and carelessly discarded garbage to which we had become so accustomed on the streets of Vung Tau. The tall buildings ringing the harbour presented a pristine purity of white silhouetted against the blue sky, while the view from the peak of Mt Victoria was simply serene and I used up an entire roll of film in trying to capture its grandeur. We booked ourselves on a couple of day tours to see the New Territories near the Chinese border and Aberdeen Harbour with its teeming flotilla of junks and water-bound humanity. Both were fascinating, while we also visited such singularly uninteresting places as the house in which the movie, 'Love Is a Many Splendored-Thing', had been filmed. The organised tours were worthwhile, but those places we reached on foot and explored at our own leisure provided the greatest thrills and most enjoyable surprises.

Away from opulent Kowloon, we wandered along miles of narrow alleyways that crisscrossed Hong Kong's shantytown. Here, tens – or perhaps hundreds of – thousands lived in abject poverty in old shacks sunk at precarious angles into the sides of hills. The inhabitants of these tin, Masonite, and mud hovels were desperately poor, yet there was a dignity in their bearing, which was lacking in the similarly poor Vietnamese we had come to know. A short journey from there or from Aberdeen Harbour back into town provided an instant comparison between the incredible social and economic divisions in the city, being home, as it was, to both the very affluent and the desperately destitute.

In other areas of this British Protectorate, we stood in awe in front of department stores bearing huge portraits of Mao Tse-Tung. My instincts somehow told me to be aware. We were, after all, participants in a war specifically against communism and we had been advised by the R&R organisers against going into them, yet the temptation to enter was stronger than all impulses to the contrary. Naturally, it was like any other large store, but the ten minutes we spent there provided a childishly satisfying thrill, as though we had been dared to do something naughty and we had secretly accepted the challenge.

The 'Suzy Wong' part of town, however, provided an entirely different kind of thrill and excitement. Here we found the movement, the life, the music, and the atmosphere about which we had dreamed. All of these fantasies of course revolved around the plethora of beautiful and available female companionship. Here we also came across hundreds of American sailors with whom we had to compete yet again. The USS *Bennington* happened to be in port unfortunately, so white shirts and bell-bottomed trousers flitted everywhere. We struck up a few short-lived friendships and went with a number of them to an American depot similar to the PX, where we bought some of our electrical goods like tape recorders and transistors.

We moved around town by bus, walked interminable distances, sailed back and forth on the ferries, rode the cable car to the top of Victoria Peak, and made at least twenty taxi trips, each of which was, to our amazement, in a very comfortable Mercedes Benz. Somehow, though, neither Gary nor I could muster the will to travel by rickshaw. They were everywhere and could be hired quite cheaply, yet the thought of sitting back regally, while another human being puffed, panted, and pulled the vehicle from up front was an unpalatable notion to both of us. We attempted to cram as much into the available time as possible. We achieved our aim very successfully, for on the last evening, as we sat in my room for a breather, we estimated that we had slept only about twenty hours since leaving 55. Being almost broke, we spent our remaining dollars on a final sumptuous meal, and, since it was around six o'clock, I made an important phone call.

The three-minute conversation with my parents, which I later discovered had been taped by them, was very difficult, disjointed, and certainly uncomfortable. I recall that my voice wavered and for uncomfortably long moments during the conversation, I suddenly found that, in spite of myriads of things I wanted to say, nothing suddenly seemed appropriate or came to mind. A similar silence from the other end, interspersed with an occasional 'yes' or 'I know', showed that my parents were in the same predicament. Despite this slight embarrassment, the sounds of their voices and the background noises I detected indicating that visitors were at the house satisfied the need I had for closer contact with those I missed so much. I think I finally managed the usual banter that we were having a great time in Hong Kong, that I had sent a letter a few days earlier on hotel stationery, and that we were heading back to Vietnam the following day. For a brief few moments, my young godson was put on the phone and my voice really quavered and shook as I tried to blurt out something of consequence to him.

There was little by way of substance in the exchange, I initially thought, but in reality it was wonderfully refreshing and just strengthened my desire for the remaining months to pass as quickly as possible.

It was also strange to hear myself speaking in Hungarian for the first time in six months, and even Gary got to say a quick hello to people he had never met.

While it was true that in Vietnam each of us kept a mental note of the number of months, weeks, and days that were left before our return home, I had secretly and foolishly refined that procedure one step further. Hidden underneath some clothing in my locker was a neatly folded sheet of paper on which I had been entering my daily tally. Dissatisfied with the knowledge that I had three months, or approximately twelve weeks – that is about eighty-four days to go – I had converted this to hours, minutes and, finally, to seconds. I fully realised the stupidity of that exercise and it was not a daily act that I wanted generally known by any of the others. Hence my secure hiding place for the sheet. I quickly became adept at multiplying the number of days left by twenty-four, multiplying that product by sixty, and again by a further sixty. Thus with twelve weeks left, I tried to fool myself into believing that the time would appear to be less if I thought of it as being seven million, two hundred and fifty-seven thousand, and six hundred seconds instead. Written in figures, 7 257 600 seconds didn't seem too long at all!

Every day I would look forward to the moment when I would enter the new total, which reduced by 86 400 each day. It really was a fool's exercise, for rather than shortening the time, I was acting like Ron, focusing too much attention on just one factor, thereby making time pass even more slowly. I knew this, of course, but continued the practice anyway. In a strange sort of way on the last night in Hong Kong, I looked forward to getting my hands on that piece of paper and being able to knock off five days' worth of seconds in one go. I had chosen Hong Kong so I wouldn't have to return to Vietnam from home, and now I still dreaded the return with a passion. That stupid piece of paper was the sole item related to our return, about which I thought with any warmth or eager satisfaction.

In spite of our wishes, prayers and hopes to the contrary, the sun did rise the following morning and a mini bus picked us up at the hotel at six. The drive back to the airport was completed in utter silence, even though all the familiar faces from the flight earlier in the week were there, too. No one wanted to speak! Almost in a daze we boarded, caught another glimpse of Hong Kong's beautiful harbour, and the plane headed southwest. The aircraft was deathly silent, as though two hundred ghosts inhabited it. Many slept or lay back in cushioned comfort, enjoying the peace and tranquillity while it was still available. There was definitely more than tiredness in the silence and icy unfriendliness of the plane. The gaiety of the previous flight was replaced by a sullen, self-imposed introspection, as the memories of the most recent happy experiences were superseded by those from before. After landing, we had a horrid seven-hour wait in Saigon before finally rattling back to Vung Tau on another RAAF transport.

A jeep picked us up at the airbase and, with an indescribable anger welling up inside me, I discovered that not only had the sun risen that morning, but 1ALSG was still there on those bloody sand dunes and I had been brought to it for a second, intolerable time. After the most cursory and probably rude greeting to those who welcomed us back, I reached for my folded sheet of paper, filled in the new, reduced tally, and was about to go to bed when I spied the letter. It had arrived during my absence and I immediately recognised the childish scrawl of Anthony Paul Jeffs. In reply to what I had written when I first received that wonderful letter from him for Fathers' Day some weeks earlier, Anthony had now written:

> *Dear Frank.*
> *I received your letter. I read it and liked it when I read the bit where it said it's good to get a letter from a small boy like me. We liked the flag, the shield, and the money. Thank you to your friends over there, and yourself, for all the things you have sent over for us. Thank you again Frank. On October the 15th, 2A and 2B are going to the RAAF Base at Richmond. We are going by bus. Do you want me to keep on writing to you? What sports do you like? (Football, socker or cricket). On October the 15th, we are going to see the planes that took the parcel over to you,*
> *Love from Anthony Jeffs.*

If ever I needed a heart-warming, supportive, and positive look, word or sign to wipe away a downcast mood, that night was it and Anthony, bless his little heart, had provided that word and that sign! Carefully, I filed this precious letter with those from my parents and my decreasing tally sheet of remaining seconds in-country, and went to bed with a half-smile, feeling much better than I otherwise would have felt.

Chapter 31

Gary and I were both exceptionally low and in the dumps for the next week. The dreariness of camp and of Vung Tau was even more pronounced after the bright lights and diversions of Hong Kong. In a weak attempt at humour, we suggested to the cook that he ought to have a supply of warm, scented towels ready for washing hands in the mess. He misunderstood or chose not to see our meaning and told us to piss off quickly in language we certainly understood. We pretended to enjoy the dehydrated fish that had been slopped on our plates, but it was an exercise in futility as were most things with which we tried to re-establish a connection. We were like fish out of water, but particularly angry about the fact that we had been forced back into our previous situation again. We felt as though we were both in love with Hong Kong and therefore anything else paled by comparison. In reality, though, we were only enamoured with the idea of Hong Kong. We could have taken R&R in a village in Outer Mongolia and still have fallen for the place, because it would have represented an escape and a respite from the enforced monotony in which we found ourselves for the second time. Consequently a new, gut-wrenching hatred of Vietnam developed and I felt even more cheated of precious time and opportunities than I had before. This was a particularly bitter and difficult period.

Surprisingly, though, a number of changes had taken place in the unit during our short absence. Since changes were a rarity, they helped make the readjustment a little easier. Andy had finally secured his transfer to Nui Dat. Although I was to miss my little mate, I was genuinely happy for him, as he had wanted the move for quite some time. He had also learned in the meantime that his application for R&R to Australia had been successful and that he would be going just prior to Christmas. I gave the earphones I had bought for him to a driver from the Dat to take to him. Ron, we were delighted to see, left on his R&R just days after our return and a week later we were thrilled to see the re-arrival of a refreshed, almost new mate who had finally reconciled problems in his mind. Wayne was of course keen to hear about our experiences while we had been away and, within weeks, his movements stirred us early one morning as he left for Singapore.

There were also three new faces in the unit, fresh blood from the tenth and eleventh intakes who were starting their twelve-month tours. I recognised in their faces the same look of quiet respect for us, similar to that which we once had for those who were about to finish Nasho. In fact, the sixth intake was being discharged in Australia around the time of our R&R, and as Nashos, Ron, Gary, and I suddenly became the army's most senior conscripted members. Gary had been promoted to corporal some weeks earlier and was now given more responsibility in the workshop, which curtailed our lunchtime running. We still managed to do it twice a week, however. Carlton won the VFL premiership, which was as good a reason as any for a further round of celebrations, and we also got the news that within six to eight weeks, we would be able to take a further break of four days. This was for rest and convalescence, or better known as R&C.

The general rule was that about a month prior to the end of a tour, a wind-down period was granted to each serviceman. For us at 1ALSG, this meant that the four days could be spent in a hostel in Vung Tau, which bore the rather fancy title of the AFV Amenities and Welfare Unit, R&C Detachment. It was really nothing more than a converted block of units, which had a number of rooms large enough to accommodate two people each. While there, we were allowed to manage our own affairs and be reasonably independent without army interference, given that we still behaved within the bounds of army regulations. While this closed off many avenues of perfectly enjoyable and fruitful behaviour, the break was always welcomed. It was, of course, much more valuable and relevant to those from Nui Dat who, coming as they did from combat situations, needed this break desperately to prepare them somewhat for the return home. The advantage to all was that we could move out of camp and lead a semi-normal life if only for a short time. Its greatest virtue for all, however, was that R&C signalled the beginning of the end.

The best news I received on returning, apart from Anthony's letter, concerned a change of job. Since its completion, Buck, a regular army man of about thirty who loved his beer and had seemed ideal for the task, had manned the 55 boozer. That single criterion and requirement would of course have qualified four-fifths of the unit, but Buck had done very well in setting up the place, stocking it with a variety of goods, painting the walls, scrounging a few pieces of furniture and serving behind the bar. Army decisions being unfathomable at the best of times, Buck was shifted to the orderly room and

I became the new barman. It was another welcome change of pace and I enjoyed the challenge it presented. Indeed, after digging trenches and counting trucks, any new task would have been a welcome challenge. The daily routine usually began with a general tidying of the bar area after the previous night's action.

I knew that many in the unit drank a lot, but it wasn't until I began to clear away the empties that the extent of the drinking became visibly apparent. I counted them on the third or fourth morning and found close to three hundred cans, which averaged out at something like four cans for each drinker the night before. I didn't bother to count empty cans each morning, but in the weeks that followed, there was little variation in the daily number of rubbish bins that were filled with them. On the occasion of someone's birthday or particularly after a departure, even more was consumed. The daily clean up was followed by a stock take. This involved the physical counting of each item on the shelves, from chewing gum, through pens, lollies, writing pads, tins of sardines, stew, tuna, spaghetti, to – of course – the full cans of beer still in stock. That count would be subtracted from the previous day's total and the difference would indicate the sales for that night. Money collected, which was held in the lieutenant's office overnight, would then have to agree with the sales calculated as per the stock take. Following this short mathematical exercise, stock sheets had to be taken to the lieutenant who checked for accuracy and counted the money. If all was well, the cash was banked at the 1ALSG cashier's office. If, on the other hand, the count disagreed violently with the money collected the lieutenant would want to know why. As a general rule of thumb, a figure that came to within a dollar or so was acceptable.

After banking, I had to load up the iceboxes for that night's trade. We usually had plenty of ice in the workshop because 55 supplied much of 1ALSG with that particularly scarce commodity. If we were short, I would take a quick trip into town to pick up four large slabs from the local ice works. By this time, I had passed my test to drive jeeps and had the glorious pleasure, on occasion, of driving into Vung Tau alone. That was the extent of the work I needed to do by way of preparation each day and it was generally finished by lunchtime. My afternoons were free, but at five, as the others ended their day, I would open the boozer and serve behind the counter till seven. At that time, someone else from the canteen committee would take over and lock up at closing time, at ten. There was little glamour or romance in the job, but its true virtue lay in the fact that it was different to what I had been doing before and as such helped me maintain and retain a continuing semblance of sanity.

Once a week I would also have to go to the ASCO warehouse and order a week's supply of new stores, based on how well certain items were selling. The extent of this purchase was also determined by the amount of money the canteen had in credit. Each unit's boozer had to remain financially independent. At times, our canteen had close to $600 in the bank, which was quite an achievement for such a small unit. Given that a can of beer sold for fifteen cents and cost us twelve to buy, and was by far the fastest selling item, a hell of a lot of cans were drunk in order to amass a profit of six hundred dollars. Within a week, I settled comfortably into the job of barman and was resigned to the fact that with time running short, my overseas duty was to consist of ditch digging, vehicle counting, security duties, and the serving of beer. I was content with that reality. But on the rarest of occasions I did wonder whatever valiant stories I would tell my grandchildren in the years to come when they would ask the inevitable question:

'Grandpa, what did you do when you were in the war in Vietnam?'

Many of us had answered the first letters we had received from the children of class 2A from Marayong Primary School. Their second and a few third letters had now arrived. In his letter, which I had appreciated and valued so much on my return from Hong Kong, Anthony had included a pastel drawing of soldiers shooting at each other, a number of cannon, and what appeared to be a fire hose but was probably a flame thrower.

His writing below the picture was a simple: *'Up the goodies, down the baddies.'*

Being influenced by early television shows which were predominantly from the US – and, in particular, American westerns – and remembering my own cowboys and Indians fetish at age nine or ten when cowboys were always supposed to be good and Indians bad, I tried to explain to Anthony in my next reply that one side in a fight was not always necessarily good or bad, right or wrong, and the message in the letter, although no doubt unsuitable for someone as young as Anthony, probably reflected my own emerging thoughts and suspicions about what was happening in Vietnam.

I wrote something along the lines that in a fight at school later on, he might become involved because of a friendship, or because he might feel that something bad had been done against him that needs to be answered. So he jumps into the fight with fists swinging, satisfied that he is doing the right thing. During the fight, as injuries start to hurt, he might begin to think that he's not right. He might even start to wish he wasn't in the fight. He might be wishing that he could suddenly change his mind and not be involved. Was the bad thing to which he had so quickly reacted really as bad as he had at first thought? Even if it was as bad as all that, was it truly worth what was now happening? Could there have been another way of solving the problem? Should he have been surer of his facts? After all, he could have made a mistake and not understood properly! But both boys who are fighting are now suffering equally and seriously and what's more important is that both of them are equally sure that each one of them is right. But wait, it's impossible for both of them to be right, so one of them at least must be a little wrong. Could both of them be a little wrong? Could he, Anthony, have been wrong all along? Could both of them be wrong? It's too late. The damage was done.

Whether any of this made sense or an impression on Anthony I don't know, for the letters stopped altogether and we received no further notes from Marayong.

Maybe that's one war story that might be worth telling my grandchildren one day, I thought to myself!

Unlike many others, I never needed a salve to soothe and nurture my pride, nor did I strive for that single heroic act which would somehow prove my manhood and justify to someone, anyone, that I had done well in the war. If I had ever felt a little guilty about the menial, seemingly unimportant tasks I performed in Vietnam, those feelings and thoughts had long disappeared. Many, however, strove to accomplish a feat that might be considered nobler, more substantial, and more noteworthy than was the norm. It was also a fact that for reasons connected with this need for manly recognition, many conveyed messages to wives and sweethearts that portrayed their actions in a much more adventurous and heroic light than was actually the case. Letters told of duties and missions that were, at best, exaggerations, and, at worst, simply nonexistent fabrications. A trip to Nui Dat might sometimes be translated into a dangerous flight to Plei Ku, or a night in the bush might become a weeklong patrol, with VC thrown in for good measure. Drivers carting bedding or food might relate a journey they undertook with a cargo of explosives, while mechanics working on jeeps and trucks suddenly told tales of their skills with armoured personnel carriers when it came to writing a letter home. While for those of us at 55, this sort of hyperbole was well nigh impossible given the fact that we were, after all, only a stores unit, there were individuals we came across who freely admitted to gilding the lily quite often.

I wasn't totally devoid of vanity, either. I sent home a photograph of myself in full battle dress with the rifle in hand, although I did point out that the photo was quite innocent and had been taken by Gary outside our hut on a Sunday, during one of our frequent, 'what the bloody hell are we going to do now,' bored afternoons.

Symbolically perhaps, the Vung Tau tip was about a mile from 1ALSG. On one occasion, we saw a huge pall of smoke rise from it as the mountain of rotting garbage was set alight. I wonder how one aspiring Audie Murphy felt later, knowing that he sent home a photo of that event, claiming it to be the result of a misdirected B52 bomb strike. An amount of boasting and exaggeration was to be expected, but I daresay that the overzealous reporting of incidents such as this caused a lot of harm and needless concern to families who perhaps accepted and believed stories in letters quite literally.

Some three weeks after I took over from Buck, a couple of carpenters decided to dress up the boozer and we selected a night for the official christening. For some reason that I never discovered, a four-foot high model of Yogi Bear was cut from Masonite and after being painted, was hung on the front wall above the bar. Appropriately, the place became known as the Yogi Bar. A framed photograph of a Qantas 707 was placed next to Yogi and a dartboard went up on the back wall. Some enterprising lad got his hands on a parachute, no doubt from an American in need of a quick buck, and that was hung in a billowing fashion from the rafters. A budding Van Gogh was let loose with brush and black paint and he sketched two gum trees on the back wall, between which lay an outstretched and comfortable-looking swaggie. With one boot on and the other off, pipe in mouth and surrounded by flies, he really was an Aussie masterpiece. An ill-directed dart would often pierce his dangling right foot. Yogi was finally dressed in a bra and a pair of crotch-less panties. A few armchairs and barstools were purchased, a fan was installed in the ceiling, and the end result was that the 55 boozer became quite a welcoming, friendly, and hospitable place.

For my part, I decided the following Monday to invest more of the canteen's profits than was normally the case. In initially setting up the boozer, Buck had purchased a line of goods that was considered essential. Apart from the pallets of Victoria Bitter and Carlton Draught that filled the storeroom next to the bar, he had bought things like cans of baked beans, stews, spaghetti, sausages, and sardines. On this particular Monday, I picked up a few cartons of KB Lager as well as Castlemaine Fourex to see if the troops would like a change of brew. I also bought several dozen beer glasses, some coasters, and packets of peanuts and cashews for that improved, pub atmosphere. I also got some samples of relatively expensive delicacies such as tinned crab, lobster, and smoked oysters. At $1.20 a can for crab, it was quite costly. The boys, however, took to these things like ducks take to water and having eaten plastic food for far too long, the high prices hardly mattered. Business boomed as never before. They appreciated the pleasure of being able to drink from a glass as opposed to sucking beer from a can, the new beer disappeared on the first night, and I had to promise to get more and a greater variety the following week. In like manner, the crab and oyster were devoured quickly and I even endeared myself to the few non-drinkers by having bought tins of orange, apricot, and peach juice, which I served chilled. My pièce de résistance was the chilling of glasses in the new freezer which had not been done before. We began to attract customers from the neighbouring boozer at 17, as well as from further afield and, overall, the canteen committee was very happy at our next monthly meeting when a considerably improved bottom line was evident on the balance sheets.

Chapter 32

2.10.68-7.11.68

You'll find that I'm quite a bit balder than when I left. I can't believe how much I'm sweating under this bush hat! My hair is falling out magnificently. Happy birthday, Greg...

Hope the package from Hongers has arrived? Thanks for your longer letters recently! I read them all thoroughly, you can be sure! I'm at sixes and sevens about what to do when I finally get back from Europe. I should really know, but I don't. Bear with me...

Today completes the twenty-eighth week here. I cut off my moustache by accident this morning. It sure feels strange without it. Haven't heard from Andy for three weeks, we haven't even been into town for about that long, it's hard to generate any interest in this place after Hong Kong really... We had some obligatory rifle practice recently. After seven months I've fired the bloody thing.

We've had a whiff about the possibility of a 17 December flight home! This is not confirmed, but would be fantastic! Your frequent letters are a constant source of enjoyment and relief and are helping me retain a certain degree of sanity, please keep writing. No, the canteen is not hard work, only longer hours, but I welcome that... The Olympics begin on Saturday; we're looking forward to some coverage on the American radio network. We hear that you might be getting direct TV pictures from Mexico City! True?

I've got a two hour lull before the five o'clock charge at the canteen, so a few lines. Strange, but since returning from HK, Gary and I have cooled somewhat towards each other. Perhaps an overdose of togetherness is all, it'll work itself out. I still haven't heard from or seen Andy, a mate of his says he's carting sand and gravel from a quarry near Nui Dat and he's not too happy about it. I see you're making plans for New Year's Eve. Hunters Lodge sounds great, but remember that December 17 is not definite.

We're not doing too well in Mexico, are we? Even Ron Clarke failed in the 10 000 metres. After all these years he does deserve an Olympic gold! The West Germans are unbelievable, though!

We had to make a quick trip to the hospital with a Vietnamese woman yesterday – she was giving birth. Lucky it was only a few minutes by truck. She had a little girl... Farewell party last night for two guys going home, it was a great night, but what a mess in the canteen! In answer to your question about a homecoming dinner, how about chicken soup with those lovely liver balls you make, pork goulash with dumplings, pancakes with cheese filling, and a decent cup of black coffee...?

The weather is heating up again, I simply loathe it! So the current round of peace talks in Paris has ended just like the previous many! Nothing new! Perhaps the American election will bring about something different...?

Gary and I start R&C on November 9. We'll be together again, but the previous problem I mentioned must have been my imagination, we're fine. Some bright news from Canberra! If a soldier signs on for a further six months, then he'll be given a thirty-day pass to travel anywhere in the non-Communist world. Sounds like a bloody good deal, but not good enough for this little black duck! The Yanks have a similar offer open to them, with the addition of a $2000 gratuity at the end of their extra service. Latest from Andy is he might be going on R&R on December 18, so there's a faint chance we might be coming home within a day of each other. Olympics finished, but the altitude sure took its toll. What about Bob Beamon's long jump, though? Fantastic...!

Finally, it's November and in some respects time has flown since 8 January when I left for Sydney. At times, though, it feels as if my entire life has been crammed into these past ten months. We're preparing for a special parade on the helipad. The area Commander, Lieutenant Colonel Gilmore, has finished his twelve-month tour and is handing over to the new OIC. We're taking bets on how many will faint in the expected 95 degree heat.

Five days till R&C. The parade went well; we even had an American band here for the handover. The new boss is loud and firm, but aren't they all? Probably nothing will change...

Melbourne Cup Day! Hope you had a good rest on the day off? I'm amazed that the package from HK still hasn't arrived. Gary's two parcels have been home for weeks...

So it's to be President Nixon for the next four years! One can only hope that it's a change for the better. Perhaps he can initiate something in Paris that his predecessor couldn't. Can you believe the conceit and idiocy of Marshal Ky in not wanting to sit at the peace conference table as long as the NLF maintains an equal representation? Who the bloody hell does he think he is? These bastards might find it easy to make grand statements from the comfort of their damned presidential palaces, but it's not easy for the poor little grunts who are dying and counting the days until this bullshit stops! Off on R&C tomorrow, I'll write again after that...

Gary and I reported at the three-storied R&C building in town and were ushered into a room with three beds. The rules as explained were simple. We were free to use the facilities for the next four days and could move about town as we wished, as long as we were back on the premises by curfew. Doors were bolted between the hours of ten at night and six in the morning, and to be caught in town during those curfew hours would result in an automatic charge and an immediate return to one's unit. We were somewhat concerned about the mention of those specific hours as that could have affected a small excursion we'd been planning for a while. Nonetheless, we nodded assent, hoping all the same that we could somehow solve the problem presented by the bolted doors.

It took only fifteen minutes to acquaint ourselves with the layout. There was a common room offering billiards and table tennis, a dartboard, and some reading material. There was a courtyard out the back for lying in the sun if one wished and we had the added comfort of having Vietnamese workers to clean our rooms. This just about summed up the R&C centre's amenities, and while it was hardly the Hong Kong President, we appreciated the change in scenery. In essence, R&C was designed to be a signal to servicemen that another period of readjustment was at hand. It was often explained in sombre monotones that departure would be more difficult than one might think. Since nearly every hour of every day was spent in the happy knowledge that, ultimately, we would leave, we scoffed at the notion that the eventual departure would be at all troublesome. We didn't yet know just how much of a problem it might be and just how significantly everything about Vietnam had become rooted in our psyche. Whether it was tolerated, loved, loathed, feared, enjoyed, or dreaded, the experience, we were told, was to colour and affect the rest of our lives. We smirked at and disbelieved such claims.

Gary and I really didn't need the delights of Vung Tau to bolster our spirits. But there were many at the R&C unit who desperately needed these quiet, private opportunities for reflection. Our time there showed us yet again that we ought not to have taken our own little problems too seriously. We saw many there with infinitely greater needs than we might have imagined we had. While we complained about boredom and monotony, we hung our heads in shame to have to listen to those who spoke of destruction, real suffering, and death. This was particularly so when the individual cried with relief at just being able to share the grief and pain that his involvement in an action had brought. We had been so cloistered inside 1ALSG that the brutalities of the war had simply passed us by, even though they had occurred only a few scant miles away. Those from Nui Dat who were on R&C enjoyed the billiards and table tennis, lay in the sun, rested, and were thrilled by the walks through town. Gary and I accepted their more senior status and kept respectfully out of their way.

We did wander through those parts of town that a few hours leave on a Sunday had not permitted before. The main boulevard skirting the bay provided a great day's sightseeing. Away from the stench of the outdoor markets and the grubby little alleys filled with massage parlours and bars, Vungers presented an attractive façade and the French influence was evident in the architecture in these more opulent sections of town. With four days of similar walks ahead of us, we retreated to our room quite often and spent hours discussing the subject which was perhaps the second dearest to our hearts, behind our first and mutually all-pervasive wish to be going home. The topic in question was just what we were going to do after the millstone of military service was lifted from our shoulders in a few months' time.

There was one absolute certainty: neither one of us was going to re-enlist. That left us with one of two other choices. We could either return to our previous places of employment, which for Gary was a tradesman's job with a Melbourne manufacturer and for me the PMG, or we could both find a new direction and begin something else. In truth, the two years of service had changed us and both of us wanted that new, something else. While Gary was restless and wanted to improve his lot in life by working for another employer, I couldn't visualise myself shuffling telephone accounts any longer either. In the final analysis, therefore, we had to come up with a satisfactory, fulfilling alternative. Exactly what that was, we didn't know. For me, the decision seemed less urgent, because I continually used the European trip as the excuse for not having to make a choice. For Gary, the time for serious decision-making was at hand. As things turned out, an answer to my situation came more easily than I had dared hope.

I wasn't able to pinpoint the moment or incident in those weeks which prompted me to decide against going to Europe the following year. I presume, therefore, that it must have been a combination of things. The yearning for home, accentuated by the dreariness of camp life would have been the largest contributing factor. Moreover, after having missed home so much for so long, I probably couldn't bear the thought of leaving it again so soon. On the financial front, although I had sufficient funds to enable me to take a six-month trip abroad, it would have meant returning in an almost penniless state. Still further, while the job at the PMG was guaranteed and waiting for me in February and March, it would not have been there in September. In any case, while I didn't really want to go back to an office job, it was reassuring to have that as an available option. Finally, I was approaching my twenty-third birthday and it probably felt inappropriate to foist myself upon the financial generosity of my parents any longer. Many boys in the unit – some of them younger than me – were returning home to wives and children and I felt, as many my age must have felt, that it was time to begin building for the future rather than squander time and opportunities by travelling overseas.

Whether this reasoning was sound or not, it played its part in determining my resolve to forego arrangements already made for the *Fairstar* and the visit to relatives. Quite unexpectedly, therefore, I found myself telling Gary on R&C that I had made a decision to enrol in a course, probably teaching, when we returned home. This was a profession for which I had always had great respect and one for which I had the necessary educational prerequisites. I had passed matriculation, but just as importantly enjoyed a good rapport with children. My sorrow for and contact with the multitudes of severely disadvantaged children I saw constantly in Vungers no doubt also contributed to this decision. Primary teaching, therefore, seemed appropriate and without too many dramatics, almost overnight, I had given myself an entirely new direction. Gary was amazed by this turn of events and thoroughly enjoyed rubbing in the fact that I had given up Cabin A1 on the Saloon Deck of the *Fairstar* which my parents had already booked, in exchange for a couple of years in Teachers' College.

It felt as though an invisible weight had been lifted off me. Having finally made the decision, I wondered why the hell I hadn't arrived at that point earlier. Now, with a finite and worthwhile goal in mind, my rotten moodiness eased and I immediately began to approach things more purposefully and with greater zest. It wasn't until then that I realised what a subconscious concern my post-army disposition had been and what a debilitating affect this had had on my behaviour. Doubts ceased, problems that had depressed me now seemed solvable, and I could clearly visualise a useful, enjoyable, and purposeful life beyond 31 January 1969.

Unfortunately, this newfound zeal and positive enthusiasm had come too late to retrieve a situation between Wayne and myself. Some weeks before R&C, the two of us had almost come to blows over the most childish, pathetically simple little misunderstanding. Lying on our adjacent beds one Sunday afternoon, we decided to get a head start on the others by sweeping and cleaning our immediate area early in preparation for the Monday inspection. After packing away several things and sweeping between the beds, we both spied, almost at the same moment, a newspaper that had fallen behind a cupboard halfway between where we stood. I'm not sure which of us spoke first, but that became irrelevant in the madness that followed. After one of us had told the other to pick up the paper and been refused, we began to argue about it until, at one point, I heard myself yell something like, 'It's your bloody paper! You pick up the damned thing!'

Wayne replied with a similarly eloquent retort, at which time I remember hurling the broom in his direction. It landed at his feet with a loud clatter on the concrete floor. I don't doubt for a moment that if several others hadn't entered the hut just then, he would have chucked it back at me. I also know that if he had, I would have flown across the narrow divide between us and would have tried to throttle him for his efforts. Within a matter of two minutes, we had changed from being amiable friends to being mortal enemies. The damned newspaper, the cause of it all, lay behind that cupboard for the next fortnight until one day it mysteriously disappeared. The space between our two beds became a virtual no man's land across which we threw icy daggers at each other. For the balance of the next two months that I remained in-country, Wayne and I didn't exchange a single word, not even to say goodbye at the end. After leaving, and as I sat in the comfort of the aeroplane, I wished wholeheartedly that I could offer an apology for such a piece of blatant stupidity, and wished that the matter would have been resolved differently, but it was too late and that outcome became the sole regret with which I left.

On the third day of R&C, we decided to put our grand plan into effect. After almost eight months of being sealed inside 1ALSG we felt we should try, at least once, to see something of the war in which we were supposedly involved. My excursion to Nui Dat had been unusual, enlightening, even adventurous, but I wanted to see a little more. Gary felt the same, so we chose the period of R&C to do something about it. As Australian servicemen, we were fairly well restricted to either one of our two bases. It was the American army machinery that had extended its tentacles throughout South Vietnam, and it was only through its transportation system that we could go anywhere outside our small corner of the country. The plan, therefore, was to hitch around Vietnam as far afield as we could in a single day, using the Yanks' helicopter network for the purpose. The idea was by no means original or unique, for many Australians had moved around Vietnam in precisely that manner. The Yanks were generally willing to pick up hikers, provided that there was room aboard their choppers at the time. They offered no guarantees about safe journeys or safe returns, nor even a promise of a return to the place of origin. If one boarded a chopper and was deposited at a location, it became the hiker's responsibility to find another chopper, which could either carry him back to his starting point, or get one to take him to a different location from where a return might be possible. Depending upon luck and the unpredictability of chopper destinations, one could travel hundreds of miles in a day seeing much of the country, or be left stranded in an isolated spot with the possibility of an overnight wait for the next leg of the journey. It was a risky business and taking unauthorised flights like these in a war zone probably bordered on the insane. However, we decided to join a long and distinguished line of other mentally unbalanced thrillseekers before us and try our luck at the game as well, in the hope that good fortune and exciting experiences would be our companions.

Swanning was the army term used to describe the business of hiking around the country in this way, and those who had done so before us warned that most troop and materiel movements from the Vung Tau airbase were normally finalised by six o'clock in the morning, and we needed to be there well before that. So, like thieves, we stole out of the R&C centre at half past four. As it turned out, the doors were not locked but only bolted, which we easily by-passed by getting someone to bolt it quietly after we left. Curfew lasted until six, so we knew that if we were caught, we'd be facing a stiff penalty. Skulking through the back streets, we reached the airbase without being spotted by MPs, and we began knocking on the doors of different flight control units. The first couple couldn't help us, while the cigar-chewing Master Sergeant at the third said he wouldn't unless we had a specific destination in mind. In truth, we hadn't considered that angle at all. We simply wanted to go further north, closer to where we thought some adventure might be found. Finally, we got the nod from one of the units which had a Chinook heading for Bien Hoa at seven. We thanked them for the offer and the coffee and sat down to wait.

The ease with which we were able to make these unusual arrangements was an indication of the Americans' disregard for simple security in 1968. Two complete strangers without authorisation were allowed aboard one of their aircraft and very few questions had been asked. Naturally, we wore the uniform of an ally, were genuine, and intended no mischief, but only we knew that, they didn't. One might have thought that greater care might have been taken with a multi-million dollar craft carrying stores and personnel in a time of war. The Americans did have a spendthrift, carefree reputation. The countryside was littered with abandoned and expensive Yankee vehicles, which normally, we would have recovered and at least tried to repair. They often did not. The VC were certainly not averse to cannibalising abandoned machinery and God only knows how much assistance the enemy was rendered by the American ethos which dictated that something broken automatically meant that it was unwanted and easily replaceable. Certainly, the old adage that a child with few toys looked after them, while one with many did not, applied to the equipment-rich American military. In one extreme case, we once heard about a sergeant betting his jeep on the fall of a card, in the confident knowledge that if he lost the bet, a replacement vehicle would always be available.

The twin-rotored Chinook lowered its rear ramp at seven and we ran on board. Pallets of stores were loaded and were being ferried to Bien Hoa, but we only saw three crewmen. In the air, we were treated again to the serenity, the lushness, the greenness, and deceptive peacefulness of the countryside as it appeared from several thousand feet. The Chinook was surprisingly cavernous inside. Although we'd seen hundreds of them take off and land from the helipad inside 1ALSG, this was our first time inside one. There was little activity during the flight, except for one crewmember who repeatedly threw pink and then blue smoke canisters out the rear, after which he watched them intently as they trailed coloured smoke earthwards. We yelled the question why he was doing this, but the roar of the motor was such that neither of us understood the animated explanation he gave, if indeed he was answering the question at all. There was definitely an aesthetic beauty to the scene as the coloured smoke left its slowly diminishing imprint in the air below. We drew deeply of the fresh, cool air, and enjoyed the slight rush of adrenalin, which resulted from not knowing what might come in the next moment. After all, we had just left the safety of home, we were without rifles as those were not allowed on R&C and if anything went wrong now, we would be without assistance and would have to fend for ourselves. It was definitely a new and heightened sensation.

Bien Hoa, north east of Saigon housed a major American base, to which was attached one of their larger airfields. As we approached, the immensity of the installation became evident. Concrete runways stretched as far as the eye could see and dotted on it were scores of metal and sandbag barriers ten or more feet high, between which were parked dozens of helicopters at rest. Like flightless birds at prayer, their stationary rotors were raised and pointing heavenward. As we neared the ground, we saw feverish activity around some of the machines, but nowhere did we see more haste and agility than from our own smoke-canister-throwing counterpart. The moment our wheels touched the ground, he jumped out, ran to a hose lying on the tarmac, and began to refuel the Chinook. As he did this, other crewmen appeared, while even more suddenly materialised and the pallets were quickly unloaded by way of the rear ramp. During the three minutes that this would have taken, other choppers either landed or took off all around us. With our motor still running, the total effect was an incredible cacophony of shrieking pistons and screaming jets, comparable only to the noise at the starting grid of a Formula 1 Grand Prix race. With the refuelling and unloading completed, our hyperactive bowser-attendant hopped back on board and we were airborne again. Gary and I glanced at each other, but there was no need to communicate in any other way. We were both thinking the same thing. If the place we had just left had been Bien Hoa and we had spent all of four or five minutes there, where the hell were we going now? Being entirely in the hands of strangers who were doing us a favour by accommodating our presence, we could hardly question what was happening or demand to be taken back. We just sat there and waited to discover what would follow.

Some thirty minutes later, the question was answered when

we landed in a veritable dustbowl. As we had approached this as yet unknown landing spot, the downdraft of the rotors created such a canopy of red dust that our vision of what was outside was completely obscured. Immediately after touching down, engines were switched off and our hearts sank as we heard the southern American twang accentuate the first word of the dreaded phrase,

'Well, boys, that's as far as we go today, so off you all get.'

Not surprisingly, the acronyms AWOL and MIA momentarily sprang to mind. Visions of being lost in enemy territory were replaced by those of capture and heinous torture. I needn't have worried, however. As soon as the dust settled, it became clear that we had landed at another large stores dump, not too dissimilar to 1ALSG. This place was much smaller and didn't have the same permanence about it, though, with only sandbag barriers protecting the tents and few stores that were spread around. There were two gigantic telescopic cranes loading several trucks, one of which took on board the pallet from our chopper. We were relieved in the next few minutes to see at least three other Chinooks take off, indicating that there was a way out after all. We had flown quite a distance from Bien Hoa and were much further west – about forty miles from the Cambodian border we were later told.

We spent a couple of hours wandering around, strangers yet totally unchallenged by anyone on the base as to our business. The temporary appearance of the installation was explained by the fact that it had only been established about a month earlier and signalled the recently perceived, new danger of Viet Cong influence in this westernmost area of Vietnam. By early afternoon, we had again begun the cap in hand task of trying to locate another chopper for the next leg of the journey. There was no possibility of a direct link from there back to Vung Tau, so we gladly accepted a ride leaving there that afternoon in a southerly direction, which was a flight to Saigon leaving at four. That, we thought, was at least in the right general direction.

The Chinook we now boarded at four was empty except for its five crewmen and ourselves. After take-off, each adopted a most business-like attitude. Two of them tested the tension in the harness-like webbing attached to either wall, while another raised and lowered the rear ramp at least three times – as though to convince himself that it really worked. We wondered why so much attention was being paid to an empty bird. When the port-side gunner loaded his M16 machine gun that was fixed near the open doorway and fired a volley of shots into the air, we suspected that there was more ahead of us than just further pallets of stores. The chopper droned on for about twenty minutes and all the time the gunner kept a watchful vigil, never taking his eyes off the terrain below. The barrel of the M16 was trained earthwards as it swivelled from left to right in its adjustable cradle. He was in radio contact with the pilot, for we heard him yell into his mouthpiece on occasion and the chopper would veer slightly one way or the other each time in response.

We had just become accustomed to the shuddering, forward motion of the craft when it suddenly lurched to the left and the M16 belched fire. The gunner had raised himself on his toes and was screaming into the headset, although none of what he said was intelligible over the combined noise of the rifle and the engines. Curiosity made us grope for a port side window and I caught sight of spurts of dust being flung upwards as the bullets from the M16 strafed the ground. The target – comprised of a small group of running men I glimpsed for a brief moment – was almost below us, because the gunner was now standing on the tips of his toes with the trigger up near his neck. The contact lasted for about thirty seconds. To the others on board, it seemed of no great import as they casually returned to their previous tasks. But Gary and I definitely paled during that short time. A minute or so later, the chopper descended further and we felt it land. The ramp had been lowered during the descent and seconds after touchdown, jungle uniforms were running up it, spilling into the chopper in a swift, but orderly manner. We flattened ourselves against a wall in order to make room, as about thirty men from the patrol filled the craft. Without a single word they sat on the floor, the first group having gone up the front and the rest blocking up from behind. Less than a minute after landing to pick them up, we were airborne again.

Only after we took off did I regain sufficient composure from this unexpected and surprising development to have a good look at the men. They were filthy, looked gaunt, and seemed physically exhausted. Judging by the stubble on their chins, they must have spent at least four days in the bush. Many of them sat reclining against the sides of the chopper, using the webbing for support, while others sat back to back, down the middle aisle. Most had their eyes closed, as if asleep, their heads lolling with the motion of the craft. Still others sat with their legs drawn up in the Vietnamese squat, with their heads resting on their knees. It would not be stretching too long a bow to suggest that their closed eyes might have been in response to prayer. Undoubtedly, they all bore signs of physical fatigue. Their camouflage-patterned jungle greens were covered in dust, beneath which were several layers of dried mud, while caked soil encircled their eyes, mouths, and nostrils. Their breathing seemed laboured because the rise and fall of their chests was more pronounced than would normally be the case and it seemed that this was not just the result of their run into the chopper. These men were, in all probability, involved in a contact with the enemy at whom the gunner had been firing minutes earlier. Before that, who knows? They may well have spent a couple of days hiding in an ambush or pursuing an enemy patrol. Whatever their previous lot, downcast and bloodshot eyes told a more meaningful story of effort and travail than any words they might have chosen to tell their story.

Not more than two yards from me sat a sergeant whose hands trembled quite excessively as he held a leash. A pair of canine eyes, still alert, followed his every move. The German shepherd, whose leash the sergeant had held continuously through the boarding process and since, had put his head across his master's lap, and although he reacted to sharp movements nearby, the dog was also utterly spent. For a moment his eyes roved over me, but they closed quickly and the animal seemed to fall into a fitful sleep. Looking around at these working soldiers, I felt a little ashamed and uncomfortable at having intruded, uninvited, upon their predicament. A medic who was tending a wounded black soldier near the back of the chopper changed the bandage on the man's thigh, revealing a deep gash running from groin to just above the knee. From where I sat, I could see the blood flowing from the wound. Shortly after, we landed in Saigon and waited till everyone had evacuated the chopper.

While there, we felt a little humbled by what we had seen. It was the briefest snippet of one event among thousands that occurred in Vietnam every day, but that tiny encounter was sufficient to satisfy our former wish of seeing something of the war. If I had difficulties in managing and tolerating my easy stay in-country, then I could only recoil in horror at how difficult a twelve-month tour must have been for the grunts who risked life and limb for much of that time. No amount of financial assistance or the bestowing of military honours could adequately recompense a person for such endurance, determination, and strength of character.

I began to wonder about my own state of mind. Why was it that in spite of repeated and substantial reminders about my personal good fortunes and lucky circumstance, I was still a self-obsessed and inwardly whining individual who wanted nothing more out of each passing day than to leave that shit-hole of a place called Vietnam? This incident with the Yank patrol should have been enough to permanently set my mind at ease! But it didn't. Even Ron, having returned from seeing his family in the Alice after R&R, had apparently reconciled his concerns. He had become a smiling, friendly and conversant person who had found the answer, had changed overnight, and had resolved his troubles – yet I couldn't and hadn't. I had no answer to my own quandary except to think that I was either going mad or was simply too selfish and couldn't therefore adequately appreciate what others were enduring.

Air traffic between Saigon and Vung Tau was regular, so we had no trouble in finding a Huey heading that way. In the interim, we walked around the airport again, to be deafened every minute or so by a jet either landing or taking-off. This airport was, for several years in the late 60s, the busiest in the world. We saw a company of South Vietnamese regulars boarding a transport plane and heading off for what appeared to be a night parachute drop. In one corner of the airfield, we approached a number of zealously-guarded Phantom jets nestled safely between solid concrete barriers as a precaution against possible rocket attacks. Foolishly, I reached for my camera, to be told in no uncertain terms by an American MP that if I didn't put it away, it would be shoved up my arse in the most uncomfortable and painful manner. Needless to say, I didn't get a close-up photo of a Phantom jet. The sun was just setting when the Huey landed in Vungers and we walked back to the R&C centre, realising that our last decent meal had been eaten twenty-four hours earlier.

Chapter 33

The remaining two days of leave were, of necessity, an anticlimax and were spent lazing around and visiting old haunts in town. We had no great desire to return to 55 on the final day, for based on what we had heard by way of rumour before R&C, we were expecting bad news about our return to Australia. It had been no more than a hint, but even the vaguest hint that we might not return home before the end of the year was enough to make us worry. The orderly room sergeant had been the one to mention almost casually as we picked up leave passes for R&C that movement between Australia and Vietnam was becoming very tight towards Christmas. At the time, I replied with the usual sour look I seemed to wear constantly and tried to shrug it off, but during our talks at the rest centre, we began to dwell on what he'd said and wondered about the outcomes if he was right. There was one and only one absolutely unquestionable fact. As Nashos of the seventh intake, we were to be discharged on the last day of January, so we had to be home by then. Otherwise our time and how we spent it was completely at the army's discretion. Generally, any accrued leave or holidays owed was taken into account when a return date was calculated and many had gone home four or five weeks early in order to take such accumulated leave before discharge. On the other hand, there was no stipulated regulation concerning this and if the army wished, we could be paid in lieu of time owed. Both Gary and I had about six weeks leave coming to us, which was why we had punted for so long on a December return home. Suddenly, we weren't so sure any more!

The bombshell was dropped two minutes after we entered the orderly room on our return. Christmas traffic was, in fact, solid, and the two of us had been slated for a return on 7 January. As we trudged up the hill to the huts after hearing this devastating bit of news, the weight of the millstone of National Service had rarely felt heavier. There was, of course, no point in protestation or in remonstration. There never was! Again, the army had screwed us and had exercised its God-given right to do so. What this meant basically was that we would have to spend three extra weeks in-country. After what we had seen on the Chinook, I was a little more understanding about this new reality than I otherwise might have been. I could easily cop another three weeks in my relatively comfortable bed and cushy job. I reluctantly grabbed my important piece of paper and added a further 1 814 400 seconds to the last total on the page, this being the number of seconds in twenty-one days. The real question was how was I going to explain this to my parents who were already making Christmas and New Year's Eve plans?

15.11.68

> I'm afraid that the news is not good. As we discussed some months ago, the army has a stranglehold on us and can usually do whatever it likes. Unfortunately, it has done it

again. Because of a shortage of planes towards the end of December, I'm sorry to say that we will not be leaving here until 7 January. The urge to scream has now passed and there is only emptiness inside. The knowledge that Christmas has to be spent here is devastating and I'm sorry that it's ruined all our plans. This affects quite a few of us from the seventh intake; we're all in the same boat. One guy had even planned to marry on the first of January and now has to postpone even that. In short, we have to add another twenty-one days to the previous count, making it fifty-three days as from today. At least this date is now a definite one and not just conjecture. I'm really wondering and concerned how this news will affect you.

Let me know.

I wrote to my parents regularly every second day and it was only on the rarest of occasions that I omitted to do so. More often than not, the act of writing was an enjoyable diversion, which enabled me to unload feelings. Sometimes, though, it felt like a bothersome chore and I would much rather have gone to see a film, or would have preferred to sleep than to sit, sweat, and write. But letters from home were arriving daily and my mother would not miss a single day when she didn't spend a short time writing to me. I therefore felt obliged to keep up my end of the commitment on alternate days, knowing that those at home were also keen to hear both the bad and the good news from me. None of the letters I wrote was more difficult to compose and finally mail than the one containing the details about 7 January.

Although I had mentioned often enough that a return date was never certain until confirmed, I had given my parents sufficient, wishful hints and reasons to make them believe that I would be home by Christmas. For all sorts of very good reasons, I had become quite sure of that fact myself. Now that it turned out to be incorrect, I felt sorrier for having put my parents in the unenviable position of having to cancel homecoming celebrations than I felt about my own loss. In a vain and stupid attempt to minimise their feeling of loss and to make them think that I wasn't in the worst of situations, I invented the non-existent, seventh intake individual that I wrote was going to marry on 1 January. There was no such person, but in writing about him I had hoped that my parents would focus more on his, rather than on the Benko household's individual loss. The intent might have been considerate, perhaps even thoughtful, but the end result of the lie was neither rewarding nor simple as things developed some weeks afterwards.

Gary and I went back to our respective jobs after R&C to see out the remaining fifty-three hot days. I didn't want to see scratches and any crossing out on my beloved tally sheet, so I drew up a new sheet of paper sporting the increased total of 4 579 200 seconds that were still left. Having to repeat twenty-one of the lovingly entered totals from the original sheet was a particularly bitter pill. Buck had taken over again in the bar while I was away. Although nothing out of the ordinary had happened, his systems differed slightly from mine and it took several days to get everything back to its usual, accustomed place. During my absence, the refrigeration mechanics had installed a larger cooler behind the bar which could hold about half the required cans for a single day's trade. This made the task of loading the two hoppers with ice much easier. This meant that I now only needed half the quantity of ice each day, whether from our own sources at 55 or from the ice works in town. I preferred town, because the short drive there gave me a few minutes of daily freedom and independence, which I valued. Within days, the monotonous, repeating pattern of camp life was re-established. I now had five weeks – or thirty-five days – to go.

Strangely, my memories of those final weeks are sketchy. Even my letters from that period provide few clues about what was happening. I do remember the strengthening and obsessive mental preoccupation I had about leaving the place, which effectively blocked out conscious registration of events that might have been occurring only a hundred yards away. In those last weeks, my world shrank even more and became the restricted confines of the barracks, the boozer, and the company of intimate friends. The only intruders allowed in were the letters from home and the persistent image of the Qantas jet that would ultimately leave Saigon on 7 January. If Ron had, in fact, gone slightly troppo some months earlier, I began to do a fair imitation of that act myself.

I can't recollect ever going to the beach again, although I must have, and even the table tennis games that Gary and I played regularly seem to have been mysteriously forgotten. Except for the daily drive into town for ice, I don't think I ever went in there again on a Sunday afternoon, and even the names of films we watched – which I would faithfully chronicle for my parents – were omitted from letters. So are any further meaningful references to 1ALSG, the Paris peace talks, the war, or future plans. As far as I was mentally concerned, the war had become a side issue, and nothing was more relevant, pertinent, or noteworthy than my private thoughts and wishes. I do recall a beer shortage in early December when, as a result of a miscalculation by the main store, supplies had run low and each man was restricted to two cans per day. Perhaps as barman, this had made a sufficiently strong impression on me to write about. Otherwise, my mind and letters dealt exclusively with those acts and images which would either follow, or were in some way connected with my going home.

Our original plan had been for me to catch a flight in Sydney upon returning and the family would be waiting at Essendon when I arrived there. Christmas and New Year's Eve would have been celebrated at home and Hunters Lodge respectively. After this, we had thought of a short, driving holiday through the Blue Mountains, via Canberra to Sydney. Part of this plan still fitted in with my delayed return in January. My parents wrote that they would postpone their intended trip by a few days and, driving straight to Sydney, would meet me there on 7 January. We could then still complete the rest of the drive as planned, albeit at the end of their holiday instead of at the beginning. Feeling somewhat responsible for having spoilt the original idea, I replied telling them that the new itinerary sounded fine. I did so even though the prospect of spending five days on the road just after getting home was not really what I wanted to be doing. My greatest desire had always been simply to arrive home, without parties, without fanfare, and without ceremony. Considering the new plan, however, being alone with the family, even if on the road, did seem like a good way of winding down. I exacted a promise from my father, however, that as from 8 January, I would do all the driving in the family car, an experience I'd sorely missed and one for which the jeep and even the Mark V truck were only poor substitutes. I also asked for several changes of civilian clothing to be brought to Sydney. The very thought of a white collar, blue jeans and sandals, after ten months of green, was the stuff of dreams. I even asked my mother to pack a tie and to bring my suit in the hope that somewhere along the way we would stop at a fancy restaurant and I would need to wear it.

We struck a further bargain in that we wouldn't send each other any gifts for Christmas. I had bought some items in Hong Kong for the family and no doubt my parents had also purchased something for me, but given the trouble we'd experienced with packages in transit, we decided to be sure and exchange presents two weeks after Christmas when we were together. My mother asked if she should withdraw some money from my account and bring it to Sydney. I explained that even though we would arrive late at night and banks would be closed, there would be special arrangements made for us to obtain cash at the airport, drawn directly from our pay books. Nearly everyone arriving home availed themselves of this, because we could only get about ten dollars of Australian currency in Vietnam and the chances were excellent that most of this would be spent on a variety of refreshments on the plane.

Although we had been quite impressed by the letters the young children had sent from Marayong Primary School and had answered them gladly, my mother's heart had been deeply touched by the gesture. Indeed, she seriously suggested that by way of repaying the kindness, we ought to take time while in NSW and visit young Anthony Jeffs at home. For some reason that I didn't immediately understand, I baulked at this suggestion and quickly pointed out by way of excuse that since we only knew the address of the school and since it would be the Christmas break, we wouldn't be able to locate him anyway. This made perfect sense and the idea was thankfully dropped.

Some days later, my mother wrote that when they were coming to Sydney to meet me, they would be with another couple whom they had befriended through Greg's involvement in fencing. I suddenly realised why the prospect of visiting Anthony had felt so wrong and why I hadn't wanted to do it. Apart from the immediate family, I didn't want to see and was not emotionally prepared to talk to or be with anyone else. I had no explanation for the feeling, but knew it to be fact. Although the couple in question were good friends and I knew them well, the pleasant family drive from Sydney to Melbourne had been soured by the knowledge that outsiders would be there. Secretly, I hoped they would change their minds, even hoped that the electrical business they had in Melbourne would run into difficulties and keep them in town, and hoped that I wouldn't end up being the centre of attraction in a situation where I'd have to relate long stories about Vietnam. The earlier, disbelieved caution that returning home would be more difficult than we thought was beginning to ring true. With only a matter of days left until the long-awaited return, a host of both real and imagined difficulties seemed to present themselves, and I began to sweat anew and became nervous about the event that I had so longed for. I began to suspect that a permanent peace of mind about everything might just not be a possibility.

I worried about this family with whom I was now forced to share precious days upon returning. I was concerned about my recent decision to take up teaching and the subsequent difficulties I might have in enrolling in Teachers' College and, of course, worried about cancelling all the arrangements that had already been made for Europe. Allied with this was the concern that if accepted into a college, I would be financially dependent on my parents for a further two years. This worried me more than most other things for, at twenty-three, I felt that it was high time that I became independent. I also agonised over the constant and disturbing news that returning servicemen were being given a hard time at home for what was seen as some sort of failure in Vietnam. I didn't know what failure this could possibly mean, apart from our failure to have won the war. Was I really to blame for that?

On the social level, I had exchanged perhaps two or three letters with a girl from home in recent weeks. She worked in the office in Melbourne with my mother, and it had been her suggestion that we contact each other. Her letters were thoughtful and kind, the photo she had sent was that of an attractive girl who was about my age and, in all respects, the correspondence between us had been great. But not having dated for well over a year and meeting her for the first time were also presenting themselves as possible sources of future angst. In all, just at the time when I should have been the happiest and most contented, I had become an even more nervous and insecure square peg, knowing that I would soon have to try to fit in a round hole. I thought that a conspiracy existed to ensure that my life needed to become as complicated and as difficult as anyone could make it.

One of the compulsory novels I read with great interest at school years earlier had been Thomas Hardy's *Tess of the d'Urbervilles*. The main character, Tess, forever finds herself in insoluble difficulties. This happens in spite of her endeavours to live life according to the strict rules that her society had laid down for people of her station in life. Hardy eventually feels sorrowful towards and takes pity on the character he's created, exclaiming when Tess has lost her life that, 'Justice was done, and the President of the Immortals, in Aeschylean phrase, had ended his sport with Tess.'

I couldn't help but recall the quote at this time – since it was the very quote from the book that the end-of-year examination paper had asked us to discuss – when it seemed that, no matter what I did, the Gods were intent on getting their full measure of sport out of me. It just seemed that anyone who had the ability to exercise power over me was determined to continuously subjugate me to his will, to the very bitter end.

The misfortune of having to spend three extra weeks in-country had apparently been accepted, in a resigned fashion, by my parents. Their first letter, in reply to mine that broke the news, was furiously caustic towards the army and its frequent, single-minded machinations. I thought that all their venom and disappointment had been expended in the composition of that letter. I didn't take at all seriously my mother's threat that she was angry enough to contact a Mr Don Chipp, our local member, to complain about our treatment. I thought it was the type of throwaway comment that people often make when they feel that an injustice has been committed, but rarely carry out. In a flippant way, I even replied that she could convey my feelings to Don, but that it wouldn't do much good since from memory, our local member was a certain Mr Suggett. I remembered incorrectly, for while Suggett was the local State MLA who had attended my high school's speech night years earlier, and from where I recollected his name, my mother had been thinking of our Federal MHR who was, in fact, Don Chipp. In any case, I thought little more about the matter for the next few weeks, until an urgent summons arrived in the boozer one afternoon that the captain wanted to see me. The money from the previous day's takings had balanced that morning and since I had little contact with the boss, I wondered what he wanted.

'Sapper Benko. Are you getting married sometime within the next three weeks?'

The question was so totally unexpected, coming as it did without any preamble, that it took several seconds of thoughtful grimacing on my part before I blurted out the definitive reply that I had no such intentions. Before I had a chance to ask why he wanted to know the answer to such a weird question, he ordered me outside and told me to wait. As I entered the orderly room from his small office, I saw that all of us from the seventh intake who were slated for a 7 January return were there. Even then, the penny hadn't dropped. Gary was called in and he reappeared thirty seconds later, casting quizzical looks in our direction, telling us that the boss wanted to know if he was getting married. The penny sure as hell dropped then! My parents must have really gone ahead and carried out the threat of contacting the local member!

There were still a couple waiting to be called by the boss and I felt like charging in there to tell him to put a halt to this stupid inquisition. I hung back, however, knowing fully well that as surely as night follows day, my presence would be demanded again. I cursed inwardly, not sure whether I was angrier at my own lie in making up that January wedding story, or at my mother's overzealous reaction in actually raising the matter with a politician. Still, I hoped against hope, that there might even then be some other obscure reason for what was happening. Naturally there wasn't, and shortly I was called back into the inner sanctum of the captain's office.

'Sapper Benko. I'm following up on a Ministerial Inquiry regarding members of this unit returning to Australia on 7 January.'

I think I broke in at this point to tell him that I probably knew the purpose behind this unusual questioning. Haltingly and with difficulty, I explained my initial disappointment with the three-week delay of RTA and the resultant letter home. Feebly, I pointed out in my defence that this had been foolish and a thoughtless bit of creative writing and that never in my wildest dreams had I imagined that matters would go this far. Thankfully, he saw the undercurrent of stupidity rather than any deviousness on my part. He rebuked me for having written such misleading crap and explained that a Ministerial Inquiry was indeed a serious matter and that the findings would be telexed back to Canberra immediately. I thanked him for his understanding, apologised for the trouble I'd caused, and with my tail between my legs I scampered from the office.

With even greater difficulty and embarrassment, I spoke to Gary, Ron and the others afterwards, explaining the reasons for the afternoon's strange developments. Happily, none of them held a grudge. They laughed the matter off. Privately, I considered the whole business to be much more serious. The thought that a Minister of the Crown had to cable Vietnam on a matter caused by my dishonest and creative writing weighed on my conscience, and was one further thorn in the foot, which persisted as a source of aggravation for the balance of my time in-country. The Gods were indeed continuing their sport with me!

5.12.68–24.12.68

It's rather early but here is the local, 1ALSG Christmas card showing the Anzac chapel. In the next few days, we'll decorate 55 a bit and get it ready for the 25th. We're buying a tree, which will go in the canteen. Again, I can't say how much your letters have meant over these months.

I had a surprise call to front the captain today. He asked me if I was getting married! It dawned on me finally that you had actually written to a politician. There was a Ministerial Inquiry as a result. It was quite embarrassing and I feigned ignorance for just a short time because it's really no laughing matter to have a Minister delving into one's affairs. I never really thought you would do it! Anyway, you will know a lot more about the whole thing than I will, for I simply won't be told much more. The result of the investigation will no doubt be forwarded to you as the people who first raised the issue. I'm very curious to know what is said…

Lionel Rose's fight against the Mexican was big news here, too. It seems he was lucky to win. Received the copy of Mr Chipp's reply. I haven't heard anything more about it from this end… Those of us returning in three weeks begin taking some sort of pill today which is supposed to clean out the system of any possible malaria, while also being a substitute for the Paludrine tablets… Lots of Christmas cards are arriving, the barracks are actually quite colourful, and the lockers are covered in them.

Andy sets out for home on R&R today, but I don't envy him! In a short five days, he has to return! Devastating thought! This letter should reach you just before Christmas, so again my love and the best wishes…

My replacement arrived today, a fellow called Youngie. I couldn't be happier. He is quite happy with the prospect of working in the canteen and he's been helping me for a few days. Since two of us are doing the work, it's finishing early, so I might take a few hours tomorrow afternoon and lie out on the sandbags behind the penthouse to get a bit of sun. I never thought I'd ever say that and actually mean it!

We have two special RAAF flights heading this way bringing goodies for Christmas dinner, we're told. Steak, chops, chickens, ham, cakes and so on. Should be a great meal by the sounds of things. Wonder how Andy is going at home? I'm determined to see him again before we leave so I'll get a ride to Nui Dat after he returns...

I never thought that I would ever get to write this sentence, but here begins my final letter to you! It's Christmas Eve and since you're leaving Melbourne on the third, there would really be no point in writing again. My letters must amount to quite a sizeable bundle by now, yours certainly do! Thanks for the telegram. I'll mention only two more things before I put in the very last full stop. I'm very glad that this is the last letter because at times they have been awfully hard to compose, given that so little of true interest has happened. Nonetheless, you've received something on a regular basis and you've known that I've been well. Secondly, my thanks again for the tons of stuff you've mailed my way – letters, cuttings, packages, food etc. They have helped enormously in keeping me somewhat sane.

Finally, here is a copy of a silly letter that's been doing the rounds here for a while. A lot of the boys are sending it home for a joke just before returning to the normal world. The countdown now stands at fourteen. As always, my love and gratitude for everything, Frank.

A LETTER OF WARNING FROM VIETNAM:
TO WHOM IT MAY CONCERN.

This is to inform you that as from ...., a certain water-soaked and slightly crazy individual known as .... is leaving our little city of NUI DAT/VUNG TAU, securely nestled among the sand hills of a semi-tropical country in the Far East known as the Republic of Vietnam. Therefore, your attention is drawn to the following advice of which you should take careful note and observance.

A. Get the women off the streets, hide all the beer, and grog, put a chain around the fridge, and lock the cow in the barn.
B. This man has survived all that the exotic east has to offer: mud, rain, heat, dust, sand, loneliness, and monsoons, not to mention a liberal sprinkling of typhoons.
C. Be he husband, sweetheart, friend, son, or brother to you, he is still yours.
D. He may look a little strange and act a little peculiar, but that is to be expected after .... gruelling months in Vietnam.
E. Pay no attention to him when he smears Soya sauce on his potatoes or mixes raw snails with his rice in the hope of making them taste better.
F. For a while, he may complain about sleeping on a mattress and at first may refuse to go to bed without a mosquito net.
G. Unless you want to risk life and limb, DO NOT ask him, 'Does it rain in Vietnam?' or 'Are the women really flat-chested?'
H. DO NOT say anything if he constantly stares at such things as chairs, smooth roads, women (with round eyes) or mutters such Vietnamese sayings as 'Choi Oy, Xinh Loi, Uc Dai Loi number one, Never Happen, or 20 Pee, no more.'
I. Further, do not ask questions or argue with him when he asks for sulphur to be put in his bath water or if he continually

flushes the toilet and gazes at it in wonder and fascination. Go along with him, he'll get over it eventually.

J. Act as if nothing has happened if he pees in the gutter, as is the local custom. If he prefers to squat on the floor and insists that everybody eats squid with him with chopsticks, pay no heed, humour him. Above all, DO NOT ask him, 'How was the mail over there?', for he will get violent and go into convulsions. If he mumbles such things in his sleep as 'Black Market', or 'You Buy Me Saigon Tea', ignore him.

K. When he is crossing the street, take care of him for he has become impartial and completely indifferent to car horns, cycles, pedestrians, water buffalo, horses, carts and other such things as are found in and on the streets of VUNG TAU, SAIGON, BIEN HOA, etc. Above all, never let him into a blue and white taxi.

L. Remember that under his tanned, rough, water-soaked and weather beaten exterior beats a heart sweet and pure, though a little wet. He may not look or act it, but he is your very own. Just allow him a few months to get used to being back in civilised living again.

M. If any problems arise that you cannot handle, please call the Vietnamese police in BARIA, SAIGON, or VUNG TAU. They won't be able to help you, but they like to use the telephone as it makes them feel important. Do not send any more letters or parcels, for he will no longer be there and much of what you've sent has been lost in the post anyway.

Cheers and the best of luck.

Chapter 34

Christmas and New Year came and went. The cooling monsoon season was now no more than a distant memory and Santa really roasted in his thick red suit, delivering presents to children in that part of the world. Apart from hearty congratulations mutually shared, which we offered each other for having successfully reached the end of another year, and the heavy drinking on both occasions, it felt less like the close to a year than I could ever remember before. We continued working as usual and, except for an extra free afternoon on the 25th, there were scant other reminders that it was indeed Christmas. That at least was my perception of the situation at the time. There were, of course, the cards, the playing of carols on the AFVN, the decorations hung in the barracks and the boozer, as well as the feast on Christmas Day. All these are the hallmarks of happy Christmases everywhere, except I was in no mood or disposition to appreciate or acknowledge any of them. I regarded them as poor substitutes for what I was missing by not being where I really wanted to be, at home with the family. It was only their absence and not the inferior nature of any celebration that made my Christmas seem miserable. It was a time that I wished I could get so thoroughly drunk that I could wake up the following morning in the full realisation that I had missed an entire day. Unfortunately, such paralytic stupor didn't eventuate, for not only could I not drink sufficient to be dead to the world, but I was on duty in the boozer and had to keep serving others who were on their way to that happy state of oblivion. Many drunks were carried to their beds that Christmas Day.

The time, however, had arrived, that with only thirteen days left, we were below the critical fortnight and so 'short', that the remaining period could have been spent, we felt, standing on one leg. My imminent departure was strengthened by the arrival of Youngie, my replacement. He was, I think, from the eleventh intake. As I noted his uncertainty and apprehension and reflected on the fact that he wouldn't be getting out of there until Christmas of the following year, my thirteen days paled into a delightful insignificance. It was also refreshing to have someone in the boozer to talk to and work with during the middle of the day, when ordinarily the place would have been deserted. He was quite happy with the idea of becoming the barkeeper and in the short time we were together formed a fairly good friendship.

The matter of the Ministerial Inquiry continued to haunt me. That the whole affair had ever happened was sufficiently troublesome in itself, but what perturbed me most was the fact that in subsequent letters to my parents, I could not bring myself to write simply and unreservedly that it had occurred on the basis of a lie. I had always enjoyed a frank and honest relationship with them. It was therefore not so much a readiness to continue deceiving them, as an unwillingness to disappoint them by telling them they had acted on a false premise that probably prevented me from clearing up the matter. I reasoned, foolishly and all too conveniently for me, that with such a short time left, I could let it slide and explain or apologise in person later on. I even assumed that we would probably laugh about it into the bargain. It was an almighty and an unsuccessful attempt at self-deception. The thing tormented my guilty conscience.

I became even more self-centred and oblivious to my surroundings as we entered the New Year. A week earlier, true to an old army custom, the officers and non-commissioned ranks had waited on the tables for us for Christmas dinner, and had served a sumptuous meal. The cook had really worked miracles, but then for the first time he had the right raw materials upon which to wave his magic wand. Fresh and freshly-delivered food had arrived from Australia. I vaguely recall an array of sea food and steak that tasted like the real thing, proper place settings, decorations, ham, cakes, and cheeses that looked totally out of place in a mess that had always specialised in dehydrated pork rings and stringy turkey. A month or even a fortnight earlier, such a change in the accustomed norm would have left its indelible mark, but the occasion, being so close to RTA, has left little more than a sketchy image. My mind was so engrossed in that 7 January flight that the only memory I have of New Year's Eve is being woken up at four in the morning by the noise of returning revellers. In our grumpy and increasingly intolerable way, I recall Gary and I bitching the following day about their lack of common courtesy and consideration.

Just as the Christmas and New Year period remains misty in my mind, so the final forty-eight hours are impressed as clearly as crystal. This was stuff obviously worthy of being committed to memory. It's difficult to describe the glee with which we returned our rifles to the Q store. The rather gruff corporal who had issued them to us nine months earlier had long gone and the new man eyed the over-oiled barrel and dust cover of my weapon suspiciously. I assured him that my reason for having applied so much oil was simply to protect the metal surfaces from rusting in case it was weeks before being issued to someone else. He didn't know just how much truth there was in the first part of that statement. I shudder, however, to think of the condition it must have been in when the next unfortunate soul got it. For the first time since our second day in-country, we walked through the unit's area without its accustomed weight hanging off our shoulders. As we did, a group passed us and they were heading to the area rifle range. We just managed to hold back the jeers and snide remarks that we could so easily have thrown their way.

Rifle practice had suddenly become an issue of high priority again. Tet, a period of national celebration, was approaching again, heralded by the beginning of the lunar New Year in mid-January. The resultant nationwide migration of a very large part of the population had occasioned a lot of fighting the year before. Some experts claimed at the time that the Tet offensive of 1968 was actually the beginning of the end. Similar trouble was expected in 1969. Consequently, the lunacy of rifle practice for cooks, clerks, and bottle washers, who would never fire a shot in anger, was considered necessary. We were, however, forty-eight hours away from boarding the freedom bird at Tan Son Nhut and concerns about Tet were far from our minds. We were enjoying a two-day winding down period during which we didn't have to do any work. Rifle ranges, canteens, trucks, paperwork, stores, forklifts, guard duty, kitchens, outboard motors, refrigeration units, and boredom were, for us, almost at an end.

I cleaned out my locker for the last time, squeezed all of

my army belongings into two sausage bags, and left out only those things which I would need at the last moment. I hung the clean set of freshly pressed polyesters in the empty locker. Lovingly, I admired the freshly-ironed creases in my shirt and trousers and thought about the cleanliness of the place in which I would wear it. Below it sat the wondrous shine on the toes of the shoes to accompany it. Together, we waited for the morning of the next day.

All had been done, nothing seemed left undone. This provided a true glow of inner warmth, of satisfaction, and of achievement. The task, no matter how hated or despised, how futile or boring, how frustrating or difficult, or how menial or meaningful – all according to one's individual outlook – had now been completed.

Chapter 35

I must have slept, but it seemed that I had been awake all night. By the time we had showered and were returning to the huts to get dressed, the first discernable light had appeared over the mountaintops on the far side of Vung Tau. The scene was picturesque and worthy of a painting, but it was gratifying to me to think that the next sunrise I'd see would be in Australia. We headed to the mess for a last meal. Even the eggs, which I forced myself to eat, tasted less of ether that morning than on other days. After several cups of coffee we went back to the huts, put on our ties, and packed away the final items that were ours to take. It was close to six and the others were stirring. For just a moment, I experienced the same feeling of guilt I had felt those many months before at Puckapunyal when I had returned to camp after my twenty-first birthday party. Then, I had been given the chance to leave camp for a party my mates hadn't shared. Now, it seemed that I was getting preferential treatment again by being allowed to leave, while others had to stay behind. The moment was only transitory and I grabbed my bags.

Farewells had been exchanged the night before and not

being very good at them anyway, I wanted to be gone quickly. Just as I was exiting through the door, Wayne swung himself out from under his mosquito net and disappeared towards the showers. He didn't even look in my direction and that purposeful act hurt more than any other insult he might have hurled my way. Without looking back, we walked down to the orderly room for the drive to the airbase.

The local populace was already on the move as we drove through town. Lambrettas chugged, straw hats bobbed up and down, the buffalo bellowed, and children squatted in front of shacks as another day was starting. We had an hour to wait before a Caribou transferred us to Saigon. We got there by nine and had another four hours to wait. We were prepared for this because we knew that RTA flights usually left in the early afternoon, timed to reach Sydney late in the evening. More and more Australian slouch hats appeared as time passed via other connecting flights and the transports from Nui Dat and from Saigon itself. By midday, the total complement of about 200 had assembled and the arrival of the Qantas 707 was accompanied by a collective sigh of relief and gratitude. The three of us were not the only grinning Cheshire cats.

The call to board came and they were really the sweetest words. After our paperwork was checked by MPs, we strode purposefully towards the steps leading into the big bird's welcoming interior. Gary, Ron, and I were among the first few to board and settled into adjacent seats near the front. Ponderously slowly, the plane filled and after an interminable wait, the doors were locked and it began to move. My heart was pumping audibly as the wheels lifted from the soil of Vietnam. It was then that the volume of conversation rose. The realisation dawned that we had finally and ultimately left.

There were mini-celebrations throughout the craft as we joyfully spent the few Australian dollars we had been given prior to departure. The first hours were spent in animated and excited talk about the families we would meet shortly. Then, as drowsiness settled in and was accentuated by the steady drone of the engines, my mind went back to 55, the place and the people who had been such a huge part and strong influence on my life in those past nine months.

Andy, bless his heart, had come down from Nui Dat on Saturday for the traditional send-off accorded to those returning on the following Tuesday. His R&R back home had been memorable and tinged with some sadness at having to leave again. It was wonderful to see him again that day. I had gone to about twenty-five of these affairs for others and had wished each time that I was the one being feted. Now that my wish had been realised, I was restless and self-conscious. The usual drinking of vast amounts was always followed by the official goodbye from one of the warrant officers or the lieutenant. On this occasion, the lieutenant was there and he thanked us individually for our various contributions before wishing us bon voyage. We responded in turn and emptied the contents of a rather copious tankard, which was kept in the boozer for that express purpose. Gary came into the canteen for our farewell and it was perhaps only the second time that he had entered the place. Naturally, he refused to drink the tankard of beer, but happily downed a like amount of orange juice.

I was the third to be called upon to speak and had the misfortune to be preceded by another who spoke along almost identical lines to those I had planned to use. In essence, he voiced the view that he had met and made outstanding friends in that place and that whenever he would remember Vietnam in the future, it would be those comradeships and ties he'd recall. He went on to say further, however, that he had enjoyed the bulk of his time in-country and would think back with pleasure on much of what had occurred.

When I stood up to speak, I completely agreed with and reiterated the first part of what he had said, but was sufficiently affronted by the rest to disagree with him. In my semi-drunken state, while I blurted out some of the niceties that were expected at such times, I finished with the truthful but ungracious statement that I hadn't enjoyed my nine months at all and had spent much of it wishing to be anywhere but in Vietnam. I voiced the rather rude and – under the circumstances – thoughtless view that if anyone truly claimed to have enjoyed their time in-country, then they must have had an awful life and a hell of a bad time at home. I thanked everyone for their friendship, wished them Godspeed away from the place, emptied the tankard, and lurched outside where Andy found me some time later, sobbing as I sat on the top of a sand hill next to the boozer. Whether it was joy, sorrow, drunkenness or the onset of mental instability that made me cry, I don't know.

By now it was quiet, except for the drone of the jet engines. Talking had ceased completely some thirty minutes earlier as everyone became distracted by private thoughts. The captain's voice crackled over the speaker and the plane banked to the left.

We automatically responded by looking out the windows in the direction he had mentioned. It was a cloudless, starlit night and the visibility was crystal clear.

'There! Over a bit further! The Sydney Harbour Bridge! All lit up! What a sight!'

I finally see it!

Part E

Discharge

Chapter 36

It was dark and the streetlights were on by the time I drove the family's Holden south down Swanston Street and through the city. We hadn't sighted the other car since leaving Albury, and not for the first time began wondering whether they were still in one piece. The narrow, winding Hume Highway had such a horrid reputation that anything was possible. My eyes were riveted as much on the other things I had sorely missed as they were on the traffic, ahead or behind. I drove past Flinders Street Railway Station, across the bridge, and onto magnificent St Kilda Road. On the left, the Shrine of Remembrance was lit up, while a short way ahead was the dangerous and busy intersection called St Kilda Junction. Casting a glance over my right shoulder, I caught a glimpse behind the football ground of Albert Park Barracks and CARO. Somewhere in that first building over there was a green piece of paper that heralded my return, soon to be followed by another which would confirm my discharge. Narrow High Street led into wider Brighton Road and we passed my old Primary School on our left, next door to the St Kilda Town Hall. Not far from there on the right was the house in which we had first lived after coming to Australia. We entered Nepean Highway, motoring past Reg Hunt, who claimed to have the largest car dealership in the Southern Hemisphere. We went under the bridge at Gardenvale and soon saw the statue of Thomas Bent, as his likeness surveyed the area he had been the first to settle. At Bentleigh High School, I had been in Bent House and we always seemed to beat Dendy, Fawkner, and Batman, especially in athletics. We halted at the traffic lights at South Road in Moorabbin and there was my old schoolmate's Marcello's barber shop where he worked for his father. A left turn into South Road took us in the direction of East Bentleigh. In preparation for the school cross-country season, Bruce Caterson and I used to run along there every morning, in all weathers. We would start from our respective homes exactly at six, meet halfway, run to the other's house, and return again, meeting in the vicinity of Chesterville Road as we pounded out the two and a half-mile run. My hands trembled slightly on the wheel as we came over the rise and saw the South Side Six Hotel. Here, a left turn at Bignell Road meant that there was only one more right, which would bring us into my street, Rae Street. As I made that right and straightened up, my parents' friends in the other car were just entering our driveway and had entered Rae Street from the opposite direction. They were safe, after all, and I was finally home.

 The reunion in Sydney had been very emotional. I lost sight of Gary and Ron in the mad rush to locate luggage after we got off the plane. We suspected this would happen and had made plans to meet each other later. The customs officers were sympathetic to our needs and hurried the obligatory search of baggage. After that, we collected money from the paymaster who had set up a banking service for our benefit. Then the security gates were opened and we were free. It was a totally joyous sensation to embrace and kiss the family who, sixteen hours earlier, had seemed so far out of reach. Many around were crying quite unashamedly as they welcomed back boys they thought they might never see again. There was a mixture of relief, joy, and delight as new fathers held babies they had never seen and as brothers, sons, and husbands returned to the fold from which they had been taken. Indeed, I had rarely felt as full of the blessings of life as I did that evening. Although my father controlled his feelings, my mother shed a tear or two in happiness. We left quickly and drove to a motel in Kings Cross, where we stayed up until the small hours unburdening ourselves of everything that we wanted to share or talk about at such a time. By about four, it was a contented exhaustion that lulled us all to sleep.

Despite the late night and a scant two hours of sleep, I woke suddenly at six to find that the closeness of the motel room was almost suffocating. Having slept near an open door and window for nine months, the sealed air in the room was stifling and close. I dressed quickly and was about to go outside when my mother stirred to ask where I was going. I told her to go back to sleep and that I was simply going for a walk. Outside, I was finally able to breathe properly. There were only a few people walking around Kings Cross at that hour of the morning. The emptiness of the streets, combined with the freedom of being able to walk in any direction, the ability to stop and gaze in peace at whatever caught my eye, the opportunity to sit and have a cup of coffee if I wished, and the reassuring sight of seeing people I didn't have to suspect or fear, were joys enough in themselves.

We left Sydney that afternoon for the three-day planned drive to Melbourne. The friends who had accompanied my parents were travelling in their car and I was glad to find that they didn't come to the airport the previous night. Later on, though, there did come the inevitable debriefing when everyone wanted to hear everything, all at the same time. Their presence was based on friendship and they had a genuine interest in my welfare, but I still found their company unnecessary, overbearing, and intrusive. I began to experience some unease and a strange lack of confidence whenever they or strangers were around. This was to haunt many others and me in the immediate future. It manifested itself in a strong desire to be alone, to be wary of things that were different and external to the accustomed norm, and to be generally distrustful of strangers. It was also accompanied, in my case at least, by an inexplicable impatience about others' wishes when these were at variance with my own. While some of these difficulties were still ahead of me and, as yet unexpected, I resented the company of my parents' friends on the drive south from Sydney and wished they hadn't come. We drove to Canberra and then through the beautiful Blue Mountains to the Victorian border. The drive down the Hume from Albury was accomplished in particularly hasty fashion. The car somehow seemed to go better and faster the closer I drove it to Melbourne.

Thankfully, many things hadn't changed and the house was just as I remembered it. The most reassuring and positive aspect of the return was to find that there were constants upon which I could rely, even if it was simply the unchanged nature of the home and the family situation. It was essential for my peace of mind to find such continuity. By comparison, it was devastating for many to discover that during their absence, wholesale changes had been effected in families or work situations. That meant that not only were they disadvantaged by being forcibly taken from comfortable homes in the first place, but that those homes were further disrupted in their absence and they had therefore lost those precious memories as well. Those families that tried to arrange new rooms or furnishings, new cars or wardrobes or new jobs for their returning sons had the best possible intentions at heart, but were probably committing an error of judgement if they thought that those changes would help the readjustment, or would be appreciated.

I was thoroughly spoilt in the first few days as the best of home-cooked food, love, and attention, were showered on me. A steady stream of visitors came to the house, asking the same questions and wanting to know pretty much the same things. I did my best to keep up with this form of well-intended but unwelcome inquisition, thinking all the time that it was, after all, a sign of people's friendship and interest and so had to be accommodated. At the same time, I was hoping madly that it would soon cease and that the situation would return to normal. Return it did, for the usual Christmas vacation ended around 17th January for most people and everyone went back to work. The novelty of a soldier back from Vietnam had worn off and I was finally left in peace and was able to collect my thoughts and sort out the immediate future.

Within a fortnight, I was to be discharged and having about four weeks of leave owing, I only needed to report on the last day of January for the official ceremony of parting. I discussed with my parents the decision to commence a profession in teaching so that bookings for the European trip were finally cancelled. To seal that fate, I went in to see the appropriate officers of the Education Department to find out how one went about becoming a teacher. Studentships for 1969 had been finalised months earlier, but in view of my very recent overseas duty, the regulations were waived and

I was offered a place in a Teachers' College that same day. It was a very heartening feeling to walk out of the office in the knowledge that a satisfying and worthwhile future was ahead of me. I was also as pleased as punch to know that my service had been valued to the extent that it had enabled such a special consideration to be made on my behalf. Finally, I visited some old mates at the PMG and resigned. Having organised the immediate future, I still had another ten free days before discharge and a further day or so after that before I was to commence a two-year course of teacher training at Frankston Teachers' College.

On 31 January 1969, I put on my army garb for the last time. In spite of my recently acquired distaste for the colour green, there was a feeling tinged with irony and even the smallest regret that it was for the last time. I enjoyed a triumphant drive that morning to Watsonia Barracks for what I thought would be a swift, painless finale. But never let it be said of the army that it deliberately lightens a soldier's load. Upon arriving and joining scores of other seventh intake Nashos there for the same reason, we were told to parade and were informed that the official discharge time would be between the hours of three and five that afternoon. The Gods were still having fun and playing their sports! In spite of a loud, collective groan, we were further told that since we had seven hours to go, we would have to weed the garden beds behind the mess. We broke ranks and headed for the canteen. Whether the sergeant who gave the order was serious or not, we never found out because we disobeyed the last lawful command that we had been given to us on a parade ground. There was one undeniable certainty. Not a single weed was pulled by any of us that day.

At four, I entered a major's office. As army regulations

required, he asked if I intended re-enlisting. A definite 'No, Sir' prompted him to sign the prepared papers on his desk. He handed them to me and I also signed them. I saluted and left the room.

Five minutes later, I drove to the control gate at the front entrance to the barracks. I noticed a young Engineer peering up the driveway in my direction. Since there was no other traffic behind me and remembering my own boredom on the security gate at 55, I decided to stop for a chat. Like Youngie, he was also from the eleventh intake and had been posted to Southern Command as a security guard. He eyed my discharge papers longingly before returning them. Seldom have I felt such a bond with and – at the same time – such a degree of pity towards a stranger as I did for him in that brief moment. Then I made the left turn into Greensborough Road away from Watsonia Barracks, out of the army, and I caught a glimpse in the rear view mirror as he lowered the boom. In spite of my momentary sympathy for this Nasho who had just closed the gate behind me, a self-satisfied grin spread across my face as I threw the discharge papers and slouch hat onto the back seat.

The duty was done and my seven hundred and thirty days were up!

Part F

With hindsight ...

Chapter 37

As a rule, I have no problems about telling people and discussing with them, should the subject arise and be raised by them, that I was a Nasho who was in Vietnam. Serving in uniform was a source of pride and of personal satisfaction at the time, and although I'm reticent to claim today that I was wrong, when at the time I believed my actions to be right, it is something I'm now compelled to do. I had done what I considered was the right thing to do in the late sixties, but that's no longer the case. I don't ever flaunt the fact that I served and when I've discussed the matter on any social occasions, whether now or in the past, I've found that invariably, I'm the one to steer the conversation away from the topic to something else. While earlier I always wondered why that might have been the case, I soon discovered the reason.

In the forty years that have passed since then, I've attended only six Anzac Day marches, have been a member of the RSL for only two years, and it even took me thirty years before I applied for the medals that I've only ever worn on those six occasions on 25 April when I've joined the thousands of others who march to the Shrine of Remembrance. Even wonderful mates I had like Gary, Andy, Ron and Barry, are absent from my life, almost discarded and neglected as remnants of a past with which I no longer wish to be a part.

When I've reflected on the bigger picture of past history and considered the awful reality of how disastrously, wantonly, and inhumanely mankind has acted and treated itself, seemingly forever, even though I find my role in that folly to have been infinitesimal, I've come to accept that it was a contributing and faulty role, which at an older, wiser age, I would never have accepted. In short and on balance, I think I was wrong to be a soldier serving in the Vietnam War and I still carry the baggage which that entails.

What I know now, and didn't when I was twenty or twenty-one, is that throughout recorded history, one of man's more accomplished and unfortunate feats has always been his ready willingness to argue, disagree, and wage war. Libraries are filled with stacks containing numerous volumes that deal exclusively with savage battles, military takeovers, partitions, revolutions, political assassinations, and territorial squabbles. Most remarkably, those wars that have the capitalised adjective 'Holy' as a prefix even seem to proclaim that the 'Word' somehow endows them with a more just cause and a higher source of righteous morality than the other, less Holy conflicts. Countless millions have died through the ages in the name of God, King, Queen, ideology, and country.

We're told by ancient historians that Pheidippides ran a long way with his important message of victory and having delivered it, lay down, and died. While this act of selfless devotion is glamorised by the twenty-six mile marathon that concludes each Olympic Games, at what cost in human lives and misery was that particular victory achieved? How many Roman citizens perished during that Empire's long and mad quest for territory? How many were sacrificed to serve the boy King, Alexander? We can read accounts of the murderous times of Genghis Khan with some fascination, or about the marauding encounters of Attila the Hun, the apparently insatiable conquests of Chinese warlords, about the tribal conflicts that have always beset Africa and New Guinea and the mortally destructive forces unleashed by the morally self-righteous Crusades.

In more recent times, history recounts the Thirty Years War, the Hundred Years War, the brutal Spanish domination of the Americas; and the spread of the British Empire around the globe, which used methods no less destructive or suppressive in nature than any other occupational force before it or since. To add to this cumulative, planetary carnage, we've had the French Revolution; the American War of Independence; and that country's internal struggle between the North and South; as well as the Russian, Japanese, and Chinese squabbles in the Far East. One can only guess at the number of victims already sacrificed at these altars of cultural, religious, racial, and territorial superiority.

Lessons had not been learned. The Boxer Rebellion and the Boer War made the historical casualty list even higher as did that war to end all wars, World War I. It hardly ended anything, of course, but was simply the forerunner to an even greater global sacrifice. At about that time, the Russians executed a Tsar and the human cost of that act, with its consequent aftermath on the peasantry of that benighted country can be hardly imagined. Soon after, warfare and disagreement became refined into the global art form which we have come to dread so fearfully in the present.

The six year duration of World War II added a further

count of dead, maimed, and broken bodies estimated to be anywhere between fifty and seventy million people.

Finally, during the past sixty years, we've seen the continuing ugliness of death in Korea and Vietnam, ethnic and religious intolerance in Ireland, Afghanistan, and Eastern Europe, and the hatred that persists between Iraq and Iran. There's an endless source of seemingly justifiable reasons why one nation's army can attack and claim that which happens to be on the other side of an arbitrary line drawn on a map.

Interspersed within this diorama of human treachery, we have been able to watch graphic, slow motion replays, and have had a bird's-eye view of the sinking of the battleships *Sheffield* and *General Belgrano* in the South Atlantic, and the pinpoint accuracy of a stealth bomber as it completed its task over Baghdad.

Combined with the brutality of dictatorships like those of Idi Amin of Uganda, Pol Pot of Cambodia, Hitler's Germany and Stalin's Russia, we live in a world and inhabit a planet whose occupants seem rarely, if ever, to be able to treat one another with mutual understanding or respect. Has history ever recorded the passage of an entire century in which there was a worldwide moratorium on war? It's doubtful!

Early man fought his neighbour for the scarce resources of the environment in order to survive. Unfortunately, that act, occasioned by necessity, has become a cultural and religious narcissism – and worse, a nationalistic conceit in later man. Sadly, these characteristics now rule the way in which we manage relationships with our neighbours.

Are we as a race so unwise, savage, and bereft of an alternative solution to a problem that the only way we can solve it is to destroy that which might stand in the way? It certainly seems to be the case!

All sorts of arguments can be summoned and found to justify the actions taken to end the ugliness of Hitler's National Socialism, or to eradicate the poisoned ideology of a Pol Pot or an Idi Amin – but to similarly justify our pursuit in Vietnam?

I cannot find any new, nor can I accept the given justifications for it and hence my persisting and bothersome baggage, baggage that has been a part of my life and that of many others for the past four decades – an inwards unease that does not hurt, but is painful nonetheless.

Perhaps the justification for the Vietnam/American War ought to be viewed, more rightly, from the other side! In the minds of the Vietnamese, in the final analysis, the more justifiable thinking might well be that the persistence and bamboo of the filthy, yet committed little mole in the underground lair who knew unreservedly that he was right, proved to be more enduring than the B52s and napalm of the self-righteous but hesitant giant in the sky, who only ever thought he might have been right some of the time, but really wasn't certain of even that most of the time!

Chapter 38

The two years I spent in the army had a profound influence on my life. It taught me about duty, perseverance, self-control, and an appreciation of all that which one should never take for granted: health and life, both of which are very transitory and never guaranteed. I look back on what I did with a feeling of some pride and achievement. Whether others view me as a defeated and bloodthirsty killer who came back from an immoral war is, to me, now partly immaterial. I know what I did and why I chose to do it. For the future, however, I will do my best to try to dissuade my son, daughter and any grandchildren, from following in my footsteps as far as military service is concerned. There just has to be a more humane, acceptable, logical, sensible and human way of solving political and territorial squabbles than that which was used in Vietnam and is, unfortunately, still being used elsewhere.

As I listened to the radio on the afternoon of 24 January 1973, the news service made a sudden, unexpected cross to the USA as the President had just announced the final, unconditional withdrawal of all troops from Vietnam. He called it a 'Peace with Honour'. As soon as his speech was over, the radio station played John Lennon's song 'Imagine'. The words and tune – with their mournful yet optimistic appeal for love, tolerance, and understanding – were almost intoxicating under the circumstances. I often think and believe that the words of Lennon's 'Imagine' give us a hint and lesson about that better way!

My strong, current opposition to our involvement in Vietnam has not always been the case. During my second year at Frankston Teachers' College, a brief year or so after my discharge, at a time when student opposition to the war was at its height, members of the College Labor Club organised a forum, which was to be a discussion and debate on the question 'Should we be in Vietnam?' As the only ex-Nasho student in the college at the time, I was not pressured, but felt naturally obliged to participate on the affirmative side, the side of the argument in which I still firmly believed.

When it was my turn to speak, I regaled the audience with a dissertation on the need to halt the spread of communism and the fully-warranted responsibility which our government had assumed to ensure Australia's security. My presentation included theoretical assumptions of an imminent victory, about which I didn't feel totally confident but mentioned anyway. I also added that in spite of the negative issues raised by the opposing speakers – that at times during the conduct of the war innocent civilians and children had been killed – I maintained that our side was still doing a magnificent job in building schools and hospitals, roads and airports, while at the same time trying to restore the power and influence of the government in order to further the progress and development of South Vietnam, which the North was constantly determined to undermine. I also spoke about the rights of a people to defend their preferred way of life and our responsibility to support that simple wish of an ally.

As a personal attack upon the protestors who had taken part in anti-Vietnam rallies, those who had marched behind red slogans and North Vietnamese flags thereby supporting the enemy, and whom we Nashos despised with a passion at the time, I also read out a diatribe which went along the following lines:

> All wars have their opponents. There are horrific accidents and unfortunate deaths suffered by civilians as a result of actions in all conflicts. A look at the history of both world wars would show plentiful evidence of extreme, unwarranted violence, terror, death, suffering and a debasement of the human spirit on both sides. It is unfortunately in the nature of war that man's worst characteristics are portrayed and that his most immoral acts take centre stage. Yet, in the end, almost as a sign of relief that it's over, the long-awaited final victory seems to lessen, if not justify the errors made. It is in fact the victory which wipes the slate cleaner and somehow, with time, cleanses the spirit. Our side has won every war in living memory and we laud, praise, and build monuments to honour the memory of those who achieved those victories. We walk with reverence and awe in those places which exist to prolong our memories of their labours, and we teach our children to think of them with affection and respect. Victory engenders acceptance. So why are you smearing us with red paint upon our return home? Are we all murderers? Would you be doing the same if the war had ended in 1968 or 1969 as a victory for our side? No, you would not! A pox on you for what you're doing to

us! While you sit in the cafes of Carlton and Darlinghurst, stroking your make-believe Fidel Castro beards, drinking cappuccino, Pimms or Bacardi and Coke, enjoying your late teenage years and composing love songs to Uncle Ho, friends of mine and your countrymen are being killed in your name by the followers of that very man you worship so! You punish and blame us for serving and paradoxically call yours the moral high ground? A real pox on you for that disingenuousness and for the kick in the guts we're getting! We don't deserve it!

We did not invent, create, or choose the situation, or the conflict. That was the work of politicians on both sides. We didn't formulate the policies under which the war is being conducted and which ultimately might even ensure that for us, victory is unattainable. That too is the work of politicians. We're fulfilling our responsibilities to our country and do our duty as asked. Can the same be said of you?

You choose to fight by pointing the finger of guilt at those who are least able to defend themselves and those, who in truth are doing the right and honourable thing by both their conscience and their country. You should, if you have a conscience, take out your anger on those who are responsible and not on those who are innocent. You have always claimed that you've occupied the high moral ground! Why? Because you maintain that your political views are superior to that of others? If so, then one can only wonder where your high-minded political views have been hiding for the past few years.

Where were your concerns and your righteous indignation for the oppressed of the world in 1956 when Hungary was swallowed up by Russian communism, or even two years ago when the same Russian bear trampled on the rights of those in Czechoslovakia? Were those not worthy of your attention and protest? Yet your silence and absence were deafening! You were nowhere to be seen! You were bloody invisible and inaudible! So don't for a moment pretend that you represent some sort of high moral standard and code when you oppose America's and our involvement in Vietnam. You are as much a pliable puppet of those you wish to follow as I might be of those I have chosen. There was and is as much justifiable right and morality, along with human omission and fault in the stance I took, as there was and is in that taken by you. We'll live with our consciences, you live with yours! But it's time you stopped blaming us and left us bloody well alone!

Had I been able to gaze into a crystal ball and seen the unfolding of events during the next several decades, I would have felt and would have been much more confident about what I had just said to the audience. Russia's actions in Afghanistan in the late 70s and in Chechnya during the 90s had remarkable parallels with those of the USA in Vietnam, and on both occasions, students' protests and opposition to Russia's involvement in those two countries were virtually non-existent.

I also planned to include, but thankfully omitted from my speech the obtuse argument that in the year of 1969, close to one thousand innocent people had died in motor and road accidents in Victoria alone, with the national figure being close to three thousand, yet I had witnessed no mass demonstration or protest against that significant waste of life. Why then, I would have asked, was there such a rabid response to the three or four hundred lives that had been lost in Vietnam over a period of the previous five years?

Needless to say, the outburst didn't endear me with the other students, some of whom would only have been nine or ten years old in 1956, or with the predominantly older, left-wing teaching staff who happened to be listening, but who would have been politically aware and active during the years I mentioned. Although it came from the heart and I meant most of every angry word, the speech contained elements that I would clearly disown now.

Only a very few returning soldiers were spat upon or had red paint splashed on them and I deliberately omitted the salient fact that we each had the choice of opting out of National Service, no matter how distressing and uncomfortable the results of that might have been. I didn't at the time admit to the nascent discovery of the suspicion regarding the validity of the Government's claims about our role and clearly, infinitely more destruction than construction was occurring in South Vietnam. All of this I knew, but chose to ignore. Time, better knowledge, and hindsight are convenient bulwarks against the embarrassments and omissions caused by youthful ignorance.

And it was the very fact that I could have, potentially, refused to serve, that began to bother me in the years soon after. Again, the lessons of history prompted me to re-think events and consider them in this new light.

When Alexander ruled the known world at the age of twenty, when Augustus was Emperor of Rome, when Hannibal crossed the Alps, when Hitler or Napoleon strove to achieve their notions of greatness, or when General Westmoreland was trying to win that increasingly unpopular war in what was previously called Indo-China, they all had one common need: they required a readily available source of manpower to achieve their military goals. We can safely assume that

Hannibal was not alone with his famous elephants while crossing the Alps, nor was Hitler aboard a German U-boat as it sank Allied shipping in the Atlantic or at the controls of a Tiger tank in the Ardennes of Belgium towards the end of the World War II in 1945. Legends do tell of Alexander's preference for leading his troops into battle while astride his favourite horse Beucephalus, but it's unlikely that Augustus led any of his centurions in person, and we know that General Westmoreland spent little time, if any, shooting at the enemy from a forward fire base in South Vietnam. Leaders and politicians generally make decisions, formulate policy, and then send others to put into effect that which they deem to be politically and militarily expedient. They then observe with some detachment as young foot soldiers, sailors, and airmen carry out their given duty of sanctioned, legalised murder.

What would have happened if men like Sir Richard Haking, who was responsible for the slaughter at Fromelles; if Field-Marshal Sir Douglas Haig, the British commander-in-chief on the western front who ordered several suicide missions, and if General James McCay, who was described as 'about the most detested officer' in the AIF, would not have had a readily-available force of tens of thousands to send charging madly at the enemy lines during the Great War? The sad and lengthy books at the Shrine of Remembrance in Melbourne, listing the names of the hundreds of thousands who died, would be comprehensively reduced. If the long list of volunteers had not materialised in defence and support of the mother country in 1915, Ypres, and Pozières would not be a part of Australia's tragic military lexicon and those same books would be even thinner. And if, on the other side, the Huns had responded in a similarly detached way, then Hindenburg and Ludendorff would have been hard-pressed to defend their much-vaunted line of defence named after the former. Thus the German list of casualties would also be considerably shortened. Indeed, would there have been a First World War at all if men on every side and every land had chosen not to serve?

All the wars, all the battles, and all the killing throughout history had been dependent upon the willingness and readiness of youngsters, like me, to become involved. Without our availability and participation, none of those wars could or would have occurred. This was a demoralising realisation when it finally hit me, but it was unfortunately a realisation three years too late, and if this now reads as though I'm advocating a form of universal pacifism in order to prevent future wars, then that is my precise intention.

Chapter 39

As a primary school teacher of thirty-five years, I've come across many students who have been violent and angry little individuals and to whom the titles of bully or miscreant would easily apply. I have witnessed, just prior to intervening, several fights which have occurred in schoolyards and there was always, without exception, a repeating pattern to how the situation was played out.

After surveying his next victim, the school bully sidles up to the poor creature and shoves him in the ribs so hard that the unfortunate soul falls in a crumpled heap on the ground. Then, slowly, in a seemingly rehearsed manner, the bully scratches a line in the dirt with the toe of his boot.

'Dare you to step over that line, you bastard,' he challenges.

Having picked himself up and tried unsuccessfully to restore some of his lost dignity, the victim looks at the crooked line on the ground, and then back at the bully.

'Well what if I do?' he mutters.

'I'll knock your block off is what,' comes the curt reply.

At this point, there are only a limited number of alternatives from which the threatened party can reasonably choose. He could perhaps ignore the challenge and walk away in the hope that the bully, having satisfied a sudden need for sport and supremacy would bother him no more. Doing that would, of course, belittle him in his own and in others' eyes. Such a lack of fortitude and guts under the circumstances might even occasion similar challenges in the future, from the same or other bullies who note this reticence for retaliation. Very few are the victims, either in schoolyards or in the international arena who opt to turn the other cheek in this manner.

The victim might also hurl himself in a wild rage across the offending line, and attempt to destroy the tormentor with an unexpected attack. By so doing, he would show the bully and himself, but most importantly the gathering throng, that he is made of sterner stuff than anyone might have imagined and that he is not to be treated so lightly. That being the case, even if the bully beats him, any injury suffered in the process would be borne and paraded with pride, as a natural consequence of having done that which he simply had to do. On balance, though, this seems an unlikely outcome, as any bully worth the name would have ensured first, in picking his mark, that he chose well and that there was little chance of such a surprising retaliation.

Thirdly, apart from the further option of telling the bully to go forth and proceed making a most unnatural form of love to himself, the victim could try a tactical withdrawal. Pretending to walk off innocently might not be such an unpalatable thing to do if he knew perfectly well that in a few minutes he could return with three mates and beat the bully's head to a pulp. In that case, what would eventuate is that a one-to-one confrontation soon becomes a skirmish involving many participants, provided that the bully can also muster support for his cause. In this scenario, it is unfortunately clear that the existing differences between the bully and the victim will remain unresolved, but a number of new hatreds will have been created among the enlisted protagonists. In the schoolyard, the conversation might go like this.

'You kneed me in the guts, you bugger!'

'I can't help it if you're a weak arsehole! Serves you right for sticking up for him in the first place!'

'Well, you also gave Tom a blood nose and he wasn't even really in the fight.'

'Serves him right, too, just for being there. He's an even bigger bastard than you.'

'I'll get you for this one day!'

'Yeah! You and who else, you turd?'

'You just wait and see! I'll get help. It'll be a bloody surprise when it comes!'

In reality unfortunately, such allegiances can be just as transitory in the schoolyard as they can often be in international relationships. Dear friends one day can turn into sinister or deadly enemies quite quickly – depending upon which of the two situations happens to better suit a changed set of circumstances. The thin veneer binding the allegiances between the Allies in the 40s and 50s devolved into the serene and tranquil battlefield of Greenham Common in 1981 on the one hand, but also into a torn and divided Germany after WW2 and the detestable Iron Curtain that separated the East and West for so long on the other. Alliances were created for momentary convenience and then discarded.

There is, of course, a further, fourth alternative that the victim might have chosen for a response, but it is one that's certainly not an option taken in schoolyards by juveniles who don't know any better, and is all too infrequently used by nations governed by adults who should.

What might have been the outcome if the victim had publicly challenged the bully to a rational, sensible explanation for the unwarranted attack? Unless an acceptable reason for the outburst was forthcoming, the transgressor would have been shown to be nothing more than a belligerent ass, who had acted on little more than momentary impulse. In front of witnesses this would sufficiently belittle the bully's standing and legitimacy. Further, if he could be made to recompense the victim for any damages caused, he would lose all the credible support he might have thought was his.

Acting responsibly and being held responsible while justifying one's actions in a public forum is the most effective system of checks and balances we have. Whether it is a group of children witnessing senseless aggression in the schoolyard and knowing it for what it really is, or the United Nations passing judgement on the unacceptability of a dictator's actions – sanctions properly and assiduously applied can bring about the desired result of revealing transgressors for what they truly are and can also redress the wrongs that have been committed.

Achieving and believing in such a degree of international responsibility, rather than slavishly accepting simple national pride as a motivating factor for our actions, is the lesson that I believe today's children – tomorrow's leaders – need to be taught. If the human race can be educated to think of itself as a race of beings with the common human purpose of pursuing a peaceful life, rather than as a disparate collection of nations and religions with different and varying life goals, a great step forward will have been taken towards arresting millennia of destructive, self-centred, national, religious and territorial greed.

Chapter 40

Since America's ignominious withdrawal – or more aptly described 'flight' from Vietnam – much has been said and written about the causes, conduct, and consequences of the Vietnam/American War. (It should not be forgotten that the people who were most adversely affected by this conflict, the Vietnamese, still insist on calling it the American War. Who could deny them that right?) Most of the judgements and commentary from our viewpoint at least has been appropriately and deservedly negative. Enduring images of the unsuccessful attempts of many desperate refugees trying to board the last aircraft leaving the American Embassy's roof in Saigon, and the footage showing helicopters being hastily dumped into the South China Sea from the decks of a carrier, make a mockery of President Nixon's claim that the US was securing a 'Peace with Honour'. That miserable finale was neither peaceful nor indicative of much honour!

It would certainly seem that the politicians who conceived and then set about pursuing this war did so dishonestly and the current, overriding conclusion seems to be that there was never an actual threat to Australia in the context of the 'Domino Theory' to which our leaders subscribed so vehemently during the 60s. Nor was there ever, more importantly, an appeal for military assistance by the South Vietnamese government as was claimed. So why then did we become so intimately involved? Serious historians and knowledgeable political theorists have already addressed that question.

Some servicemen like me simply feel cheated and duped to have had our loyalty and willingness to serve our country so shamelessly abused!

A lot has also been said and written about the effects of the war on us as individuals. Some were spat upon and castigated as child-killers on their return to Australia. I have to be honest and say that it didn't happen to me. Some returned and found that they could not resume work with their previous employer for a variety of reasons. I was not so unlucky. Many found that after arriving home, wives or girlfriends had forsaken them and the difficulties of readjustment therefore became increasingly harder. Again, I was not in that unfortunate situation. Others found that the stress-related conditions resulting from their service caused severe insomnia, restlessness, the inability to retain or maintain previous levels of concentration and therefore to resume their careers or continue relationships. In extreme cases, the more recently diagnosed effects of PTSD (Post-Traumatic Stress Disorder) have seen many attempt and some succeed in ending it all by suicide. I thank blind luck or whatever greater power oversees such outcomes for the fact that I haven't been down that road either. Some are still suffering from anxiety, depression, from a variety of skin disorders or bouts of unprovoked anger that they cannot explain or justify even to themselves. Again, I am grateful for my unfamiliarity. Above all else, there are indications that even the children of Vietnam veterans might be disproportionately represented in national studies of inherited, genetic disorders. Thankfully, our children seem not to fall into that category, although our son's persistent eczema, which we were assured he would grow out of by his teens, remains into his late twenties. Who knows exactly what the real answers are?

But there is a bothersome negative from which I cannot claim to be free. That is the ever-present feeling of guilt. To have been part of that unjustifiable war and, more importantly, a lost war has left its indelible mark. Not only have those at the sharper end, who did the actual fighting, felt it. Others in administrative and support roles like many in my unit also carry it as a constant reminder. During my time in Vietnam I never shot at another person; killed no one; neither raped, violated nor hurt anyone; but tried always to act in a supportive manner towards my mates. In fact, I did my duty as asked and should be feeling pride, not guilt, in the knowledge that I chose to serve, while many others who could and should have done so, didn't!

So, then, why do I have this feeling of guilt?

Until two years ago, when I had a chance telephone conversation with a mate, I could never rationalise the feeling. Was it a feeling of guilt about the eventual military loss? Was it guilt about having been ultimately shown to be in the wrong? Was it guilt about the hidden suspicion that I knew I was being duped at the time – yet still willingly participating? These were some of my faulty conclusions. Speaking to John Rodgers at that time, who had been a clerk at 55, clarified the matter. Buck, as he was affectionately called – without knowing that he did so – explained my unknown guilt feelings as he described his own when he said simply that, 'although he had not shot at anyone either and didn't actually feel like the terrorist who blew up a bus thereby killing dozens, he did, however, feel like the driver of the bus that conveyed the bomber to his destination.' For me, as well, that is the crux of the matter!

Try as we might to rationalise our individual roles in the whole sordid affair, simply having been involved carries with it varying degrees of associated responsibility and culpability and those will live with us for as long as memory insists on being a constant reminder of that reality. No matter how trivial or insignificant my role, I cannot pretend to feel exonerated from all guilt because I was, after all, party to an episode that has resulted in untold misery. During America's and our long tenure in South Vietnam, some 60 000 foreign troops were to die on that country's soil. 300 000 were wounded and about $150 billion (in 1960s money) was spent on the overall effort. Some 240 000 South Vietnamese gave their lives and over 1 000 000 were wounded. On the other side, experts say that an estimate of 1.5 million dead seems conservative, while the wounded might be as high as four times that number. What possible justification can there be for such a mammoth and horrendous waste of human lives? How many of the world's poor could have been fed, clothed, housed, and educated with the money that was so readily spent?

How can a participant in such an enterprise internalise and then pigeonhole this thing into the basket labelled *'I'm not really accountable or responsible, because I simply did what I was ordered to do'* and not be adversely affected?

In over thirty-five years, I haven't been able to do so and I doubt that I ever will.

Chapter 41

On 28 September 2007, close to one hundred ex-members of 55 AESS/EWPS met again and held a happy, yet poignant reunion in Canberra. We remembered the unit's fortieth anniversary since being formed in Vietnam in 1967 and recalled with joy the ending of hostilities in Vietnam in 1975.

It was the first of the unit's reunions that I had chosen to attend. On previous occasions, I had either been too busy at work to travel to the various destinations like Alice Springs where the boys had gathered previously, or had simply been unwilling to participate. The desire to meet with old army acquaintances again was never very strong and I always justified my absence on the basis of unreasonable cost or inappropriate timing.

I could not have been more wrong!

On this occasion, however, my wife and I drove up to Canberra, and despite earlier concerns about being out of place and perhaps having nothing in common any more with those who might be there, I'm delighted to have been part of that reunion.

About fourteen years earlier, an ex-member of 55, Ray

Seymour, decided that it would be timely to try to contact as many members of the unit as possible and form a club or association whereby those who wanted could get in contact with each other and meet if they wished. He began a nationwide search of the 450 or so men who had at one time been part of 55, and collated a long list of names, addresses, and contact details of those equally keen to resume friendships. Having this list, Tony de Bont, one of 55's commanding officers, took over the task of producing a newsletter for the members of the unit and the first of those was simply several A4 pages stapled together, containing names, contact details, and a few scant bits of general information. That mailing became Volume 1.1 of the newsletter and was sent to us in January 1994. Since then, the '55 Newsletter' has grown into a thirty or forty page, biannual, Australia Post Registered Newspaper. It contains a host of useful information along with many members' contributions. At the time of writing, edition 14.2 has been circulated and I'm pleased to have on file, a copy of each edition published so far. The work that Tony has done, in terms of editing and compiling, printing, publishing and distributing the paper, has been nothing short of wonderful. I know that it provides many with important information and contacts, without which their lives would be measurably poorer. Tony's knowledge about army protocols and its inner, legal workings has also helped many needing that sort of advice.

Suffice to say that in September of 2007, Tony, Ray, Bert Hagel, and John Sahariv – all ex-members of the unit – acted as an organising committee for the gathering in Canberra and close to one hundred of us, most with spouses, sat around a formal dinner table on the Saturday night. Also present were the recently widowed wife of one of our mates, accompanied by her adult son. Our mate had led a troubled life since Vietnam and had died under difficult circumstances. That morning, we had participated in a solemn ceremony at the Australian War Memorial, with a plaque being dedicated to the unit and placed on permanent display at the Memorial. The following morning we were to assemble at the Vietnam Memorial in Anzac Parade for a remembrance parade for old, lost mates.

That evening, however, there were over seventy small candles on the dinner tables. Tony and John read the names of over seventy of our comrades who, since Vietnam, had passed away. As the names were read, one of us raised a hand in turn to signify that the person was present and then extinguished the candle in memory of each. There were tears in the room! The candle and name card closest to where I sat belonged to George Mahoney who served with 55 from August 1969 until June 1970. That was almost a full year after I had left Vietnam, so I had no personal knowledge of George, nor of his circumstances. Nonetheless, my heart went out to him and to his family, and my hands trembled slightly as I picked up the candle to blow out the flame. As Tony said afterwards (if indeed such a thing needed saying), 'That number of missing mates in such a brief time was a massive loss and nothing short of a needless and untimely tragedy.'

Since the end of my seven hundred and thirty days in the army and eventual discharge from it, some wonderful things have happened in the world and to me personally.

In that time, we've witnessed the disappearance of the Iron Curtain and the dismantling of the Berlin Wall. Along with that came the demise of the old Soviet Union, a slowing of the maddening military rivalry between East and West and the end of the Cold War, the reunification of Germany and the swift growth of the European Economic Community which has helped bind, what was up till then, a disparate collection of competing nations. The experts who claim to know and who monitor such things were loud in their declarations at the time that the Doomsday Clock had been wound backwards considerably from the apocalyptic midnight that it had been fast approaching.

Then followed a slight easing of tensions between India and Pakistan, some of which still persists, while unbelievably, as we've witnessed in recent times, even the leaders of the two Koreas have decided that some contact is better then none and, at the time of writing, have held one round of amicable talks. China has also changed dramatically and in spite of the crushing of the student-led democratic protests of Tiananmen Square in 1989, she, too, has adopted a more open style of leadership and has become an economic giant, with some saying that China could become the powerhouse to drive the world's future fiscal markets. Political, social and economic co-operation have now started to exist in places where dissent and distrust had always been the norm.

Who, back in 1975, could have thought such things would happen?

On a personal level, I married a wonderful, loving, and understanding girl. Kris understands and tolerates my periodically moody behaviour which I try hard to control. We have both had fulfilling professional careers and have now retired. We have two wonderful children, Danielle and Stephen. Our daughter is married, while our son is to marry within months. Personally, my status in life has been gradually elevating ever since my army days – from a recruit to a sapper in 1967, to a teacher in 1972, to a husband in 1974, to a father in 1977 and 1980 (Danielle and Stephen, respectively), and it's been recently raised further to the dizzy heights of a grandfather to Ethan in 2006.

But all of the socio-political progress has been more than outweighed by continuing mayhem. At a time when 'global warming' and 'climate change' have become the current catchcries of impending catastrophe, the Middle East is still in tatters. The Israelis and Palestinians continue to fight for their respective recognitions and rights to exist, Lebanon remains strife-torn, while Syria and Iran play deceitful baiting games with their neighbours. Cuba still languishes in an economic and social backwater, Tibet still suffers according to her master's will, many African countries are still torn asunder by endless dictatorships, Burma is continually on a knife edge, and there is no end in sight to the poverty and hunger that bedevil half of mankind. Not a pretty picture!

As an example of our shameful capacity for wanton policy-making and ultra risky leadership, I often hang my head in disbelief about this single, political gamble. During the 1970s, when Russia and America already possessed a combined nuclear arsenal of sufficient size to obliterate all human life on Earth seven or eight times over, and at a time when millions were dying of hunger in Ethiopia and Asia, what did those two superpowers choose to do? Each scurried to spend extra billions on building more powerful and even deadlier bombs! Did they truly think that obliterating all life fifteen times over was a preferable course of action? In fairness to the creators of that policy, I should point out the seldom-argued and ironic fact that this course of action might have actually helped arrest the arms race – but the reality that it took an absolute guarantee of our annihilation for us to step back and reposition priorities says a lot about human shortcomings. MAD (Mutually Assured Destruction) was the acronym so glibly assigned to this potential genocide of humanity and mad indeed was the world at the time! Now, when millions still continue to starve in Africa and Asia, vast sums are being spent on storing or dismantling that very arsenal. This bears the stench of such wanton waste and therefore of human debasement, that future generations will, and ought to hold mine responsible for allowing it to happen!

However, can we boast about fresh enlightenment now? Sadly, no! In the interim we've had no less than two Gulf Wars, incessant religious persecution, racial tensions in Africa and East Timor, ethnic genocide on a pitiful scale in the Balkans, and countless acts of brutal terrorism worldwide, one of which has become recognised universally and simply as 9/11. What that unleashed is now playing out its miserable sequel in Afghanistan and Iraq. Today, 13 October 2007, we witnessed the arrival back home of the body of the second Australian soldier to have made the supreme sacrifice in Afghanistan. His wife, children, and family mourned his tragic and untimely death.

Forty years ago, we might have thought that Pearl Harbour, the Somme, Hiroshima, Nagasaki, Auschwitz, Dresden, Changi, and Sharpeville were placenames of shame, follies from which we should have really learned. Unfortunately, we haven't!

Rather, together with My Lai, Londonderry, and Soweto, they have just about been superseded, by virtue of their infamy in a placename 'hall of shame' by such more recent ones as Srebrenica, Darfur, Guantanamo Bay, Beslan, Omagh, Ground Zero, Rwanda, and Halabja.

Who, back in 1975, could have thought things like that would continue to happen?

Until such time as we all insist on rattling our sabres, on

waving our national, political, religious, and military symbols defiantly rather than proudly in the faces of those opposite who happen to hold differing views, with each proclaiming to have the right to impose his supposedly superior symbols on the other, we will continue to be at odds,to wage war based on those differences and children will continue to mourn the untimely deaths of their fathers.

And won't that continue to be a massive, tragic, and unnecessary loss!

Where is the present or future leader, the Mahatma Gandhi or the Nelson Mandela of the twenty-first century with the will, skill, knowledge, and foresight; the statesman with the ideals and agenda that could act as the circuit breaker in arresting this eternal lunge, parry and thrust; this endless bloody cycle of distrust, conflict and pointless retribution that seem to persist like cancer infecting our human tribes?

Wherever you are, we need you desperately!

New Releases... also from Sid Harta Publishers

OTHER BEST SELLING SID HARTA TITLES CAN BE FOUND AT
http://sidharta.com.au   http://Anzac.sidharta.com
***
HAVE YOU WRITTEN A STORY?
http://publisher-guidelines.com

New Releases… also from Sid Harta Publishers

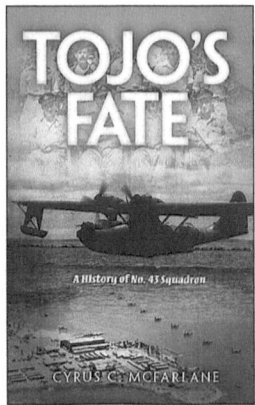

OTHER BEST SELLING SID HARTA TITLES CAN BE FOUND AT
http://sidharta.com.au   http://Anzac.sidharta.com
***
HAVE YOU WRITTEN A STORY?
http://publisher-guidelines.com

Best-selling titles by Kerry B. Collison

Readers are invited to visit our publishing websites at:
http://sidharta.com.au
http://publisher-guidelines.com/

Kerry B. Collison's home pages:
http://www.authorsden.com/visit/author.asp?AuthorID=2239
http://www.expat.or.id/sponsors/collison.html
email: author@sidharta.com.au

Purchase Sid Harta titles online at:
http://sidharta.com.au

New Releases... also from Sid Harta Publishers

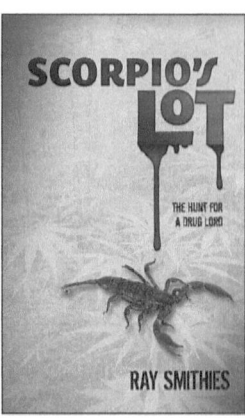
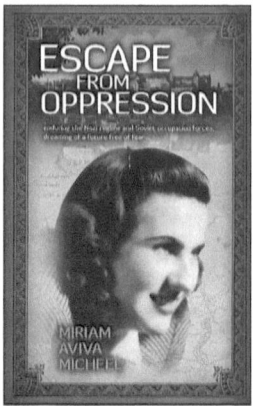

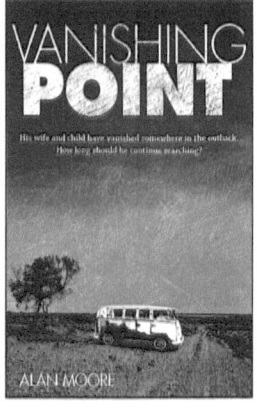

OTHER BEST SELLING SID HARTA TITLES CAN BE FOUND AT
http://sidharta.com.au   http://Anzac.sidharta.com
***
HAVE YOU WRITTEN A STORY?
http://publisher-guidelines.com